With the Tsar against Napoleon

Louis Victor Léon Rochechouart

With the Tsar Against Napoleon

The Recollections of Louis Rochechouart with Russian Forces during the Revolutionary & Napoleonic Period

ILLUSTRATED WITH MAPS & PICTURES

Louis Rochechouart

Translated by
Frances Jackson

LEONAUR

With the Tsar Against Napoleon
The Recollections of Louis Rochechouart with Russian Forces during the Revolutionary &
Napoleonic Period
by Louis Rochechouart
Translated by Frances Jackson

ILLUSTRATED WITH MAPS & PICTURES

First published under the title
Memoirs of the Count de Rochechouart

Leonaur is an imprint of Oakpast Ltd

Copyright in this form © 2017 Oakpast Ltd

ISBN: 978-1-78282-682-8 (hardcover)
ISBN: 978-1-78282-683-5 (softcover)

http://www.leonaur.com

Publisher's Notes

Contents

PART 4: IN THE SERVICE OF LOUIS XVIII

Introduction

Born in 1788, that is to say, on the eve of the Great Revolution, I was exposed, from my earliest childhood, to hunger, cold, and all the miseries of humanity. Left an orphan when very young, without friend or fortune, I found in the Duc de Richelieu a protector who gave me shelter, and helped me up the first steps of my military career, a second father, who never ceased to show me the most tender affection. I shall ever feel the deepest gratitude to him, and this is my reason for publishing this book. I wish to make known the private life of this eminent statesman, his kindness, simplicity, charity, integrity, his love of duty and of his country.

Nearly every town in France has raised a statue in honour of some man of greater or less celebrity; not one has remembered the minister who was at the head of affairs from 1815 to 1819, who freed France from the Armies of Occupation, and restored her credit to such a degree that whereas the *rente* was valueless in 1816, it had risen to seventy-five *francs* in 1818; the minister who made over to the sick poor the sum voted to him by the Chamber. Not one historian has been attracted by this noble figure. I shall begin by showing what he was in private life, hoping that some writer better qualified than I am, will one day make known the services he has rendered to his country.

I shall follow M. de Richelieu from the time when I joined him at Odessa, through his creation of Odessa, his expeditions into Circassia, his inspection of the troops, and of the colonies, scattered over the three provinces of his vast Government of New Russia; and, finally, through his two Ministries in France under the Restoration, and to his death, in May, 1822. I have, so to speak, never left him; I directed his household, and as his relative, his secretary and friend, I received his most intimate confidences; no one knew him so well, unless it were his confessor.

Separated from him from the end of 1812 to the middle of 1814, we kept up a regular correspondence, in spite of the stirring times and difficulties of communication, a correspondence which shows in every line his kindness and his patriotism. During these eighteen months, I was attached as *aide-de-camp* to the person of Alexander I, and took part in all the events from the crossing of the Beresina to the entry of the Allied Armies into Paris. My duties bringing me into communication with the general staff, I was at the centre of all reports and information, honoured by His Majesty's confidence, and entrusted by him with some important missions; I am thus in a position to supply details, hitherto unknown, or little known, and bring my humble tribute to the memorable campaigns of Saxony and of France.

But, I repeat, my main object in publishing this volume is to obtain recognition of the virtues of the Duc de Richelieu, to bear testimony to his memory with truly filial affection, to pay the debt of gratitude that fills my heart, to teach my children to reverence my benefactor, and to bring my fellow-countrymen to repent of the oblivion in which they have left one who loved them so truly and rendered them such great services.

I ought, therefore, to have begun my narrative with my arrival at Odessa, and to have ended it in 1822, with the death of the Duc de Richelieu, but I thought it would be of interest to narrate the severe trials of my childhood. . . .

★★★★★★

The Comte de Rochechouart adds: "And to end with an account of my visit to The Hague, and the missions entrusted to me by the Duchess de Berry in 1833 and 1834." But as these details would be of little interest to the English reader, they have been omitted in the translation.

★★★★★★

The idea of writing came into my head when I was twelve years old, not that I thought of writing memoirs, but merely of jotting down anything that happened to me. Continuing to keep this sort of diary, I unconsciously wrote these *Memoirs*.

The varied phases of my youth took me to many lands, brought me into contact with eminent persons, and made me a witness of important events. As a child, the impression left by my adventures was sufficiently strong to induce me to write them down; later, I continued the practice in order to make known the virtues of my benefactor.

In writing out in full the notes of my journal, I have left the style just as it was, correcting only the grossest faults, eliminating the high-flown phrases that interrupted the narrative., But, I shall be asked, how is it possible to write, even tolerably, when twelve years old? What thoughts can a child of that age put on paper? Is he capable of passing any sort of judgment on the simplest events of life? To this I reply: No teacher is so good as adversity, when it does not brutalise. Both distress of mind and physical suffering leave indelible marks on the memory; many things are learned in that school without books. Left to my own resources very early, compelled to support myself, I was forced to reflect, at an age when other boys play at ball or prison-bars. . . .

General Count de Rochechouart.

Jumilhac, December, 1857.

CHAPTER 1

Early Years

Louis-Pierre-Jules-César de Rochechouart, Colonel of the Armagnac Infantry, married, in 1775, Elizabeth Armide Durey de Morsan. They had the following children:—

1. Victor, born in 1776, died at Port-au-Prince in 1802.
2. Philippe, born in 1779, died in 1791.
3. Louis, born in 1782, killed at Brienne in 1814.
4. Cornélie, born in 1784, died in 1794.
5. Myself, Louis-Victor-Leon, born September 14th, 1788.

As a youngest son, I was destined for the Church or for the navy. Cardinal de Rochechouart, Bishop of Laon, and my great-uncle, the Bishop of Bayeux, who had both died only a few years before, had opened for me the way to ecclesiastical honours. The navy offered me the chance of rapid promotion, as two of my cousins held high positions in it. The Vicomte de Rochechouart, Chevalier du Saint-Esprit, and in command of a squadron, had won distinction at the siege of Gibraltar in 1782; his flagship of seventy-four guns, the *Majestic*, passing through the line of the British Fleet. The Vicomte de Mortemart had won great renown in the battle delivered by M. de Grasse on April 12th, 1782. He braved three British men-of-war in order to rescue his ship, the *Glorieux*, totally disabled. There is a picture representing the incident in the Ministry of Marine at Paris.

Events decided my career otherwise.

I was put out to nurse with a worthy farmer's wife at Saint-Germain en Laye, and remained there until 1794, so I was six years old when I returned to my father's house.

My mother, as a friend of the Duchesse de Polignac, was admitted into the intimate circle whom the queen, Marie Antoinette, gathered around her at the Petit Trianon, by way of recreation from the official receptions of the court. Having thus been privileged to see this sovereign's affability in private life, my mother was deeply grieved when she saw her queen defamed, harassed and condemned to death upon the scaffold; she resolved to risk everything in the attempt to rescue her. She joined the conspiracy of the Baron de Batz, and advanced a great part of the sum necessary to hire assistance. The *Moniteur Universelle* of the 18th *germinal* of the year III (the 7th April, 1795), No. 175, gives the following description of the plot:—

> There has been a conspiracy to rescue the queen; it was projected by the former Comtesse de Rochechouart and the notorious Hébert, called Père Duchêne. The Allies paid Hébert, who demanded two million *francs*. One million had been paid down and the other was to be paid after the project had been carried out, but Hébert was seized with panic, and became a denunciator.

To bribe the warders and convey the necessary information to the prisoner was a task which called for great prudence as well as great courage; my mother had only the latter. She threw herself blindly into the enterprise, without taking account of the danger or the chance of success.

From the first the queen had declared that, unless her children could be delivered at the same time, she would prefer to suffer the rigour of her lot.

The attempt failed; there was a search for the authors, and their names soon became known. My mother's name was one of the first on the list. It was learned, at the same time, that the Abbé Edgeworth, who accompanied the king to the scaffold, and gave him religious consolation, was living, under the name of Essex, at my father's country house of Montigny, near Pithiviers. A warrant of arrest was at once issued against the former Comtesse de Rochechouart, charged with conspiracy, etc.

My mother was living at Passy with my brother Louis, my sister Cornélie, and me; she went to Paris nearly every day to arrange various matters. My father was at Montigny and my brother Victor with the army of the Prince de Condé.

The warrant for my mother's arrest was issued so quickly and so secretly that no one was able to warn her of the danger. The municipality of Passy presented themselves at her house, escorted by *gendarmes*, who had been instructed to guard all the doors and convey the *aristocrate* to prison.

After a minute search, they were satisfied that she was absent; they then seized all her papers, silver, jewellery and lace; these things were to serve as evidence at the trial, but they took possession of them without an inventory and divided them among themselves. I was informed of this fact later at the registry. The honourable citizens, disappointed at the absence of the former countess, conferred together as to their course of action; one was for carrying off the children; this idea was abandoned. There was no mention of them on the warrant. The concierge and servants were subjected to a long interrogatory, and it was decided to wait until the time when the *suspecte* should return home to dinner, that is to say, between two and three in the afternoon. The *gendarmes* also went into the house, in order not to arouse the suspicion of the former countess.

No one had taken any notice of my brother Louis, who had heard and understood everything. He slipped into the garden, climbed on to the wall and jumped down into a deserted side street. He ran towards the barrier, met my mother coming home on foot, and told her all that had happened. Thanks to his intelligence and devotion, she escaped certain death. Instead of returning to Passy, she took Louis with her, and went back to Paris, where she concealed herself in the Hôtel Grange-Batelière under the name of Durey. A few days later she sent a trustworthy person to fetch me.

Fearing that at any moment she might be discovered, my mother set out for Caen with my brother and me, leaving my sister at school at Passy; later on, she was to go to my grandmother, Françoise d'Albignac, Comtesse de Morsan, who was living at Villecresne near Grosbois.

I will at once tell the sad story of what befell my poor little sister Cornélie. The schoolmistress was denounced as a *suspecte*, arrested, tried, and guillotined, and the children turned out of the house. Imagine the bewilderment of this little child. She knew her mother was away from Paris, and her father thirty leagues distant in the country; she was without money and half dead with fear in her loneliness. There was only her grandmother with whom she could take shelter, and she hardly knew where she lived. All she remembered was that she would have to go out of Paris by the barrier de Charenton, or de la Grande-Pinte. Trembling, she set out in the direction of the other side of the town, scarcely daring to ask her way, for fear of attracting attention.

After wandering for two days in Paris and the environs, she fell fainting from exhaustion and want of food, in a ditch by the roadside. Here she was found by a kind lady, who, struck by the refined style of her dress, in spite of its disorder, and by her beautiful features, worn by suffering, tried to restore her to life. From what the child told her, she placed her under the care of Mme. de Morsan, for the place happened to be near Villecresne. In spite of every care, my poor sister died in her grandmother's arms two days later. Fatigue, want of food, and terror had exhausted her and given her a death-blow. She was then ten years old.

To return to our journey. When we reached Caen, we alighted at a bathing establishment kept by a M. Dussaussais, who let furnished rooms. I shall never forget his name, for it was at his house that I served my apprenticeship in poverty.

Very soon after, my mother providentially overheard (from a letter that was read aloud in the street as she was passing) that her hiding-place had been discovered, and that Citizen Pomme, a representative of the people, had arrived from Paris to arrest her. The warning was too serious to be neglected, and she resolved to leave at once. She had a passport for Switzerland, perfectly in order, but it was necessary to avoid exciting suspicion. The Abbé Geard, one of our friends, who was also in hiding at Caen, advised her to set out on foot, and to continue her journey in this way for several days. My brother was in bed with broken chilblains, and as I was only six years old, I could not walk far; so, she left us to the mercy of God, as they say.

She told M. Dussaussais that she was going to stay with friends in the neighbourhood, and begged him to take care of us while she was away, and she paid for our board and lodging for a month in advance. Then, taking us aside, she charged us never to tell anyone our name, but always to say we were called Durey, which was her maiden name. She left us at five o'clock in the morning, and two hours later Citizen Pomme arrived to arrest her. He subjected us to a long interrogatory, and ordered a *gendarme* to watch us night and day, as he was convinced that my mother would come to seek us. At the end of a week, as it seemed unnecessary to keep a *gendarme* employed in watching two children, he was recalled.

Thereupon Mme. Dussaussais seized upon us and our clothes. She had just sent away her servant, and she made us take her place. We had to wait on the bathers, to warm and fetch their towels, to pump water to fill the tank and the large boiler; in a word, we were simply bath attendants. But all this was nothing compared to the sufferings we were to endure in the severe winter of 1794-1795.

In October, finding she had an opportunity of letting our room, Mme. Dussaussais made us move into the attic. The roof was in a bad state, and the rain, and later the snow, fell on our bed. She pretended that, as there were two of us in one bed, it was more healthy to have a little air. The good lady allowed us three shirts between us. "They are not too many," she said, "but they are enough for lads like those." Then she arranged our day in the following manner: Get up at noon, so there was no question of breakfast; punctually at one o'clock we had for dinner very thin soup, and what was left of some badly-cooked boiled meat, with plenty of haricot beans, some barley bread and very thick cider that nobody cared for; bed at six, a novel but simple way of dispensing with supper; our meals were reduced to the simplest expression. It was thus we were treated during four long months.

The situation of the Hôtel des bains Nationaux was ideal for a bathing establishment. It was built in the old moat of the town and surrounded on three sides with water. When the snow melted, the water rapidly rose to the first floor. Mme. Dussaussais then prudently retired to the house of one of her friends in the upper part of the town, leaving us, with a manservant, in charge of the establishment. We were sheltered in our attic, and all communications cut off. On the third day, our bread fell short; fortunately, there were plenty of apples left in the fruit-store, and these formed our only food for six days. What was our delight, then, when we were able to set foot on land, and have something warm to eat! With the return of spring, bathers appeared in great numbers, and the pump again called for our exertions.

Seeing no way out of our predicament, my brother resolved to write to my father, who he supposed was still at Montigny. We did not know whether he had emigrated; our letter was sent off secretly, and we put our trust in God, the refuge of the unhappy.

During our long winter nights, my brother, who was twelve years old and fairly well educated for his age, taught me what he knew of French history, sacred history, geography, grammar and sums. I said my lesson in the evening, and for every slip of the memory I received a fillip on the nose, and was not allowed to go to sleep until I had said my lesson perfectly. Thanks to this method, I made rapid progress.

Our patience was exhausted, and we were thinking of running

away, and in our boyish heads were arranging a splendid plan of escape, when one day my brother heard a woman asking for Messieurs de Rochechouart. She said she was the wife of our father's house-steward. Words fail to describe our joy; it is impossible for anyone to realise the delight of such a change unless he has been in a similar position.

Mme. Dinjean, for that was the name of our deliverer, told us that our father, having learned where we were from my brother's letter, had obtained a passport for us and for herself, so that she might take us to him. We had been nearly nine months at the house of Mme. Dussaussais, and were impatient to see the last of her. The old shrew had the effrontery to claim the sum agreed upon by our mother, as if we had been housed and fed in accordance with those terms. Mme. Dinjean succeeded in arranging everything amicably. She paid Mme. Dussaussais the half of what she had asked; it was much more than was due to her, but then we had to remember that her roof had sheltered us when we were abandoned. What would have become of us if we had been turned out into the street?

This thought made us part good friends, without resentment on our part; we were even grateful to her for not having pitilessly driven away the children of an *émigrée*. When we reached Paris, Mme. Dinjean took us to Villecresne to see our grandmother, who then told us of our sister's sad death. Mme. de Morsan had not known what had become of us. The story of our sufferings reminded her of Cornélie's sad and cruel end, and she insisted on keeping one of us with her. My brother stayed, and I left for Montigny with Mme. Dinjean. The time I spent at the *château* had an indescribable effect on me. The place seemed delightful, the food exquisite; I began to enjoy life after so many humiliations and privations. My great-uncle, the Bishop of Bayeux, had ended his days at Montigny, beloved by everyone in the village. Out of reverence for his memory, my father had never been molested, even at the height of the revolutionary turmoil; the villagers would even have protected him if he had been denounced.

Four months later I was called away from this sweet, peaceful life by a letter from my mother. She announced her return to France, and begged my father to send me to her at once, which he did, to my great regret. He would only consent to part with me on condition that my brother Victor should take my place. Victor had left Condé's army, and recently returned to France, but had not been able to get his name struck off the list of *émigrés*.

My mother could not remain long in the same place. She had just returned from England, and was going to Switzerland, but she said she had so many things to settle that she would send us on before her. She gave my brother Louis the money necessary for this long journey, with directions as to the route he should take to reach Fribourg, where two of our aunts had taken refuge during the Reign of Terror. She promised over and over again that she would soon rejoin us.

My brother, who was only thirteen, found his task a very difficult one. I do not know how he could have accomplished it, if God had not come to our aid in Franche-Comté, by causing us to meet a Swiss who was returning to Neufchâtel. This man took pity on two children travelling alone, and allowed us to go in his carriage, sharing the expense. It was the end of January, a very bad time of the year for travelling in the mountains; besides, the roads were almost impassable, owing to the little care taken to repair them, and to the transport of cannon, in spite of the rains, which made the roads full of ruts and quagmires. Our travelling companion was taking home a beautiful, but very light, carriage; he had bought it to serve as a model to the carriage-makers of his country. It was not strong enough to withstand the jolting, and after having been overturned three times, it reached its destination, but quite unfit for use.

At Neufchâtel, we found an opportunity of going to Berne. Our mother had given us a letter to one of her friends, M. d'Erlach, who lived there, begging him to look after us, and to send us on to Fribourg, where we should find Mesdames de Besse and de Rochechouart, the daughters of one of my grandfather's brothers. We arrived there in the evening when they were receiving some friends in the drawing-room. As we had come from France, we were overwhelmed with questions, which we were unable to answer as we were so young. One must have been an *émigré* to form an idea of the value of every bit of news to our poor, aged and infirm countrymen, who were unfit for service in Condé's army.

My mother had promised to join us shortly; but weeks passed, and we did not even receive any letters from her.

One day, an unexpected event threw us into the greatest perplexity. We had been three months at Fribourg, studying under a French priest, as our aunts had arranged that he should teach us, when one morning the servant announced a deputation from the Committee of the *Émigrés*. They came to order us to leave the Canton of Fribourg within twenty-four hours, on the singular pretext that we had brought "suspicious papers" and "impious opinions" from France. They said we should receive permission to remain if we could find an influential citizen to be surety for us; otherwise, no mitigation or delay. It was impossible to reason with, people who would drive us away on such a pretext.

We did not know what had become of our mother; and our family council sought in vain any way of avoiding this abrupt dismissal, not knowing where to send us. The time was passing rapidly, and we were beginning to lose all hope, when a much respected citizen, the Dean of the Chapter and head priest of Fribourg, touched with pity, came to rescue us from our cruel position, to console us, and take us to the Hotel de Ville, where he became our surety. Only that morning he had heard, in the sacristy of the Collegiate Church, of the incredible decision that had been taken with regard to us. We had no words to tell this good priest how greatly we were touched by this truly Christian act, but we were deeply grateful to him.

M. Allois, the President of the Committee of the *Émigrés*, a coarse, hard man, said to the venerable Abbé Seydoux: "Dean, since you are so kind as to be surety for these little vagabonds, you must take them into your house to see that they behave themselves."

"Very well, I will do it with pleasure," replied the good priest. We went with him to our aunts, to tell them of M. Allois's irrevocable decision. M. Seydoux asked fifty *louis* a year for the maintenance of the two of us, and said that with this he would be responsible for all our expenses, even our clothes.

His housekeeper, an old French lady, loaded us with kindness, and all the while we were at the Presbytery she never ceased to be a mother to us.

Thus, once again, we, poor deserted children, found a shelter, but, this time, with a loving welcome.

The Town Council of Fribourg took every opportunity of worrying the poor little innocent outlaws who had taken refuge in their town; and did not foresee the revolutionary storm that was to break out, and overwhelm their country.

Every day brought out some new good quality of our host and his old friend. It was not long before an opportunity occurred of putting their kindness to the test. We had been barely two months at the Presbytery, when we heard that our aunts had left Fribourg, and returned to France, without telling us anything about it, thus leaving us without any news of our mother, or provision for our support. My mother had sent them thirty *louis* on our arrival, but this sum had been exhausted some days before, and not being in a position to help us further, they thought it best not to grieve us by telling us before they went away. This new difficulty only redoubled the good priest's care of us. He exerted himself to give us instruction, both in religion and in secular knowledge, for events had caused our education to be much neglected.

Although I was very young—only nine—he thought me old enough to make my First Communion; trouble had developed my mind and character. He wished us to go to the old Jesuit school that only took day-scholars, but it was necessary to pass an entrance examination; he therefore gave us a very clever young priest as a coach. I will say nothing as to my own success at the Fribourg school, but my brother made great progress; as for me, I found myself very backward compared with the boys of my class.

On her arrival in France, Mme. de Besse wrote to tell us that our mother was in England; she sent us her address, and advised us to write to her. We wrote at once, but received no answer.

The Revolution in Switzerland added to the difficulties of our position. I shall not be expected, at my age, to explain the Swiss Revolution. Suffice it to say, that on March 15th, 1798, General Brune entered Switzerland with three French divisions. He came to give liberty to a country that was certainly not "subject to feudal slavery," according to the saying of those days. Severe fighting ensued. The Swiss could with difficulty be prevailed upon to accept the blessings brought by the French Army.

These events, at last, induced our mother to concern herself about us, and to write to us. She had just returned to France, and told us to set off at once to join her in Paris. With her letter, she sent us a draft for 2,000 *francs* on a bank at Bâle. She thought this sum would be sufficient to pay the expenses of our journey, and whatever might be owing. She had not allowed for our having lived for two years with the priest of Fribourg. Our aunts had only paid for the first term; so, we owed nearly 2,000 *francs*, the amount of the draft less the discount. The good dean was satisfied with 1,200 *francs*, leaving the rest for our journey and some necessary purchases; he was sure our mother would soon repay him what she owed.

We very gladly spent another fortnight with the venerable priest; both he and his housekeeper, Miss Codray, had a personal affection for us, as if we belonged to them. At last, we tore ourselves from their arms, after bidding them farewell for ever.

We left Fribourg with heavy hearts in the early days of May, 1798, after having lived there twenty-seven months, and we reached Paris in six days, without any mishap, travelling by way of Berne and Bâle.

CHAPTER 2

London and Altona

After her delight at finding we had grown so tall, and were looking so well, our mother could not help laughing at our appearance. Our hair was out short, standing up like a brush, with an immense pigtail, without any powder. We each wore a sort of dress-coat with long skirt, of a material half wool, half thread, with green, yellow and white stripes; the cut resembled that of 'the revolutionaries of 1793; we had black silk waistcoats, short breeches of grey cloth, spotted stockings, and shoes with large copper buckles. In addition to this elegant costume, we had a most countrified appearance. Before she let anyone see us, our mother sent for a tailor and a hairdresser, so that we might not look like Auvergne peasants in their Sunday best.

Our mother was mixed up in a plot with the English Government, the consequences of which were soon to plunge us into the greatest misfortunes. As she was obliged to return to London, she obtained, with some difficulty, a passport for Antwerp. We left Paris on the day that news was received of the taking of Malta by General Buonaparte, without resistance; the island was necessary for his expedition to Egypt. From Antwerp, we went to Rotterdam, and crossed to England in a Swedish brig. We landed at Dover, after a voyage of six days, and arrived in London on July 5th.

We spent seven months in England, during which time I learned to speak English fairly well. We went with our mother to visit the Countess of Staremberg, wife of the Austrian Ambassador, who was living at Richmond, and who had been her schoolfellow at the convent. We also went to Staines, near Windsor, where the Duchesse de Mortemart was living in retirement with her children, in a charming cottage belonging to the Duc d'Harcourt.

★★★★★★

Victurnien Jean-Baptiste de Rochechouart, Duc de Mortemart, born in 1752, had married Gabrielle d'Harcourt in 1772, and had three daughters; left a widower, he married, as his second wife, in 1782, Pauline de Cossé-Brissac, by, whom he had Casimir, born in 1786, and three daughters.

★★★★★★

From this visit dates our friendship with Casimir de Mortemart; as we were almost of the same age, we were put to sleep in the same bed during the whole of our stay at the cottage... I will try to explain the object of our visit to London. While we were in Switzerland, my mother, instead of joining us, had gone to England. At that time, her affairs in France were in a prosperous state, and she had many friends. She was asked if she would be willing to be of use to Louis XVIII. With her pronounced Royalist views, and her leaning for political intrigue, she replied that she was devoted to the king, and ready to act.

In an interview with the Duke of Portland, then Minister for Foreign Affairs, she insisted, first, that she should have a letter from the Count d'Artois (to whom Louis XVIII, who was in Russia, had given full powers, with the title of Lieut.-General of the Kingdom) expressing approval of what she was about to do. Secondly, that she should have a formal declaration from the English Government that everything was to be done in the name of the King of France. Provided with these two important documents, and a letter of credit for £1,000 on Mr. Pope, a rich banker of Hamburg, my mother returned to France. She set to work at once, and was on the point of succeeding in her mission. As I was so young, I never knew the details of this mission; I only knew that it was a question of gaining over certain personages to the king's cause.

Having spent all the ready money at her disposal, my mother had recourse to the letter of credit. To her amazement, it was returned to her a month later:

The drawer has no account with Pope's Bank.

With the help of her friends, and by making use of her remaining resources, she got over the difficulty. Then she wrote to England, asking for an explanation of this breach of faith, and announcing that her mission had been entirely successful. While waiting for a reply, she sent for us from Switzerland; she wished to take us with her to England, so that she might settle there until she should be able to return to France with the king. As the reply that she was daily expecting from London never came, she took the course of going to England in person, intending at the same time to give an account of her mission. As soon as she reached London, she asked for an interview with the Duke of Portland, and he sent the under-secretary, who explained to her that the English Government had changed its plans, and would have nothing more to do with the affair.

He added:

You may expect, *Madame*, to receive the order to leave the United Kingdom. You will be able to return to France, where you seem to have such brilliant connexions.

Now, my mother, after leaving Caen, had met this secretary in Switzerland, where he was *Chargé d'Affaires*, and being merely an *émigrée*, she had made some jests at his expense, which he never forgave. When she accepted the mission described above, it appears, he had not been informed, and only heard of it from her letters. He represented to the Duke of Portland that he was being deceived, and that my mother was taking part with Talleyrand against the Royalists—hence orders were given to cancel the letter of credit. My mother only learned these details long afterwards.

She took the fatal resolution of making the public judge of the quarrel. She would have done far better to have left it alone, and to have sacrificed the 30,000 *francs* she had advanced. She received the order to leave England. She feigned illness and had leeches applied to her chest. Thus, she obtained a month's delay, then that of a second month. Being under strict surveillance all the time, she was unable to take any steps to justify herself. Finally, she was given her choice, either to go to Hamburg at her own expense, or to be sent from Yarmouth, with other expelled criminals, at the expense of the State. She left for Hamburg.

We set out from London in December, 1798, and landed at Cuxhaven, where we remained until the following March, when we left for Altona. My mother preferred this quiet town to Hamburg, which, at that time, was crowded with French *émigrés*, some living in affluence, others reduced to great poverty.

She did not lay aside her project of revenge. She drew up a memorandum against the English Government, spent a large sum in having it printed, and gave another large sum to the captain of the packet-boat, who undertook to deliver the copies to a bookseller belonging to the Opposition, in London. All these expenses exhausted our means, and we were obliged to work for our living.

My mother drew extremely well, and made little pictures to ornament fans, work-bags (called reticules) and boxes of all sizes. My brother and I undertook the pasting and mounting; we also made ladies' straw hats. As the younger son, it fell to my lot to offer the articles manufactured in our workshop at the fancy depositories in Hamburg and Altona. In order to praise up my wares, I had to learn German. I often met with rebuffs from these worthy Germans, who naturally tried to get the goods I offered as cheaply as possible. I held out as long as I could, knowing the value of my merchandise from the time and trouble it had taken to make.

One day, I was unable to sell a single thing. I went home with everything I had taken out. There was not a halfpenny left in our purse, and the butchers and bakers allowed no credit to *émigrés*. In order, not to think about our hunger, we had to walk about until it was time to go to the Marquise de Brouille's reception; this lady gave a supper every evening. That night, the guests wondered at our appetite, and our poor mother was as hungry as we were.

This kind of life brought many reflections; poverty is a sad thing. My mother's courage and resignation were admirable. Imagine, one of the most attractive ladies of the court, brought up to expect a large fortune—she had a dowry of a million *francs*, an immense sum in those days—clever and accomplished, suddenly fallen to a position not far removed from beggary. Yet she did not allow herself to be cast down for a moment; her courage redoubled her physical strength. After the trials of the day, she would appear in society in the evening with all her wonted vivacity and wit.

We had made the acquaintance of Prince Louis of Prussia, the son of Ferdinand, brother of Frederick the Great. The prince was celebrated for his wit, his good looks, and wild behaviour. When speaking of the Duke of York's reverses in Holland, he remarked jestingly: "My cousin of York is like a drum, he makes no noise in the world unless he is beaten." The Prussian prince invited us to spend a few days at his *château* at Bremen, and entertained us most hospitably; he gave a ball in our mother's honour. He would often come to our humble lodgings, attracted by the wit and animated conversation of the poor *émigrée*.

He offered to take me as a cadet in his own regiment, which was in garrison at Hamburg, and assured me of rapid promotion. I was only eleven, and my mother would not hear of my beginning my military career so young.

During our hours of work, she delighted us every day with some new story of court life, so we became familiar with all the intrigues that she had known. She constantly spoke of our family, of the duties belonging to a great name, and gave us a taste for good manners and good society.

One day, I forget exactly what led to it, there was mention of the wine of Tokay, the estate of the Emperor of Austria, as King of Hungary. She told us by what strange chance she had come into possession of fifty bottles.

The Emperor Joseph II had come to France to return the visit of his sister. Queen Marie Antoinette; he was travelling under the name of the Comte de Falkenstein.

Our mother said:

At this time, I was obliged to go to see the Controller of the King's Household, the Baron de Breteuil. Your father, who was in the army on the other side of the Rhine, was soliciting an appointment, and he wrote to me to make haste in putting forward the request, as another person was seeking the same favour. Knowing that the Baron de Breteuil was a very early riser, I decided to be at his office by six o'clock in the morning. With this in view, I went to Versailles overnight, and asked a lady whom I knew, and who lived at the castle, to allow me to sleep in her rooms. I had chosen an unfortunate day, for the minister was engaged with his *premiers commis*, the name given to the head clerks.

I determined to wait until they had gone, and the usher, who knew me, showed me into a room where I could wait without attracting attention. I was two mortal hours waiting in this charming room, and, to keep myself awake, I walked up and down studying the pictures on the wainscoting. They were very well done, and represented the love affairs of the pagan gods, not a very proper subject. I was so much absorbed in my study of the pictures that I did not hear the door open behind me; I only heard a voice whisper these words in my ear: '*Madame* is apparently going through a course of study of the human form,' and at the same moment I was seized round the waist.

I turned, much abashed, and saw the Emperor Francis Joseph.

25

Recovering my self-possession, I replied at once: 'No, *M. le Comte*, but I invite you to attend a course on good manners,' and I fled.

The emperor inquired my name from the usher, and the next day he wrote me a very polite note. The Comte de Falkenstein begged me to allow him to begin his course of good manners at my house, and to tell him on what day I could receive him at supper.

I told him that next day, arrayed in doctor's cap and gown, I would receive him and put him through his first examination in the presence of several of my intimate friends. I did, in fact, invite five or six of my friends, among them Prince Max des Deux-Ponts.

Punctual to the moment my illustrious guest arrived, and, after kissing my hand, he said: 'I have come to ask a double pardon.' As to the first, he had the good taste not to refer to it, but with regard to the second, he said he had acquired in Germany the execrable habit of being able only to drink a particular kind of wine, so he had taken the liberty of having a case of it brought to my house.

My butler in announcing, '*Madame la Comtesse*, supper is served,' told me in an undertone that a hamper containing fifty bottles of Tokay had been left with the porter. The supper was as merry as possible, and free from etiquette, out of regard for the Emperor's *incognito*.

Another time, our mother related a conversation between the Duc d'Orléans and the Duchesse de Brionne. It took place in the evening after a drive to Longchamps, where, as is well known, all society gathered in splendid carriages and exquisite dresses. The queen asked her cousin to describe the ladies he had seen. He answered, "*Madame*, there were two kinds, the passables, and the *passées*."

The Duchesse de Brionne, who was no longer young, and had been to Longchamps that day, took the latter part of the description as applying to herself; exasperated at his rudeness, and detesting the Duc d'Orléans as much as he disliked her, she replied, "It seems *Monseigneur* is more at home in *signalements* (descriptions) than in signals."

The allusion was to the Battle of Ushant, where it was said the Duc d'Orléans would not allow his vessel to reply to the signal of the Comte d'Orvilliers, the admiral in command of the French fleet. After

BATTLE OF USHANT,

this reply, the queen rose to pass into the State apartments. The Duc d'Orléans followed her, but when he reached the door he stepped aside to allow the Duchesse de Brionne to go in before him, and, as he did so, he added, in a mocking tone, "*Beauté passez.*"

The duchess, unruffled, made him a low curtsey, saying, in an undertone, "Like your reputation, *Monseigneur.*"

I could fill a volume with all these stories, but I forbear, as I only wished to give a sketch of my mother's conversation while we were working. We became as familiar with the Courts of Louis XV and Louis XVI as if we had lived there ourselves.

Almost every evening we met, at some house or other, the Comte de Gand, who was in great request on account of his wit and power of repartee. One evening, he told us he was going to Spain to rejoin his brother, who was in command of the Bourbon Regiment. I begged him to let me go with him, feeling sure that his brother would admit me as a cadet into the regiment. I felt I was a heavy burden on my mother, and hoped she would be able to get over her difficulties better without me.

M. de Gand agreed, but confessed that he was himself very short of money, and could only afford to take me if I could provide at least twenty-five *louis* for my journey. I told my mother of the plan; necessity overcame her affection, and she consented. M. de Septeuil, formerly the King's First Valet, lent her thirty *louis.* I took twenty, and told M. de Gand that I could not get any more. The remaining ten *louis* were to enable my mother and brother to make their escape from this abode of poverty.

I set off on August 1st, 1800. It was very painful to me to leave my mother and brother. When should we meet again? I had taken a childish pleasure in the prospect of being my own master and escaping from our miserable surroundings, but I had never thought of this parting. If some unforeseen event had occurred at the last moment to prevent my going, I should have been delighted. I had gone too far now to draw back.

As I spoke German fairly well, my travelling companion asked me to find a ship. I soon found a Hamburg schooner about to sail for Bilbao. The captain agreed to take us for eight *louis* each, to include our board. This was not dear, and M. de Gand congratulated me warmly.

A dead calm for five days, and then a terrible tempest off the coast of Holland—such was the beginning of our voyage. After having been exposed to rough weather for twenty-eight days, our ship was badly damaged—leaks, masts broken, sails torn, rudder carried away; when we were on the point of sinking, we met an English pilot. He towed us into the port of Weymouth, and charged eighty guineas for his act of charity in saving our lives.

Though we were far away from Spain, we were delighted to find ourselves on land again, and in a good hotel. A week after our shipwreck, the captain came to tell us that it would be impossible for him to put to sea for three months, the time necessary for the repairs. This prospect was to the last degree annoying to us. A fortnight passed in uncertainty as to what we should do. M. de Gand eventually decided to go to Falmouth and embark for Portugal, passing from there to Spain. This was the only course open to us, but there was a slight difficulty—we had no ready money; with the exception of a few gold and silver coins, we had only bills of exchange on Bilbao, and it was impossible to negotiate them as England and Spain were at war.

I began to suspect, but too late, that I had chosen a wretched mentor, incapable of guiding me, and likely soon to drag me into great difficulties. Our three weeks at the hotel, together with some not very moral expenses on the part of M. de Gand, had involved us in a debt of nearly fifty pounds. How were we to pay it? My companion wrote to the Comte d'Artois, who was in London, as he knew. Having formerly held the position of Gentleman-in-Waiting to the prince, he was able to appeal to his kindness. *Monsieur* sent him, by the next courier, a note for fifty pounds, all His Royal Highness could do for him.

But this was not enough to pay all our debts, so we remained in a most difficult position. I found a French priest, living at the house of a Catholic nobleman as tutor to his children. I suggested to M. de Gand that we should go and see him, if only to ask his advice; he refused to go with me. So, I went alone to the castle where the Abbé Derby was living. No sooner had I mentioned my name than he said, "I will do everything in my power to oblige you, for I owe the pleasant position I now hold to one of your relatives, the Duc de Mortemart."

I explained our difficulties in a few words, and begged him to accompany me to M. de Gand to help him with his advice. He came at once, and offered M. de Gand forty guineas, saying he could do without them for a time and begging him to accept them and return them when he should be able to do so. M. de Gand, astonished at this generous act, wrote out an "IOU" without a single gracious word. I felt ashamed at the extraordinary way in which he accepted the good priest's offer; if I had been in his place, I should quickly have found words of acknowledgment of the great and most disinterested service he had rendered. I doubt whether M. de Gand ever returned those forty guineas.

After giving the money, the Abbé Derby withdrew, telling me again how glad he was to have been of service to a relative of his benefactor. Thus, for the second time, Heaven had sent someone to rescue me from almost desperate straits. The first had been the good *Curé* of Fribourg.

We hastened to pay our debts and to take our places in the coach for Falmouth; but our money failed again at Exeter, and we had not even enough to pay for our supper. Up to this time, M. de Gand had concealed his trouble from me, and, above all, the cause of his trouble, for it was brought about by his own misconduct; he confessed to me that before leaving Weymouth he had been obliged to pay a certain sum to two women of doubtful character. M. de Gand, who did not know a word of English, felt that he could not extricate himself from the false position in which he had again placed himself without my aid.

Having finished our supper, we had to pay for it; I begged the conductor of the stagecoach to lend us four guineas on the security of my companion's gold watch; M. de Gand gladly gave it up, having quite lost his head; I explained to the conductor that we had miscalculated the expenses of our journey. The watch, with its chain and seals and charms, was worth at least thirty guineas. The conductor made no difficulty, and we were able to continue our journey.

When we reached Falmouth, I wondered how M. de Gand expected to manage the sea voyage. I knew by this time that he had little prudence and less presence of mind, and not a halfpenny in his purse. He explained that he intended to ask the captain of the packet that was to take us to Lisbon, to allow us to pay on our arrival; we should then have no difficulty in cashing our drafts on Bilbao. This seemed practicable, and I went with him to the packet-office. Our suggestion was not at all well received; we were told it was usual to pay on embarking, and they mentioned a banker who would probably negotiate our drafts.

M. de Grand lost what little courage he had left; he shut himself in his room at the hotel to give way to his grief. As for me, I was younger, and had been the spoilt child of Providence, who had always sent me help when affairs seemed desperate. I ordered tea in the coffee-room, and, while taking my meal, I saw a man that I knew, though I could not remember his name, nor where I had seen him before.

The traveller also noticed me, and said in English, "You are a foreigner?"

I replied in French, "*Oui.*"

Then "*Parlons français,*" he said, and asked me where I was going and where I came from. I answered his questions and told him my name, when he said he had often met my mother at Lady Craven's in Altona. I also mentioned the name of my travelling companion, when the Englishman exclaimed, "Why, he is an intimate friend of mine! Take me to him."

No sooner had we entered the room than M. de Gand exclaimed, "Ah! my dear Griffits!" (Probably Griffiths.—Tr.)

Then I remembered his name quite well. M. de Gand related our adventures at great length, omitting some personal details, and merely speaking of our voyage to Portugal and our present difficulties.

"Don't worry," answered Mr. Griffits, "I am going there too with my wife and daughter. I have taken the large cabin of a boat sailing for Lisbon. There will be room for you two; I shall be delighted to oblige you in this way."

He placed his purse at his friend's disposal, and M. de Gand took from it what was necessary to redeem his watch, and to pay our expenses at the hotel until we sailed. Six days later, when the wind was favourable, we went on board a large three-masted Hamburgher. We were most hospitably entertained, and the society of the Griffits helped to pass our long voyage pleasantly; owing to contrary winds we were twenty-four days at sea.

I was anxious to get away from M. de Gand. I was afraid he might land me in a position from which I could not extricate myself. I made up my mind to go into the army. An opportunity soon presented itself. There were three regiments of French *émigrés* at Lisbon; they had retained the white cockade though in the pay of England, and one of them was commanded by the Duc de Mortemart.

Two days after we landed, I sought out Lieutenant-Colonel the Marquis de Mortemart. My mother had introduced me to him when he was passing through Altona on his way to Portugal, after leaving Condé's army. (The author explains later that the Duc de Mortemart was absent in England, and had left the regiment under the command of his brother.—Tr.) He received me very kindly, and admitted me into his regiment as a *chasseur noble* until I could receive a better appointment. With great delight, I went that very day to the barracks of the Val de Preïro, and slept in the room with the other soldiers.

Thus, I became a soldier when I was twelve years and three months old. What a rough experience!

What a dangerous position! Without anyone to guide me, with no father or mother at hand, no one but strangers who, as superior officers, were separated from a private like me. The night of December 20th, 1800, was the first that I spent in barracks.

CHAPTER 3

In Portugal

As we have seen, my military career began early, and I passed
through all the grades, entering the army as a private. Our uniform
was red, facings and collar of black velvet, white woollen lace, silver buttons stamped with three *fleurs-de-lis*, a red felt cap, the white
cockade, and the words "regiment of Mortemart" inscribed on the
plate of our shoulder-belt. I carried out all my duties, mounted guard,
went to drill at four o'clock in the morning, was present at parade
in the morning and afternoon; but, after the wretchedness of Altona,
I thought myself the happiest soldier in the regiment. When on the
march, or at manoeuvres, the *Chasseurs Nobles* were on the left of the
regiment; at other times, we fulfilled the duties of sergeants, bearing
their badge, and receiving their pay, a ration of bread, meat and wine,
and thirty-five *sous* a day.

Nearly all the *Chasseurs Nobles* had been officers, and our three
officers had been field-officers; we had eleven Chevaliers de St. Louis
in our ranks. An old sergeant was selected to instruct me; he taught
me theory, fencing, the use of arms, and the tone in which to give the
word of command. I enjoyed this life for four months, never dreaming,
or wishing, that my lot should be any better, and enchanted with my
new profession.

The Duc de Mortemart had been, travelling in England, leaving
his brother, the Marquis de Mortemart, in command of the regiment.

One day, when I was going to my post as orderly at the door of the
barracks, I met the sergeant-major of my company who told me that
another *chasseur* would take my place, and that I had been promoted
to be sub-lieutenant. At first, I thought it a stupid joke, but I was convinced when I heard my name mentioned in the order-of-the-day.
I went at once to thank the Marquis de Mortemart, and to ask him

how I had come by such a favour. He told me that a sub-lieutenant, M. de Verteuil, had been suddenly called away to the colonies to succeed to an estate; according to the English custom, he wished to sell his commission; he asked seventy *louis*. No sergeant, or *Chasseur Noble*, had such a sum in hand, and it must be paid ready money. M. de Mortemart had bought the commission for me, "delighted to render this service to a cousin belonging to the elder branch of the family."

He told me to order my uniform at once from the tailor of the regiment; my reception was fixed for the following Sunday, at parade, before Mass.

I returned to my quarters in a state of joy, bordering on delirium. During my whole life, I had met with nothing but misfortunes and poverty; I found myself suddenly delivered from both. I shall never forget the date, March 13th, 1801. There was still one difficulty to be got over. According to the English regulations, no one could be an officer till he was sixteen, and I was only twelve and a few months. But my eventful life had made me look old for my years, and I five foot high; so neither the officer who inspected the regiment at the end of every quarter, nor any of the other officers, took any notice of me.

By a singular chance, I was in the pay of England, wearing the white cockade, in a regiment stationed in Portugal under the command of one of my cousins. My captain, M. de Murat, was a brother of the Marquise de Pesay, an intimate friend of my mother, and my lieutenant, the Chevalier de Manny, had formerly served as captain in the Armagnac regiment under my father's command. So, I was most kindly treated by the officers in spite of the great difference of age.

England had three regiments in Portugal wearing the white cockade, and named after the colonels in command: Castries, Mortemart, and La Châtre, the latter also known by the name of the Loyal-*Emigré*.

A few months after my promotion, there was talk of war; we were to go by sea to Oporto, the Government fearing that this important post might be taken and destroyed by the Franco-Spanish army assembled on the frontier. We were crowded together on merchantmen of all nations, hired as transports by the English Government. After a week, however, the plan of campaign was changed, and we were disembarked, and ordered back to barracks. Three weeks later, we came out again, under orders to join the Portuguese Army encamped at Elva, twenty-five leagues from Lisbon, on the Spanish frontier. The Duc de la Foënça, Marshal-General of the Kingdom, a descendant of the Royal Family of Braganza, was in command of the Portuguese

Army. He was more than eighty years of age and in failing health, and led his little army from Alentejo with great caution, without firing a shot, although his forces were superior in numbers to those of the Spanish Army.

I must call this campaign a journey, as we were never under fire; no historian, no newspaper, has ever mentioned it; this silence, so distressing to my self-love, shall be broken. I will be the historian of my own glory, and instruct posterity; this explains why I insert this campaign in the list of those in which I served.

Marching with a regiment, I had an advantage over the travellers who preceded me, in that I had always food and lodging, and, above all, I was not robbed by brigands. What I say of Portugal applies also to Spain, which was no whit behind her neighbour in the matter of roads, hotels and brigands.

The three regiments of *émigrés* received orders to march at the end of June, 1801, when the heat was excessive. The first six leagues we went by boat, half a company in each boat. I was in command of the *Fregata*, and we set sail for some port the name of which I have forgotten; and followed the flower-decked banks of the Tagus, till we cast anchor at six o 'clock in the evening. In my inexperience as a sailor I had forgotten to take fresh water, and we suffered much from thirst, as the water of the Tagus is impure.

When the flotilla had assembled, the signal was given to land; the Mortemart Regiment went to Vallada, about half a league away, where we were to sleep. The Portuguese staff officers had not appeared, or sent word of our coming, so nothing was prepared, neither food nor billets. Half the regiment had to sleep in a large stable, the other half in the Corn Market; a granary over the market was assigned to the officers, and some Grey Friars gave hospitality to the staff officers and the band. It was late when everything was arranged, and we all settled down to sleep as best we could. Before four o'clock in the morning the drums beat the reveille, and we set off on a march of five leagues in beautiful sunshine.

We had scarcely left Vallada when we entered a most fertile plain, at least twelve leagues wide, watered by many canals fed by the Tagus, and protected by high wooded hills on the north and east. The pretty town of Santarem is situated in the midst of this plain. We were to remain there several days in order to give time for the English division to join us. It consisted of three regiments of *émigrés*, a battalion of artillery, also *émigrés*, commanded by M. de Rothalier, and five hundred

Light Horse; General Frazer was in command of this division, which formed the advance-guard of the Portuguese Army. Arriving at Santarem at eleven o'clock in the morning, under a broiling sun, we were amply compensated for our night at Vallada by the reception given to us in this charming town of eight thousand inhabitants.

We were drawn up in order of battle on the principal square, and surrounded by a curious and kindly population. We were assigned our billets. I was billeted at the house of Joao d'Alteca, who received me most hospitably, and made me promise, and even give my word of honour, that I would not take any meal away from his house. I yielded without much persuasion. Towards six o'clock in the evening, after parade, my host took me to see one of his friends who had a charming wife and two pretty daughters. Astonished at my youth, they asked me if there were many officers of my age in the regiment. After an excellent supper, a young *abbé* sat down to the piano, and sang some delightful *modinhas*, Portuguese ballads, then we danced. At midnight, we took leave of this amiable family, and I promised to come again the next night to a grand ball given in my honour.

I left Santarem with much regret, after having spent three days there. We passed on to Abrantes, halting one night on the way, and following the banks of the Tagus. At Abrantes I met with an adventure which wounded my pride. Arriving on the Saturday, we were all assembled at Mass on Sunday in the principal church of the town. The novelty of our troops, the splendour of our uniform, and, above all, the reputation of French soldiers for gallantry, had attracted many ladies out of curiosity to the Mass of the regiment. I noticed a remarkably beautiful lady among the crowd, and thought from her look that she was not indifferent to me, and, so vain was I, that I could not help relating it to one of my comrades, the Chevalier du Repaire, who was much older than I was; he had formerly been one of the Guard of Louis XVI, and had been seriously wounded at the door of the queen's apartments on the night of the 5th October.

He resolved to give me a lesson, both to moderate my good opinion of myself, and to teach me discretion in affairs of the kind. So, after the Mass, when I was assembling my company, he sent me a little note, written in Portuguese, saying that a lady who had taken a fancy to me wished to know if I would follow the bearer who had been charged to show me the way. I was to answer *si* or *naô*. I never doubted for a moment that it was the beautiful lady I had noticed at the Mass, and I answered, without hesitation, *si*. Carried away with the thought of my first good fortune, I asked no question of my guide. He stopped in front of a fine house and told me to go up the steps; going on before me, he led me into an anteroom full of lacqueys, very badly dressed, as is the custom in Portugal.

One of them opened the folding doors without announcing me, and I found myself in a large drawing-room, where I saw the Chevalier du Repaire, who introduced me to the Comtesse de Misquitella, at whose house he was billeted, a charming woman, but seventy years old. I was mortified at first. A little rascal of thirteen who thought he was going to his first tryst! I consoled myself with taking my share of a very good dinner; the countess overwhelmed me with kindness, partly because I was related to our colonel, and, still more, because she had known my mother very well, when she was staying with the Comtesse de Fonza, Mademoiselle de Canillac, who was a near relation of ours, and had married the Portuguese Ambassador in France.

We left Abrantes three, days later to join the Portuguese Army encamped near Ocrato, on the Spanish frontier. After remaining there, a fortnight, without making any advance or receiving intelligence of the enemy, there was talk of a retreat. This surprised us very much, as the Spaniards opposed to us were inferior in force, and had no thought of attacking, but on the contrary feared our advance. The Duc de Foënça, hearing that we were dissatisfied, assigned to us the most honourable post in a retreat, the rear-guard.

The retreat having been decided upon, it was our duty to manoeuvre to mask it. Our English dragoons were reinforced by six squadrons of heavy Portuguese cavalry. The latter galloped away at the sight of some Spanish scouts who had come to reconnoitre, and who fled when they saw our troops on the gallop. The Spanish Army, believing it was attacked, beat a hasty retreat.

In spite of there being no fighting, as the two armies had turned their backs on each other, we were seventeen hours on the march; there was no beaten track, and having no guides, we had lost our way.

When we reached Abrantes, we were stationed on the further side of the Tagus, with orders to defend the bridgehead, constructed by the English engineers. For a whole month, we stood resolutely awaiting the Spanish attack; at the end of this time we were informed that peace had been signed at Madrid through the mediation of Prince Lucien Buonaparte.

We gladly set out again for Lisbon. As we passed Santarem I did not fail to go to see my former host, Don Joao. Instead of embarking on the Tagus, the column followed the main road past Sacavem, and crossed the town of Lisbon, without halting, in order to take up winter quarters at Luz, about a league farther on.

Such was my first campaign; if it did not train me in the art of war, at least it enabled me to make a delightful tour in the interior of Portugal.

France and England having signed the Peace of Amiens, in which it was provided that regiments bearing the white cockade should be disbanded, we received orders to embark for Portsmouth, where we were to be disarmed; owing to continual storms the voyage was long.

The English carried out the disbandment with a generosity bordering on ostentation. Each officer received two years' pay and a donation of ten guineas; moreover, they were to be conveyed on English transports to some port on the continent. I received for my share £260. Every non-commissioned officer and private received two months' pay and a donation of two guineas.

CHAPTER 4

Paris and Odessa

The Duc de Mortemart asked me what were my plans. I replied that I was going back to France in the hope of finding my father, my grandmother de Morsan, or, at least, some member of my family.

I left Southampton for Havre in July, 1802, with the Marquis de Mortemart; a packet plied between these. ports once a week. The Marquise de Mortemart and her mother were awaiting us at their Château of Orcher, two leagues from Havre. I accompanied them to the Château de Meilleraye, nearer Rouen, and spent nearly a month with them. Then I went on to Paris to learn what had become of my people. The news was very sad. My father had died, November 3rd, 1801; my grandmother had left Villecresne, and was living in retirement with her nephew, d'Albignac; my mother and my brother Louis were at Odessa; my brother Victor had died of yellow fever in March, 1802, at Jacmel, in the Isle of San Domingo.

My father's affairs were in the hands of a lawyer. I went to see him, but as I was a minor and had no power of attorney from my mother or my brother Louis, and no certificate of my brother Victor's death, he sent me about my business. I wrote to my mother telling her of my arrival in Paris, and of all our misfortunes, and while awaiting her reply, I lived on the money I had received from the English War Office. I met the Marquis de la Tour du Pin, just arrived from St. Petersburg, and he confirmed the news that my brother Louis was sub-lieutenant attached to the staff at Odessa, and that my mother was living with him. I wrote a second letter, giving an account of my life since I left Hamburg, and I begged her to say if I should join her.

News of the important events had just reached Paris—the assassination of the Duc d'Enghien, the conspiracy of Georges Cadoudal, the tragic end of General Pichegru, the trial of General Moreau. The police, seeing plots everywhere, required that every citizen should be provided with a *carte-de-sûreté*. Now, in the matter of papers, I had my brevet of sub-lieutenant of the Regiment of Mortemart in the pay of England; less than this would have been enough to land me in prison.

I had discovered two great-aunts, sisters of my grandfather: Louise de Rochechouart, married to the Comte de La Touche; Camille de Rochechouart, married to the Baron de Montboissier, and a daughter of Mme. de Montboissier, the Comtesse de Mirepoix; they were all three living in the Château de Cersay in Brie, seeing only a few intimate friends. I asked if I might stay with them. I went out of Paris on Sunday afternoon, as if I were merely going for a walk, and no one took any notice of me at the barrier. After staying six weeks with these good aunts, I returned to Paris duly provided with a *carte-de-sûreté* quite in order, from the municipality of Cersay.

I put up in a little hotel at the corner of the Rue du Bac and the Rue de Grenelle, and on the following day, I received a letter from the notary of the Duchesse de Richelieu asking me to go and see him. I went at once. He gave me a letter from my brother Louis, saying that he had been appointed *aide-de-camp* to the Duc de Richelieu, and that my mother was in Poland with the Duchess de Nassau, and was very anxious that I should join her there. I set to work to try and procure a passport for Russia. The Russian Ambassador had just left Paris, and owing to the quarrel between the two countries passports were no longer given to Frenchmen for Russia; then I asked for one for Trieste.

Napoleon had just assumed the title of Emperor. Lists still remained open at all the municipal offices to receive the votes of the citizens. The lists bore at the top of the sheet on the left *No* in small letters, on that on the right *Yes* in a line by itself. You were asked to put your name on one of the sheets, and you did not obtain a passport for a foreign country until the Commissary of Police had certified your identity and good conduct. To put myself in order, I went to the commissary of my district. He suggested that before leaving I should record my vote. I hastened to sign Léon de Rochechouart on the page *Yes*; as soon as I had signed, my certificate was handed to me. Thus, I was one of the vast majority who elected Napoleon Emperor.

My passport being in order, I paid my debts, and left Paris on my birthday, September 14th, 1804, after having lived in Paris two years and two months. I was then sixteen. I was about to undertake a long journey across Europe to find the only remaining members of my family, with thirty-four *louis* in my pocket, what was left of my donation when I was demobilised; it never occurred to me that it would be impossible for me to take so long a journey with such slender means; however, in spite of my youth, my way of life had given me a certain amount of experience.

To husband my resources, I established myself in the panier of the diligence that was to take me to Milan; the name panier was given to the part of the coach now used for luggage, with this difference that, whereas the travelling trunks are protected by a large awning, the panier had no protection whatever. You lay full length beside the conductor, on straw more or less fresh; I had represented that I could not travel in a close atmosphere without being ill. The inns where the coach stopped were too dear for my purse, so I confided to the conductor that I had to be economical, and every time we stopped for a meal he pointed out a public-house where I fared very well and much more cheaply.

I passed the night in my *panier*, where, thanks to my youth, I slept better than I should have done in an uncomfortable hotel bed, with damp or dirty sheets. In spite of all these precautions and privations of all kinds, when I examined my purse on arriving at Milan I found I had spent eighteen *louis*, more than half my fortune, and I was far from being half way through my journey.

I had heard of the magnificent theatre of La Scala and the excellence of the acting; I went to the play. During the interval, I went up to the green-room, and was dazzled by the sight of twenty gaming tables all covered with gold. As it was impossible for me to get to Russia with sixteen *louis*, I resolved to hazard two *louis*; if I lost, I would go to Verona, and enlist in the Austrian Army. They were playing *faro*; I chose the knave of hearts, and thought of putting six *francs* on it, but the banker repulsed me scornfully, saying: "They only play for gold at my table."

Rather nettled, I said, "All right!" and put down a *louis*. My knave of hearts won the first time; I doubled the stake and won again. I left the whole a third time, with the same luck. I wanted to get back my eight *louis*, but there was a crowd around the table and I was not in time, especially as the banker had his own reasons for wanting me to try a fourth chance, when by the law of probabilities I ought to have lost. The knave of hearts came up a fourth time. I gathered up my sixteen *louis* and went on playing with insolent luck. "When I left the theatre, I had won forty *louis*, so I treated myself to a good supper.

Not wishing to tempt fortune too far, I made inquiries about leaving for Padua at once; the waiter knew a posting-master who was starting at three o'clock the next day and had a vacant place. I struck the bargain that very night, and then went to bed. The next day, before leaving, I visited the magnificent cathedral, the museum and the town.

On the following day, after luncheon at Cremona, we arrived in good time at Mantua, where we were to pass the night. Encouraged by my success at Milan I went to the Casino; they were playing *bitibi*; the bank, not so exclusive as that at Milan, accepted both silver and gold. My good luck continued, and I filled my pockets with gold and silver pieces of all sizes. An officer, standing near me, whispered to me: "I advise you not to play anymore, and to take care of your pockets as you go home."

I thanked him for his advice, and asked him to go back to the hotel with me, and stay for supper. He accepted without much pressing, and I ordered the best supper I could get, with Bordeaux and champagne. The waiter, who had seen me empty my pockets, promptly carried out my order.

Arriving at Verona next day, I spent the afternoon in visiting the antiquities of the town, which are very curious, especially the arenas. Thinking I had enough money to take me to Russia, I did not visit the Casino at Verona."

At Vicenza, a young Italian applied for the fourth seat in our carriage, in place of a traveller left at Verona. He spoke French very well, and as he was a native of the country, he knew it perfectly, and became my guide. I was truly grateful for his unwearied kindness; I paid rather dearly for it, as will be seen later. Thanks to my guide, I saw all the objects of interest in the pretty town of Vicenza; then, those of Padua, where we remained four days waiting for the boat for Venice. My companion's name was Luigi Capello; his mother, brother and four sisters were living at Padua; his father, formerly a doctor, had died a year ago, and he himself was returning from Pisa where he had completed his studies and taken the degree of doctor of medicine. He introduced me to his family, and as he had not yet begun to practise, he suggested that he should accompany me to Venice.

We embarked on the *Brenta* and had a most delightful journey. This canal passes by hundreds of villas where noble Venetians were living. They had lost their former greatness, but not their wealth. Thus, passing from one enchanting scene to another, we arrived at Venice, following the Grand Canal. We put up at the Scudio di Francia, one of the best hotels in the town. My companion bargained with the innkeeper that we should pay 4*fr.* 5*c.* each, per day, for board and lodging. We had a room on the first floor facing the Slavonian Quay—luncheon, dinner, and supper, all very well served;, living was cheap in Venice at that time.

The next day we began our sight-seeing, and thanks to my clever guide, I think I saw everything there was to be seen. The Doges' Palace and Senate House took up a whole day. I still recall the impression made upon me by the Great Council Chamber, with the seats still arranged round the table, and the papers placed before them. I visited St. Mark's, and other very beautiful churches, and the public and private museums. At the end of four days the quantity of fruit and ices I had consumed brought on an attack of fever, followed by two other attacks.

I was taken great care of by Dr. Capello, who thoroughly understood that kind of fever, which is very common in Italy in the autumn. When I was nearly convalescent I took my passage on the packet for Trieste; the young Capello took an affectionate leave of me, saying: "I am sorry I cannot go on with you to Trieste, I must return to my patients at Padua." Then, wishing me a pleasant voyage, he left me, with tears in his eyes. I felt the separation very much, as it deprived me of an amiable and cultivated companion. I thought I was deeply indebted to him, not only for his attention during my recent illness, but for the economical way in which he had managed my expenses at Venice.

While still under the influence of these feelings I went down to my cabin to unpack a few things. I had a large dressing-case in which I kept my money. When I arrived in Venice I had 62 *louis*; what was my surprise to find I had only 24 left! My expenses at Venice amounted to 4 *louis*, so 34 were missing; it could only be accounted for by clever pilfering on the part of Signor Capello. I remembered that, in the height of my fever, I had given him, without hesitation, the key of my dressing-case so that he might pay for medicine at the chemist's. My amiable Italian, with too much delicacy to take all my money, had deducted his fees as doctor and guide. I resolved to be less confiding another time.

I had hoped to embark at Trieste for Odessa, but as it was so late in the year no boats were running for the Black Sea, or even for Constantinople. The only course open to me was to turn northward again, and go to Vienna, and thence by Galicia and Volhynia to Russia; and, thanks to the charming Luigi, I had only 24 *louis*. I entrusted myself, without fear, to the good star that had protected me hitherto.

I at once began to look out for an opportunity of going to Vienna; in the course of my wanderings I met the Comte de Tilly. He had come from Lemberg, having left the Austrian Army in order to enter that of Naples. I told him my plans, and he very courteously offered me letters of introduction to some French officers of his former regiment. I accepted them with delight.

Having obtained a place in a *land-kutsche*, I left for Vienna. The journey by short stages from Trieste to Vienna was very long; but I met with no adventures or mishaps by the way, merely beating down the landlord's charges at every inn we came to, as I was much concerned at the state of my purse. But what an undertaking to go from Paris to Odessa, passing Venice and Vienna on the way, with only 36 *louis* when I started. (Only thirty-four *louis*, in fact, as mentioned earlier.—Tr.) In spite of the length of the journey, and my slender resources, I arrived at last. I should therefore be most ungrateful if I did not acknowledge the watchful care of Providence over me.

I was hoping to find an old friend of my mother, the Prince de Ligne at Vienna, but he was living with his daughter, the Princesse de Clary, at the Castle of Töplitz, in Bohemia. I only remained twenty-four hours in Vienna, and took the first opportunity of going to Cracow. When I arrived there, my purse was empty; I sold my watch and a few trinkets to a Jew, and was able to reach Lemberg half frozen; I had no cloak or cape, only a light overcoat, not warm enough for December. After paying the diligence I had only 38 *francs* left, and 350 more leagues to go!

The Comte de Tilly had especially spoken of the kindness of his intimate friend, the Chevalier de Bavière. I inquired where he lived, and as soon as he saw me he told me he had been captain in the regiment d'Armagnac, under my father's command. He greeted me affectionately, and asked me where I came from, where I was going, and if I were in want of money. I answered him quite frankly. Then he said: "Leave your inn, write to your mother, and come and stay with me while waiting for her answer; you will share my bed; as for food, we will arrange about that; it is settled, is it not!"

I thanked him from the bottom of my heart. This is exactly the fourth person that Heaven sent to my aid at most critical moments. I cannot speak too highly of the welcome given be by the Chevalier de Bavière, and the delicate manner in which the officers of the regiment treated me. They were nearly all *émigrés*, and messed together in a very humble way. They passed the word round, and I was the guest of each in turn, so that I should receive my mother's answer before I had exhausted their invitations.

I went to the police station to obtain a permit to remain in the town. The official, a young Pole, told me that my mother was just then staying with the Princess de Nassau at Kraminieck in Russian Poland. I wrote to her at once, telling her of my arrival, and the reason why I was detained in Lemberg. A few days later, a banker in the town informed me that I could draw upon his bank up to 100 *ducats*, about 1,200 *francs*; at the same time, he told me my mother would come to Lemberg soon. I continued to share the Chevalier's room and bed, but I did my utmost to return the hospitality of the officers who had invited me.

As the custom of the country required that every man of good family should be in uniform, I ordered a uniform of sub-lieutenant of the regiment of Mortemart.

A week later one of the Prince of Nassau's carriages appeared to take me to a *château* belonging to the princess, about a league from Lemberg, where I should find my mother. I threw myself into her arms; at first, she could not recognise in the young officer the little boy who had left her at Hamburg. After the first outpourings of affection we sat and talked until four in the morning; we had so much to say, and so many questions to ask each other. The nest day I returned to Lemberg with my mother; I was anxious to introduce the Chevalier de Bavière to her. She greeted him as a mother should greet her son's deliverer.

In 1815, I was fortunately able to obtain for this best of friends the post of Lord Lieutenant, at Condé, a position he had greatly desired.

A few days later we went to Tynna, in Podolia, the estate of the Princess of Nassau, the last descendant of the illustrious family of Sobieski; here we passed the rest of the winter. The good princess, wishing to show her affection for my mother, and her sympathy with her in her misfortunes, entrusted to her the government of two villages which belonged to her in the Crimea, on the banks of the Dnieper, and she gave her 400 *ducats* for the expense of establishing herself there. The rent-roll of these two villages could be reckoned at 500 *ducats*.

CHAPTER 5

At Odessa

The thaw having set in, we left to take possession of the property; the shortest route was by way of Odessa, which we reached after a three days' journey through the *steppes*. The Duc de Richelieu was at St. Petersburg, but I found my brother again, the companion in so many troubles of the past. My mother was eager to enter into possession of her estate, and set out at once. I remained with my brother, waiting for the return of M. de Richelieu, as I was unwilling to. do anything without consulting him.

In accordance with a custom of those days, the Duc de Richelieu had been betrothed, when only fifteen, to one of my cousins, the daughter of Count Louis de Rochechouart. The young Count de Chinon was to leave immediately after the betrothal ceremony, and travel for three years, accompanied by his tutor, the Ven. Abbé Labdan, whose advice, happily for the count, was very different from that of his grandfather. The Marshal de Richelieu, that sceptic *par excellence* in an unbelieving age, that spendthrift, who literally threw money out of the window—money not always too scrupulously obtained—had insisted upon taking charge of his grandson's education. The following anecdote was told me by M. de Richelieu himself.

One day, when he was eight years old, he went into his grandfather's study to wish him "Good morning." The marshal, who had been lucky at cards, at the king's table the night before, kissed the boy, saying: "See, here is a purse with forty *louis* for your little amusements." A fortnight later, in the same room, the marshal said: "I will fill up your purse; it must be empty."

"No, grandfather, I have still the forty *louis* you gave me."

The marshal opens the window, and seeing a beggar passing by, throws the purse to him, saying: "Look, my good man, here are forty *louis* that my grandson could not spend in a fortnight."

Thanks to the teaching of the Abbé Labdan, M. de Richelieu, always the great nobleman, knew how to be generous when occasion required; but—just the opposite to the marshal, who was called by his soldiers "the first marauder in France"—his integrity and straightforward conduct have remained proverbial in Russia.

The three years' absence having expired, the Count de Chinon returned to Paris, and found his betrothed wife a hunchback. The marriage ceremony took place all the same, usage demanded it; but when the bridegroom left the church he set out alone for Austria and Russia.

In 1790, when, on the death of his grandfather, he had become Duc de Fronsac, he obtained leave from the Empress Catherine II (with the consent of Louis XVI) to serve as a volunteer in the Russian Army, which was about to assault the fortress of Ismail; the Prince de Ligne, and two French officers, the Count de Langeron and Count Roger de Damas, had already arrived with the same object in view.

M. de Richelieu joined them at the camp in the evening of November 30th. The next day, accompanied by a Russian general, he went, very early in the morning, to pay his respects to the commander-in-chief. When he reached the camp, he saw a group of soldiers surrounding a naked figure that was jumping about and indulging in violent gymnastics on the grass, although there was an icy fog.

"Who is that madman?" asked M. de Richelieu of his companion.

"The *generalissimo*, Count Suvaroff."

The count, noticing a foreigner, for M. de Richelieu was in the uniform of the French Hussars, beckoned to him to approach. "You are a Frenchman, I see?"

"Yes, *mon Général.*"

"Your name?"

"The Duc de Fronsac."

"Ah! The grandson of the Marshal de Richelieu. Well, what do you think of my way of taking open-air exercise? There is nothing better for the health. I advise you, young man, to follow my example. It is a certain way to avoid rheumatism."

The general made two or three more capers and then returned to his tent, leaving his companion amazed at his reception.

On December 22nd, after a preliminary bombardment by a thousand cannon, the *generalissimo* sent forward his assaulting troops before daybreak. M. de Fronsac met a company who had lost their way, and had no officer to lead them. He took the command, and went to the support of General Lascy, who had been unable to take the bastion Hassan Pasha. Thanks to this help and above all to the bravery of the leader of the new corps, the position was carried and General Lascy entered the fort at the same time as the other assaulting columns. The heroic defence of the Turks exasperated the Russians, and according to historians 38,860 Turks were put to the sword, or otherwise slain. The Duc de Fronsac rescued the daughter of the *seraskier* (Turkish commander), but the unhappy girl, placed with a convoy of prisoners, was ruthlessly killed by the Cossacks, with her companions.

This carnage of defenceless people revolted the Duc de Fronsac, and after the victory he was nowhere to be found. Although General Lascy made many inquiries he was unable to learn the name of the officer who had come to his aid, and could not, therefore, recommend him for promotion. A few months later he met him at Prince Potemkin's, and at once drew up a special memorandum. The empress conferred on the Duc de Fronsac the title of Knight of St. George, of the Third Class, and in addition gave him a golden sword inscribed "For Valour."

Later, Paul I. appointed him colonel of a regiment of cuirassiers at St. Petersburg, and it was at this time that he became attached to the Tzarewich, Alexander. One night, learning that a village in the neighbourhood was on fire, the duke, without waiting for orders, went with his regiment to the assistance of the unhappy people. Paul I., regarding this as a breach of discipline, deprived him of his command, whereupon the duke rejoined Condé's army.

Not long after this the Emperor Paul was assassinated, and Alexander wrote to his friend, who had congratulated him on his accession, as follows:

> My Dear Duke, as I have a few minutes of leisure I employ them in writing to tell you how greatly I am touched by all you say in your letter. You know my feelings and my esteem for you, and may judge how glad I should be to see you in St. Petersburg, and to know that you were in the service of Russia, where you would be so useful. Receive the assurance of my most sincere attachment.
>
> Alexander
>
> Peterhof, June 17th.

In 1803, the new emperor entrusted to the Duc de Richelieu the government of the infant colony of Odessa. When I arrived there, he had just been called away to St. Petersburg, and we learned soon after that he had been appointed Governor-General of New Russia, a province as large as France, extending as far as the Caucasus, and comprising three Governments: Kherson, Ekaterinoslaff, and Taurida or the Crimea.

M. de Richelieu returned to Odessa on April 27th, 1805. My brother presented me to this kindest of cousins, who gave me a warm welcome. I at once began to call him "Uncle," a title which seemed to me more respectful. He asked news of his sisters, Mme. de Montcalm and Mme. de Jumilhac, and then questioned me as to my plans. I told him of my wish to enter the Russian Army. He replied: "I will attend to you as soon as the grave matters that will occupy all my time, are in order. Meanwhile arrange with your brother to take up your quarters here."

Relying on my brother to let me know when I ought to return to Odessa, I decided to rejoin my mother. She had written to us several times, and seemed well satisfied with her position. I passed Kherson, unhappily without stopping, and reached Achyllée, the village where my mother was living. She was from home. Her maid said: "*Madame* the Countess was not feeling well, and has gone to Kherson to see an Italian doctor; she took a young girl from the village with her, to wait on her. We have been expecting *Madame* every moment."

I spent the day in going over the property with the steward, who explained the various improvements in view. As my mother did not return I left the next day for Kherson, and stopped at the first tavern I came to, to inquire where I should be able to find her. No sooner had I entered than a terrible sight met my eyes. My poor mother lay dead, with her face uncovered (according to the Russian custom), on a sort of *catafalque*, covered with white sheets, and surrounded with candles. . . . . I had only learned that she was ill a few hours ago. Startled and terrified, I fainted away and did not recover consciousness till six hours later.

A French merchant, who had heard my servant mention my name, had me carried to his house, and his wife was watching by my bedside when I regained consciousness. He had seen my mother, and thinking her very ill, had written to us at Odessa; his letter must have arrived soon after I left. He undertook the arrangements for the funeral on the following day, and, though scarcely able to stand, I followed the coffin to the cemetery.

I was deeply grieved, although I had not been much with her. We were looking forward—my brother and I—to her being settled near us, so that we might console her declining years with our tender care. I regretted keenly that I had not been present during her last moments. She had died, surrounded by strangers, in a wretched Jewish inn, deprived of the consolations of her religion, and unable to embrace her children or give them her blessing. She had lost the power of speech, and succumbed in a few hours to a malignant fever; an Italian priest had been hastily summoned, and had given her extreme unction, but she was unconscious. She died on the 10th May, 1805, at the age of forty-eight and a few months.

I returned to Odessa, to mourn with my brother. Then we went back to Kherson to arrange all our mother's affairs, and especially to restore Achyllée to the Prince de Nassau. As we had informed him of our mother's death he sent an estate agent with full powers.

When I returned to Odessa, the Duc de Richelieu sent for me and said:

My dear cousin, I am going to make arrangements for you to join the Russian Army. Stay with me, like your brother. In a few months, I shall know what you will be fit for; meanwhile, learn Russian and distract your mind.

From this time, until his death, I never left the duke, except during the campaigns of 1813 and 1814, and I managed his household all the time.

When we had wound up our mother's affairs my brother and I had each 200 *ducats*. The Duc de Richelieu provided me with food and lodging, so there was no need for me to hurry.

CHAPTER 1

In the Service of Russia

In the spring (1806), there was talk of war with Turkey. A great Council met at Odessa to discuss the plan of campaign. Several generals, or *aides-de-camp* of the Emperor Alexander, were staying with M. de Richelieu. The day was devoted to affairs of State; in the evening, they played cards and smoked until midnight; the Russians even then smoked a great deal.

It was at this time that M. de Richelieu wrote to the Minister of War, at St. Petersburg, mentioning my brevet of sub-lieutenant of the regiment of Mortemart, asking that I should be admitted as sub-lieutenant into the Russian Army, but that I should remain with him as *aide-de-camp*. As it took six weeks to obtain an answer, he suggested that I should avail myself of my last weeks of freedom to visit Constantinople with the two sons of General Fenshaw. He said: "Make the most of your opportunity. Here are 100 *ducats* for the little expedition."

General Fenshaw, who was English by birth, had entered the Russian service when very young, and had been appointed Commander-in-Chief by the Empress Catherine II. Now retired, he held the post of Civil Governor of Kaffa, the ancient Theodosia. I had met his sons during the wedding festivities of d'Olonne, and, as we were about the same age, we became great friends.

The boat left the next day for Constantinople; the crossing of the Black Sea was rather rough, but as we entered the Bosphorus the waves suddenly became calm, and the current carried us rapidly towards Pera, where the channel widens and becomes an immense lake; we were enraptured with the view that lay before us. As soon as we had cast anchor opposite the arsenal of Top-Khaneh, a sloop conveyed us to the quay, with our luggage; for this barbarous people do not require a foreigner to submit to any quarantine, or formalities of custom-house, police, health, etc.; no question is asked; no one takes any notice of you.

After we had landed and were settled in our hotel we called on the Russian Ambassador M. d'Italinski, who undertook to obtain for us the firman necessary to enable Franks (a word used to denote all who were not Mussulmans) to see the mosques. A field-officer of the *janissaries* and two *janissaries* accompanied us on our tour. The pleasure of seeing this strange town is dearly bought; first of all, you must make a handsome present to the officer, and then, proportionate presents to every custodian. It cost us each 180 *francs* to see four mosques, including St. Sophia, the courtyard of the palace, called the Old Serail, and the menagerie which is there.

My stay in Constantinople was prolonged as the Russian Ambassador wished me to take back important dispatches. I was in no way reluctant, and availed myself of the opportunity to make some delightful excursions in the town and neighbourhood, and even in Asia Minor. Every evening we had a dinner, a ball, or theatricals, at the house of some consul, or European merchant, and this, although war between Russia and Turkey threatened to break out at any moment.

One evening, as I was going to Pera to dine, M. d'Italinski sent for me and said:

Here are dispatches for Odessa of the highest importance; send word to your servant to finish packing your trunks, while I give you some instructions. A Russian brig of war is waiting for you; the wind is favourable for going up the Bosphorus.

Three hours later I was sailing towards Odessa in delightful weather, and on a calm sea. My dispatches were landed. As for me, I had to undergo a thirty days' quarantine, which the Duc de Richelieu rigorously enforced, because some cases of plague had been reported at Constantinople. After taking me to the *lazaretto* the brig continued its course to Sebastopol, the port to which it belonged.

The dispatches were indeed of the first importance; diplomatic relations between Russia and Turkey were to be broken off. . . . When I left the *lazaretto* I found my commission of sub-lieutenant, and a letter from the Minister of War appointing me *aide-de-camp* to the Duc de Richelieu.

Three days later we entered upon a campaign against Turkey. The forces under General Michelson were divided into three distinct army corps; the first, under the Duc de Richelieu, with the Count de Venanson as Chief of Staff; the second, under General de Meyendorff, the third, under the orders of the commander-in-chief.

Our column crossed the Dniester by a bridge of boats, constructed under my brother's direction, entered Bessarabia, and occupied the Turkish fort Akkerman, without firing a shot. . . . At the same time Yusuf Pacha opened the gates of Bender to General Meyendorff; the commander-in-chief entered Moldavia; Bessarabia and the Boudjak remained in the hands of Russia, with the exception of the fortress of Ismail. Orders from St. Petersburg forbade the attack being pushed further. Two army corps remained, the one on the Pruth and the other on the Danube. M. de Richelieu returned to Odessa with his staff, leaving the Count de Langeron in command.

In February, 1807, three Moldavian *boyars* came, as an embassy from their council, to ask the Duc de Richelieu "to honour their capital with his august presence"—the exact words, written in French. He accepted the invitation, and they returned in all haste to make preparations.

M. de Richelieu's suite consisted of two *aides-de-camp* (a young Livonian and myself), a French physician. Dr. Scudéry, a Russian Secretary, and seven servants; we were conveyed in three carriages, with six horses each. Leaving Odessa, we spent the night at Tyraspol, on the Dniester, opposite Bender; the next day we went on to Kishenev, the chief town of Moldavia, where MM. Balche and Canons were waiting, charged by the council to welcome the Duc de Richelieu and escort him to Yassy; also, to order the post-horses required for our carriages.

Moldavia is a delightful country; the soil is very fertile and the people afford an interesting study; they are of Roman origin, as may easily be seen from the beauty and regularity of their features and their robust constitution, especially in the case of the peasants. Were it not for their language, it would be difficult to recognise the descendants of the rulers of the world in these people with their meek, timid, and cringing manners—the result of long servitude. The ordinary language of Moldavia is a mixture of Latin with Turkish, Slav and Greek words, introduced by their conquerors.

Before reaching Yassy, we went to see the famous wall of Trajan, a rampart twenty-five leagues long, behind a wide moat, built by those indefatigable Roman *legions* as a barrier between their soldier-colonists and the neighbouring hordes.

At Yassy, we stayed at the residence of M. Costaki Balche, a brother of the deputy who had come to meet us. The town was full of generals and staff-officers of all ranks for the Russians still carried on warfare in the ancient manner. The troops took up their winter quarters, and during the interval of rest, the list of officers, the effectives, and the military stores were reorganised. Napoleon, unsparing of men as he was, could not adapt himself to this method, too slow for his great genius; he called it out of date and fought at all seasons of the year when it seemed to his advantage. He paid a terrible penalty five years later. Had he followed the old method at the time of his expedition to Russia and taken up winter quarters at Smolensk, he would have been spared the disaster that overtook his hitherto invincible army.

Happily, for us, this method had not reached the banks of the Pruth, and for a whole month balls, concerts, theatricals and most *recherché* dinners followed one another without interruption.

I will try to give an idea of society at Yassy at that time. The men had long beards and wore *kalpaks*, a sort of turban in fur; they were clad in the richest stuffs, and shod with yellow Turkish slippers; in a word they followed Oriental customs. They retained the wearisome gravity of the Turk, but in imitation of European civilisation, they allowed (contrary to their wishes and their customs) unlimited freedom to their women, who did not fail to abuse it. They adopted the latest fashions from Paris or Vienna—even their furniture came from Paris—and they imitated the manners of the ladies of the Court of the former Kings of France.

One day, Mme. Costaki Balche received us at noon in bed, under pretence of migraine. She wore a *coquettish* cap, an embroidered jacket adorned with magnificent lace, and rose-coloured bows; a priceless cashmere shawl, covered the bed, and in every corner of the room were beautiful porcelain vases filled with rare flowers; a skilfully arranged half-light completed the dramatic effect. . . . At the end of three weeks we began to think of returning to our duties. Important military operations were to begin in a few days on several points simultaneously.

Before returning to Odessa, M. de Richelieu wished to see the fort of Ismail, the scene of his first campaign. Leaving Yassy, we passed through Bessarabia and the Boudjack, to Faltchi and Tobak, crossing the Danube at Kilia, and following the right bank of the river until almost opposite Ismail. General Meyendorff was blockading the fortress with 10,000 men, the remainder of his army corps occupying important positions. The Count de Langeron was in command of a division encamped on the right bank of the Danube, with the flotilla under his orders. He established his headquarters on the largest of these gunboats, thus having a much more healthy abode than on the banks of the river, which is wide and muddy in this part; the vapour arising from the marshes, which are covered every night with an icy mist, is a frequent cause of fever. M. de Langeron assigned us a gunboat to live in.

We arrived in time to witness the attack on Tchétal Island, formed by two arms of the Danube, and situated opposite the fort. . . . My brother, who held the post of engineer on the staff of M. de Langeron, had been charged to place a battery to silence the enemy artillery that protected the island. He did this during the night, and at daybreak, the Duc de Richelieu and the Count de Langeron, with a numerous staff, arrived. The officer in command of the battery at once gave the signal to fire; the Turks, surprised at first, quickly replied from the bastion of Hassam-Pacha with guns of large calibre.

Some of our soldiers, hearing the whistling of the balls over their heads, ducked, and I might have done the same, going under fire for the first time, if I had not been warned by my brother. Being on my guard, and thinking of nothing else, I did not follow my neighbours' example. The Duc de Richelieu, glancing at me and seeing my correct attitude, said:

This is your baptism of fire. Now you know what it is like, it will not affect you.

I left the battery to accompany the commander-in-chief on a reconnaissance; he wished to get near the ramparts, and form an idea of their strength. We reached the glacis without meeting any scouts or advanced posts; the town might have been deserted—when suddenly a hundred horsemen, splendidly mounted, came out at a gallop. They made our Cossack scouts fall back. At the same moment we were greeted with several volleys from the guns; the balls passed over our heads. . . . There were several cavalry charges on both sides, without result.

I saw then, for the first time, what I often witnessed later during our expeditions to the Caucasus—the desperate valour of the Turkish cavalry. Five or six hundred horse tried to break our infantry, which was formed in two squares. Vigorously repulsed by a fire at close range, they turned round, but re-formed a short distance away, to attack another face of the square. Receiving another volley, and exasperated at being unable to make a breach in this human wall, ten of the most intrepid rushed forward as far as the bayonets of the first line; turning their horses round, they made them back, rearing so as to throw both men and horses upon our soldiers, thus hoping to make a way for their comrades; but they fell victims to their heroism without being followed. . . . The weakness of our artillery and effective force obliged us to defer the attack of the Isle of Tchétal for a time. The Duc de Richelieu returned to Odessa, to take the command of an expedition on the coast of the Black Sea, on the borders of Circassia.

General Meyendorff's army not being large enough to defend the vast extent of territory that had fallen so quickly into his hands, he could not rely on the Christians of Moldavia and Wallachia, and must have distrusted the Mussulmans in the event of a reverse. He therefore adopted a very rigorous course, treating these poor Tatars—shepherds and small farmers, with their wives and children and flocks—as if they were soldiers who had surrendered. The entire population, regarded as prisoners of war, and escorted by three regiments of irregular Cossacks, were deported in the depth of winter to Kursk, 800 leagues away.

Out of 15,000 souls, divided in three columns, who were thus sent to the North-East of Russia, only two-fifths reached their destination; the rest perished on the way from fatigue, privation and cold. This course was by no means necessary. The Tatars of the Boudjak, a very peaceful people, would never have attacked the Russians, even in the event of a retreat.

CHAPTER 2

In Circassia

We were to attack Anapa by land, and the fleet under the Marquis de Traverset was to leave Sebastopol, and bombard the town from the sea. The Great Russian Black Sea Fleet, as well as the fine naval bases of this part of the Empire—Nicolaïeff, the dockyards of Kherson and Sebastopol—were under the Marquis de Traverset. Thus, two Frenchmen governed this great province for the *Tzar*. Alexander had given them the fullest powers, convinced as he was of their talents, their loyalty, and above all, of their strict integrity. He had even given them *carte blanche* in certain cases, a rare favour on the part of an absolute Sovereign, so jealous of his authority. The telegraph informed us at Taman that the fleet of twelve vessels had sailed.

M. de Richelieu, at the head of his division, immediately crossed the Kuban—a river with a strong current which forms the boundary between Russia and Circassia—without encountering the least resistance. He marched on Anapa along a level shore, firm enough to bear the weight of the artillery; his right was protected by the sea, his left skirted the most beautiful meadow land. It was in the middle of May, in glorious weather, under the rays of an Eastern sun, the air laden with the scent of the flowers that abound in these meadows in spring. All this, and the thought that I was entering Asia, impressed my youthful mind with a delight that will never fade from my memory.

The army marched during the night and halted, at sunrise, four *versts* from the fort—a *verst* corresponds to our *kilometre*; it then left the shore, and went up a gentle slope to a plateau commanding the town. The infantry drew up in order of battle, facing the sea; the cavalry on the left flank, the artillery massed in the centre.

The admiral, on board a corvette, came forward beyond the line of battle and gave the signal; the rear-admiral replied; at once, all the vessels began to approach the fort and defiled, firing a broadside at about half a cannon's range of the fortifications, the upper town, and the port. Each vessel, having executed this manoeuvre, stood out to sea, tacked about, and returned to salute the unhappy town with a second volley. This terrible bombardment annihilated the batteries, ramparts, houses and public buildings, and blew up two powder magazines. The *pacha* had not expected the attack; he withdrew with the garrison into the thickets of some woods about a *verst* from the town, and the whole population followed.

A third broadside was about to be fired, when the admiral discovered, by means of his telescope, that the town was deserted. Instead of giving us the signal agreed upon, he ordered two companies of marines to land, wishing to give the navy the glory of completing the victory. . . . But our Cossacks, the best scouts in the world, signalled to us that the town was evacuated. Then the Duc de Richelieu put himself at the head of his cavalry, and set off at a gallop, ordering the infantry to follow as quickly as possible. He entered the town at the same moment as the marines. Blinded by the smoke of the burning town, which prevented the cavalry and marines from recognising each other, a few shots were exchanged, fortunately without killing anybody, though eight or ten men were wounded; a bullet rebounded and struck the flap of my saddle as I was trying to stop our men from firing.

Our first care was to extinguish the flames, and save as many houses as we could so that we might billet our troops. The great mosque was undamaged by the fire, and M. de Richelieu and his staff took up their quarters there. For my share of the booty, I picked up a magnificent copy of the *Koran*, a MS. with illuminated letters, adorned with vignettes and arabesques of extreme delicacy, and bound in a very original manner. A few years later, Ramis-Pacha was passing through Odessa, and I had the unlucky idea of showing him my book. He had scarcely glanced at it, when he said:

> Give me this book. It belonged to a holy man who has enriched it with pious reflections; it ought to be in the hands of a believer.

He made his request to the Duc de Richelieu so urgently that I had to surrender my prize.

The town was still burning, and we could not account for the perfume that filled the air; an extraordinary thing, for a burning town has generally a most intolerable smell. It came from the palisades of cedar wood and rosewood, such as we use for making lead pencils. High columns of smoke scented the air. It was with difficulty that we checked the fire that was destroying these precious palisades. I picked up a huge piece of one of them, and when I got back to Odessa I had it made into a dressing-case by a French cabinet maker. I lost this dressing-case, which I greatly prized, during the crossing of the Berezina in November, 1812.

It is difficult to form an idea of the appearance of this great town, deserted by all its inhabitants; the houses and shops open, and choked with furniture and goods that the owners had not been able to take with them. With the exception of cats, we did not find a living creature; dogs, horses, cattle and sheep had followed the inhabitants.

Leaving a garrison to defend the town, the Duc de Richelieu returned to Odessa. The emperor had just assigned to him the duty of provisioning the Army of Moldavia, and this necessitated his being on the spot. I asked him to let me remain with General Gangueloff, who had been left in command of the Expeditionary Force, with orders, now that Anapa was taken, to go into the interior of the country to give a severe lesson to all the little independent princes whose warlike habits recalled those of our feudal chiefs in the thirteenth and fourteenth centuries. Regardless of treaties, signed two years before, and without any declaration of war, they had improvised a claim on the lands of the Zaporogue Cossacks, carried off many head of cattle, and seized some of their wives and children and sold them in Cabardie.

M. de Richelieu hesitated. He had just received a dispatch from the commander-in-chief of the Army of the Caucasus, announcing that the eldest son of the Duc d'Aumont (brother-in-law to the Duchesse de Richelieu) had been killed during the assault of a miserable little town. As captain of a regiment of infantry forming the advance-guard, Ernest d'Aumont was leading his troops up the ladder, when a stone hurled from the top of the wall fell on his head.

M. de Richelieu told me at the same time of the death of Halbrecht, his first *aide-de-camp*, who had been attached to his person for five years. Halbrecht had obtained permission to remain with my brother before Ismaïl, and had just fallen in a night attack on the Isle of Tchétal; the attack had failed, the scaling ladders having proved too short.

All this bad news made a deep impression on the kind duke. I was his only *aide-de-camp* left, and his relative. My youth appealed to his sympathy; he feared an accident, yet wished to see me rise in the army; it seemed a favourable opportunity; the expedition could only last a few days on account of the small quantity of food and ammunition we could take with us. At last he consented to let me accompany General Gangueloff.

We left Anapa in the evening. M. de Richelieu parted from us at the end of the first league, and took the road back to Taman, while we turned to the right and entered the interior of the country. It was the end of June, and the stifling heat compelled us to march by night. For guides through this unknown country, bristling with mountains and covered with thick woods, we had the Cherkesse princes, enemies of those we were about to chastise, the *murzas*, Tatar nobles, and, above all, the valiant Haslam-Gheraï.

A little before sunrise we halted in a delightful meadow, watered by the Atacoum River, in order to allow the infantry to rest. Although the Cossack scouts had not signalled the presence of the enemy, the general took every precaution; he had fought for some years in the Caucasus, and knew how the warlike inhabitants of the mountains take advantage of the least imprudence to fall upon the unwary troops and annihilate them.

An old Circassian, Peck Murza, said to us:

We are not far from the residence of Seffer-Bey, the head of the expedition that carried off the Cossacks' wives and cattle. The meadowland, where we are resting, belongs to him. The *aoul* (Tatar village) is well worth pillaging.

The general ordered me to take fifty *chasseurs* and as many Cossacks, and raid this village. He said:

Be prudent. Do not attack with your whole force; send Cossack scouts to reconnoitre the village, and ascertain the presence, or absence, of the inhabitants. Beware of ambuscades. Always keep a strong reserve with you. Above all, do not despise your enemy, if he should attempt the least resistance. I warn you, these fellows are brave and past masters in the art of war. Go, and may God protect you! I will keep a detachment ready to extricate you in case you should have too many Cherkesses on your hands.

The general knew I was taking command for the first time in face of the enemy, and that I was unaccustomed to warfare in the Caucasus. The responsibility led me to make it a point of duty to follow his wise counsel.

On leaving the camp, my guide took a path to the left. Soon after, I entered a thick wood, which fortunately became less dense within a short time. We then found ourselves among large trees, sufficiently far apart to enable us to see what was happening around us. Three Cossacks went in front with the guide; four others followed within pistol range. Six Cossacks on each side covered the flanks. I marched thus for about half a league, when I came in sight of the village. My seven Cossacks of the advance guard entered with their lances lowered. Being prudent, they did not alight, though hungering for pillage. They wished to find out if the houses were deserted or not.

It was well they did this, for after they had passed the first house a shot was heard, and a young man leaped from the flat roof with a shrill cry that rang in my ears for a long time. "It is the cry of alarm," said my guide. "Be on your guard."

I at once ordered my little troop to have their muskets ready. Scarcely had this been done, when a lively fusillade broke out between my soldiers and some thirty Circassians who were much more expert than my skirmishers. I ordered half of my Cossacks to dismount and leave their horses in charge of one or two of their comrades in the centre . . . in a moment four of my men were wounded; the enemy could take aim deliberately from behind the trees.

I asked my guide if the other side of the village were not more open. He replied that about a hundred paces farther on there was a large field without trees. I gave the order to cease firing, and sent a non-commissioned officer and fifteen *chasseurs* to occupy the field. I followed with, the rest of the troop. This manoeuvre entailed further losses; my bravest sergeant was killed and six *chasseurs* (or Cossacks) wounded by a *mollah* in a green turban; his son loaded one gun while he fired with the other. My poor sergeant was shot in the heart, while trying to capture the wretched *mollah*. His death was quickly avenged; taking advantage of the moment when the *mollah* was changing his gun, a Cossack ran him through with his lance.

This fiend being killed, his companions gave way. I left the wood in hot pursuit of the remaining combatants, and gained the meadowland where I was in comparative safety; soon they disappeared altogether. Fearing lest I might make another false step, I halted surrounded by my skirmishers and sent twenty Cossacks to search the village, bring away what they could and set fire to the houses. As they were setting fire to them, cries showed that the women were still there; I sent to rescue them. We took 30 cattle, 6 horses, 150 sheep and a quantity of barley; also 8 women, 5 babies in arms, and 3 men who were ill, among them the brother of the chief of the *aoul*—such was the result of my expedition.

The *chasseurs* and Cossacks divided the clothing and equipment among them; for my share, I kept the poignard found at the girdle of the terrible *mollah*. The village having been reduced to ashes, I collected the booty and began the retreat. I was anxious to get out of the wood, where comparatively small forces might have stopped us. The wounded were able to walk; the body of the dead sergeant was placed on a stretcher hastily formed of branches. General Gangueloff, having heard the firing, sent me a company as reinforcements, together with a surgeon and a wagon for our wounded and for the booty that might be a difficulty to me. The soldiers wished to carry the stretcher on which lay the body of their sergeant; in spite of their fatigue, they insisted on paying him this mark of respect as far as the camp.

On my return, the general congratulated me on the complete success of the expedition. The capture of three men, including the brother of Seffer-Bey, gave promise of a favourable exchange of prisoners. As for the women prisoners, I had looked forward to seeing some beautiful Circassians. Complete disillusionment! They were all old and ugly. One of them was recognised as the wife of a Cossack, carried away some months before.

We left our bivouac a little before midnight on a punitive expedition to the territory of Khalabat-Aglou, the assassin of our friend Haslam's father and the principal author of the last disaster to the Cossacks. The total absence of roads rendered the march very fatiguing; we had to clear our way through woods and dense thickets and to construct a sort of bridge for the artillery over every stream. At last, at nine o 'clock in the morning, we came in sight of the chief's house. The Cossacks attacked the main village without waiting for the general's orders, and set fire to it in several places at once. All the inhabitants fled to the neighbouring woods. After having set fire to several more villages and captured a great many horses, cattle and sheep, we recrossed the Couban and returned to Russia eight days after we left Anapa.

Leaving General Gangueloff's force, I made my way to Odessa, having been entrusted by the general with the report of the expedition. We had burned more than 300 houses, captured 500 head of cattle and brought back 106 prisoners of both sexes, destined to be exchanged for Russians who had been carried into captivity during previous raids. To these details he added the amount of our losses, and recommendations for promotion. I was recommended for the rank of lieutenant.

CHAPTER 3

Life in Odessa and the Provinces

On returning to Odessa, I resumed my duties in attendance on M. de Richelieu. A nephew of General Cobley, *commandant* of the town of Odessa, named Stempkowski, took the place of Halbrecht, who had been killed before Ismail. We divided the work as follows: the first *aide-de-camp*, a captain, was military secretary; he received the reports of the troops under the command of the governor-general. I was second *aide-de-camp*, and directed the personal affairs of the duke, his correspondence in French, his finances, his household and stables, also the works of the improvement of Odessa, paving the streets, planting trees, laying out walks and the management of the Casino. Stempkowski took the third place, with no definite duties; he was an excellent comrade, and I shall often have occasion to speak of him.

During my wandering and unhappy life, my education had been much neglected. I had only a very superficial knowledge of history and literature. The town of Odessa possessed a magnificent library, which supplied me with books. In my leisure time I studied French, English, Italian, German and Russian literature. I spoke all these languages fluently. I also studied ancient and modern history. My time was fully occupied.

The Duc de Richelieu arranged his day as follows: he rose at six, summer and winter, and took a cup of *café au lait* at eight o 'clock; then, except on Sundays and festivals, he gave audience for an hour to anyone who wished to see him; after this he worked with his three civil secretaries till 12.30. At one he dined, then worked, or went out, until evening; he had supper at nine, and went to bed at eleven.

We took breakfast privately, each in his own room; at dinner covers were laid for twenty, of whom fourteen were members of the household, *viz.*, the three civil secretaries for the Governments of Kherson,

Ekaterinoslaff and Taurida, the secretary for the town of Odessa, the chief of staff of the division with two officers, three *aides-de-camp*, a French doctor, named Scudéry, who lived with us, my brother, and lastly the venerable Abbé Labdan, formerly tutor to the duke.

After having completed the education of the Duc de Richelieu, this excellent priest took charge of that of the Duc d'Enghien. He became insane on receiving news of the execution of his pupil. M. de Richelieu received him at Odessa, and took the most affectionate care of him. The other guests were foreign consuls, distinguished visitors to the town, or merchants. There were not so many at supper, and it was possible then to talk more freely with the duke; the secretaries for civil affairs and the staff were not present, but the duke always invited some of the residents of Odessa.

I had the direction of many servants for the upkeep of the house. There were fifteen horses in the stables, and I had also the management of the vegetable and pleasure gardens, situated about a *verst* from the town. I was very young, and surrounded by dependents who literally paid court to me as the nephew of the governor-general; they begged my influence with the duke, and sought to gain it; they offered me their services. What a dangerous position! What a temptation to take advantage of it, and even abuse it! If I had not had constantly before my eyes the example of the strictest integrity and the most perfect disinterestedness!

During my stay at Odessa I had sent an excellent French cook to M. de Richelieu to take the place of one Schultz, whose story I will tell later. Food was very cheap at Odessa; butcher's meat of excellent quality was three *sous* the pound; plenty of fish came from the Black Sea, game from the *steppes*, fruit and vegetables from the Crimea, a country deservedly celebrated for their production. Later on, the garden, laid out under my direction, amply supplied all our needs. Wines from France and Spain were admitted without any duty.

I spent the autumn in laying out the garden and arranging the salt-water baths, which were already attracting numerous visitors. (The frequent reference to baths throughout the narrative shows that the author had never forgotten his experiences as a child at Caen.—Tr.) During the winter, I built a theatre and assembly-rooms.

In the spring of 1808 the Duc de Richelieu resolved to travel through the provinces under his rule in order to visit the colonies, settle the civil government of each province, and inspect the troops encamped in New Russia, who formed (including the Cossacks) an effective force of 40,000 men. He appointed me to accompany him.

He began his tour by inspecting the colonies near Odessa, who numbered 15,000 souls, distributed as follows: 14,000 lived in villages within a radius of five leagues of the town, all bearing German names that reminded the colonists of their native land—Maintz, Strasburg, Marienthal, etc.; the remaining thousand lived in the suburbs of Odessa; their houses were all built alike, each with a garden; this arrangement had been very expensive, it is true, but it brought these colonists—locksmiths, carpenters, masons, etc.—close to the town, which was an advantage to everyone.

In order to people her immense *steppes*, the Empress Catherine II had attracted numerous colonists by granting them very advantageous conditions. To obtain agriculturists, or artisans, she had agents along the banks of the Rhine, empowered to provide emigrants with money to enable them to make the journey, packed in their large German wagons, drawn by four horses. On their arrival in Russia, the committee for the colonies gave to each household a stone-built house, a cow, a yoke of oxen, and a cart, and, in addition, a payment for the first year of their settlement, that is to say, until the head of the family should be in a position to supply the needs of his household by means of his harvests, or his work.

The father received so much a day, the mother rather less, and the children in proportion to their ages. At the end of ten years the house, garden and lands became their property. The committee then rendered an account of all that had been supplied, and the colonists paid interest on it, at 5 *per cent.*, for fourteen years. They were not subject to conscription for twenty-five years, and were not even obliged to allow the soldiers passing through the village to be billeted on them. The Mnémonists came to Russia with all their riches, and a decree of the emperor exempted them for ever from military service. When a certain number of families had formed a village, they chose a name for it, and elected a *burgomaster*, who, once in office, conducted the correspondence with the colonial committee.

This committee consisted of a president, treasurer, secretary and eight councillors; it sat at Ekaterinoslaff, the centre of the German immigration; a sub-committee at Odessa administered the affairs of the colonies in that town and in the civil government of Kherson.

Nearly all the colonists were German—from Swabia, Baden or Würtemberg. The Mnémonists belonged to the Anabaptist sect, known in Germany by the name of the Moravian Brothers; they came from Königsberg in East Prussia. Their religion expressly forbade them to kill a man, and therefore to make war. They were very rich, many of them possessed a hundred thousand *thalers*; the King of Prussia only granted them permission to sell their land on condition that they paid to the State a twentieth part of the produce of the sale.

The Duc de Richelieu had been instrumental in settling the Tatars Nogaïs; there was a special administration for them, presided over by the Comte de Maisons, formerly President of the *Parlement* of Rouen, who devoted the last thirty years of his life to their welfare. He was untiring in his constant care of them, and would never receive either salary or compensation. The emperor asked him what he could do to show his appreciation of his services.

The count replied: "I should like to give my name of Mesnil-Maisons to the principal village of these good Tatar Nogaïs."

The Tatars were never able to pronounce these two French words; a special *ukase* was issued translating them into the Tatar language. In order to induce these nomads—descendants of the ancient Moguls, conquerors of the East—to settle down, M. de Richelieu had a mosque and a house for the *mollah* and his family built in each of their camps. Each horde had a *mollah*, and, not wishing to leave him, they settled down near him and the mosque; then the government built houses for these nomads, who possessed many flocks. Instead of providing them with cattle, as in the case of the other colonists, the government bought cattle from them to give to the Germans; the money they thus received was a further inducement to them to accept a settled life.

Finally, there were Russian colonists belonging to different religious sects, some Bulgarians driven out of their country by the exactions of the Turks, and some Greeks. Altogether they formed 203 villages, distributed as follows: 106 German, 30 Tatar-Nogaïs, 13 Bulgarian, 21 Russian dissenters, 25 Greek and 6 Jewish, (apparently the Count de Rochechouart has omitted two villages from his list, as these only number 201), making altogether a population of 300,000. To these must be added the artisans settled in the towns of Kherson, Odessa, Ekaterinoslaff, Theodosia and Taganrog.

Each colony preserved the free exercise of its religion, and the municipal organisation in use in their native land; thus the Germans nominated their pastors and *burgomasters*, the Mohammedans, their *muphtis*, or *mollahs*, and their *cadis*. All their lawsuits were heard in the Russian courts, but always through the medium of the colonial committee.

I have tried to give an idea of the organisation and importance of the colonies established in New Russia. I now pass on to describe the inspection. The Tatar-Nogaïs were the first visited, then the Swabians, the Mnémonists, etc. It is impossible to give an idea of the impression made upon us by the sudden contrast of the dress, manners and customs of the Tatars, and these Germans with their huge blue coats reaching down some way below their knee, with well-burnished copper buttons as large as a turkey's egg, sheep-skin breeches, long red waistcoats, blue stockings, shoes with immense silver buckles, low beaver hats, the sides of which were turned up, forming a perfect triangle. They drove us, having first attached four large Mecklenburg horses to our carriage by means of enormously long traces. When we took their first relay we had just left the Tatars, whose team consisted of six little horses, two in front with a postilion, and four attached to the carriage according to the Russian custom, all going full gallop.

In his report to the emperor, the Duc de Richelieu wrote as follows:

> Never, Sire, in any part of the world, have there been nations so different in manners, language, customs and dress living within so restricted a space. The Nogaï's occupy the left bank of the Molotschna, families from Great Russia, the right bank, then, higher up, are the Mnémonists, facing the Germans, half Lutheran, half Catholic; higher up again at Tolmak, the Little Russians, members of the Greek religion, then a Russian sect, the Dukaboitzi.

The Mnémonists interested us greatly. This colony, composed of agricultural capitalists, had prospered within a very short time, partly on account of the capital they had brought in, but chiefly on account of their sobriety and purity of life. Their religion was based on Christian charity, hence they had no quarrels or lawsuits, but a patriarchal life as depicted in the Bible. At the time of the inspection, they had just begun a great work of clearing the land, which would add immensely to their well-being.

The Greek colonies, established twenty-four years before around Mariapol, were no longer subject to annual inspection. We went to see them, however, because, having now attained prosperity, they would be a guide to us as to the future of the more recent colonies. The Duc de Richelieu was much pleased with the flourishing condition of the colonies, and asked the Emperor to bestow honorary rewards on the enlightened governors entrusted with the management of all these colonies.

When the inspection was over, we made our way to Taganrog, on the Sea of Azov, at the mouth of the Don. The town was within the Province of Ekaterinoslaff, but had a governor of its own; Baron Campenhausen held the post at this time. He showed us everything of interest in the port and town, and especially the vast storehouses, or granaries. Peter the Great had founded Taganrog in 1706; he fortified it, and constructed two ports, one for military purposes, the other for commerce. The military port had died out, but the port for commerce was flourishing. After Odessa, Taganrog was the principal Russian port on the Black Sea for the export of grain.

On leaving Taganrog, we went to Nakhetchevan, a town on the right bank of the Don, built in 1780 by the Empress Catherine II. She had intended it for all the Armenians scattered over the Crimea. They welcomed us with great delight; it was the first time a governor-general had visited them since the town was founded. Their manners, customs and dress still retained their Asiatic character, slightly modified by intercourse with Europeans. The town is beautifully situated and surrounded by delightful gardens. We would gladly have spent some days there, but the *gorodnitche*, Chief of the Police, warned us that nine-tenths of the population, rich and poor, young and old, had been suffering for some years from an hereditary skin disease. This unpleasant "indisposition" as they called it, which had permanently infected the town, was caused by their extreme want of cleanliness, for, contrary to Eastern customs, they never take baths. The fear of contracting the disease hastened our departure.

After a rapid drive, we reached Azov, built on the site of the ancient Tana or Tanaïs, a celebrated Greek colony, whose ruins bear witness to its former splendour. This town received the name of Tana in 1203, when the Venetians took possession of it. In the hands of these clever and dauntless merchants, half traders, half warriors, its commerce quickly became a source of great wealth. Every year many vessels left Venice for Tana, which thus became the emporium of the products of Europe and the merchandise of India, brought to Tana by caravans. All its riches disappeared after its conquest by the Tatars; and the total destruction of the town followed upon the coming of the barbarian hordes. On the site of Tana, was built the fort of Azov, now a wretched straggling village, without present or future.

After the inspection, we took the road to Ekaterinodar, the chief town of the Zaporogue Cossacks, or Cossacks of the Black Sea. The Duc de Richelieu was to inspect it in great detail.

The Zaporogue Cossacks received their present organisation from the Empress Catherine II in 1770. After the destruction of the Zaporogues, a Tatar horde, she formed the Cossack Corps, and gave them the country which they have occupied ever since. Their capital took the name of Ekaterinodar, or Gift of Catherine, to perpetuate among them the memory of this great sovereign. She entrusted to them the defence of the frontier against the Circassians. She conceded to these new soldier-agriculturists a vast extent of territory, up to that time an immense solitude, now one of the most fertile provinces.

As the intended visit of the governor-general had been announced some days beforehand, the Cossacks had been able to prepare the relays of horses necessary to convey us to their headquarters; our carriage was drawn by six horses, and fifty Cossacks escorted us from one place to another.

Azov was forty leagues from Ekaterinodar, and, but for the escort, we might have been carried away by the Circassians; the country we passed through was desert and the roads almost impassable for a carriage. We were stopped by the absence of bridges at every stream we came to, and the Cossacks literally carried our carriage to the other side. Not being able to travel by night, we bivouacked at a little Cossack outpost, in the midst of a dangerous swamp, formed by the overflowing of the Kuban. We should have suffered greatly from hunger, if we had not taken the precaution to bring provisions, which our escort shared with us.

Two years later, when M. de Richelieu was making the same tour of inspection, he was very nearly carried off by the Circassians, who had received information of his approach. A hundred of them lay in ambush in a marsh, full of reeds seven feet high; they had had the power of endurance to remain hidden for thirty-eight hours, without moving, and with the water up to their armpits. The spot was well chosen; the troops had to march two by two along a narrow causeway over the marsh. The aim of the Circassians was to cut off the escort, and seize the governor-general.

The Duke de Richelieu was saved by the purest chance. A Cossack of the advance-guard, suddenly seized with intense pain, threw himself on one side at the very point where the Circassians were hidden among the reeds. Thinking they were discovered, they moved, and the Cossack, in his surprise, forgot his pain, and fired a pistol at a venture. At the sound, the whole escort came up at a gallop, and began a fusillade into the reeds. The Circassians, wet as they were, returned the fire as they came out of the ambush; but the combat was unequal. The more so, as a fresh escort and relay of horses were awaiting the governor-general only two *versts* away. At the sound of the fusillade, it was an affair of a moment for these bold horsemen to gallop to the scene of the combat.

Encouraged by the presence of the governor-general, the Cossacks fought magnificently, and soon overcame these adventurers, who left thirty of their men on the field; the rest were taken prisoners, with the exception of five or six, who escaped over the marsh. On the side of the Russians, one officer and twelve men wounded, showed that it had been a hard fight. The prisoners avowed their project of capturing the governor; they wished to take him alive, and counted upon demanding a heavy ransom. I relate this story here, as I was not with M. de Richelieu on that occasion, having been detained at Odessa by important affairs.

To return to our journey of 1808. In spite of all the delays caused by the bad roads we reached Ekaterinodar towards evening, having taken twenty hours to drive forty leagues, without counting the night when we bivouacked. The *attaman*, the name given to the Cossack chief, received us with the highest military honours, and the greatest care for our quartering and for our meals, which were prolonged indefinitely and became very fatiguing. We sat at table three hours, and that twice a day; in order not to hurt the *attaman's* feelings it was necessary to eat and drink a great deal. The banquet was made much longer, as our host — no doubt with the intention of pleasing us—ordered that every course should be served three times; thus, soup three times, roast meat three times, *entrées* three times, salad three times, etc., etc.

"In honour of the Blessed Trinity Whom I now invoke," he said, and his words were answered by three cannon shots, and three hurrahs from the Cossacks present and those on guard before the house. Before going to bed we must drink three cups of tea and three glasses of rum. What a diet! The master of the house set us an example. It is impossible for anyone who had not been present at the banquet to imagine how much he was able to eat and drink; he was, however, a Colossus, sixty years of age, but looked not more than forty. In his youth, he had fought with an ox, and conquered. The Circassians feared him; more than once they had felt the strength of his arm.

He was the father of a numerous family, but did not rightly estimate their importance. M. de Richelieu asked him: "*Attaman*, how many children have you?"

He turned to the Cossack who was waiting on him: "Trophimus, how many children have I?"

"Eleven, General," was the reply.

"All boys?" said the Duc de Richelieu to hide the laughter that was choking him.

"Trophimus, how many daughters have I?" continued the *attaman* in the same tone.

"Four, General," said the Cossack with the utmost gravity.

No doubt the quantity of meat and drink consumed by the *attaman* accounted to some extent for the loss of memory with regard to his own family; still the comedy of it all, and especially the gravity of Trophimus, amused us for a long time.

The *attaman's* name was Boursak; it had been given to him at the Foundling Hospital at Kieff, where he had been brought up at the expense of the government.

The inspection began the day after our arrival. The *attaman* paraded twenty regiments of six hundred men each, less those stationed in the redoubts along the Couban on the frontier, and in addition four batteries of eight. Each Cossack must have three horses, so the effectives numbered 11,000 men under arms, and nearly 40,000 horses, including those with the artillery, and the baggage and the officers' horses. This military Republic also comprised old men, priests, women and children, all under the direct rule of the *attaman*.

M. de Richelieu devoted five whole days to the inspection of these marvellous troops, certainly the best in Europe as vedettes and scouts. I shall have occasion to give numerous proofs. Their horses are as well trained as dogs. At a sign from their master, they will lie down, or get up, understanding all that he wishes them to do.

CHAPTER 4

Inspection of Troops in the Crimea

Our next duty was to inspect the troops in the Crimea, the famous Taurida of antiquity. . . .

Thirty-six hours after leaving Ekaterinodar, we reached Taman, the ancient Phanagoria, the last town occupied by the Zaporogue Cossacks, who had not exploited its ruins, in spite of their great value. The houses all retain some vestiges of their former splendour—fluted columns, finely sculptured capitals, stones engraved with Greek inscriptions, magnificent *bas-relievos*—masterpieces abandoned, mutilated, in any case lost to art. My horse ate his oats out of a white marble sarcophagus with exquisitely carved mouldings.

A large boat, belonging to the Admiralty, was waiting to take us across the Cimmerian Bosphorus, called by some the Straits of Taman, by others the Straits of Kertch, by others again the Straits of Yeni-Kalén. After two hours, we landed at Kertch, formerly the capital of the Bosphorians, described by Strabo under the name of Panticapaeum.

This town, strangely fallen into ruin, is still of some importance on account of its situation. The population is Greek; the ground is covered with precious ruins, marbles of all colours, and broken statues; one has literally but to stoop down to collect them. Just below the soil are found medals in gold, silver, bronze, etc.; the government has erected a museum for all these treasures. Two days before our arrival, on opening a tomb, called the Tomb of Monima, which was in the way of some building operations, they found medals of the ancient Kings of Pontus, gold bracelets, cameos, and other women's jewels, and some statuettes; they offered me a bronze statuette, strongly oxidised, and another in pale blue marble, very rare; both represented Egyptian gods; I bought several medals.

Before inspecting the troops in the citadel of Kertch we had to visit those at Yeni-Kalé, in the Tatar language—a new port, three leagues from Kertch, at the extreme point of the Crimea, where the channel leading from the Sea of Azov to the Black Sea is narrowest.

On our return from Kertch, General Fenshaw, whose sons had accompanied me to Constantinople, was expecting us to dine with him at Kaffa. He was now seventy years old and on the retired list, and held the post of Civil Governor of Theodosia; the troops forming the garrison remained under the orders of the Duc de Richelieu, the Governor-General and Military Governor of New Russia. General Fenshaw made a point of offering hospitality to strangers travelling through his province. After our reception by the Nogaïs and the Cossacks, our kind host's unremitting attention, his exquisite dinners, the conversation of his wife, who must have been very beautiful and was very entertaining, the society of amiable young people; in a word, after having studied the manners of the Tatars, the return to civilisation had many charms for us.

The town of Theodosia owes its name to the sister of Leucon; the Genoese had made it their principal mart; they had erected the fortifications that are still standing, and a wall, strengthened with towers rather near to one another, around the town, which, under the Genoese, had recovered its former wealth. The excellent state of preservation of these ramparts shows the immense sum that had been spent on them, and the importance attached to the defence of the town. Nothing could be more picturesque than the embattled girdle following all the undulations of the ground, now climbing to a peak on a high rock, now diving to the depths of a ravine, now following the windings of a stream. Kaffa has a fine port and square, and streets that had been widened, and straightened, under the care of General Fenshaw, a beautiful old mosque, now used as a church of the Greek rite, and a splendid promenade overlooking the sea. The commercial importance of Kaffa has considerably diminished since the rise of Taganrog, and, still more, of Odessa.

The Duc de Richelieu had arranged to begin his journey along the southern coast, the mountainous region of the Taurida, as soon as he had inspected a regiment of dragoons at Karassu-Bazar, a little town about five leagues from Kaffa. The roads being impracticable for driving, he left his carriage and all the accessories of the inspection at Kaffa, with orders to rejoin him at Simferopol. The younger Fenshaw obtained leave to accompany us on this expedition, which was the more interesting as it was made with the governor-general of the province. Tom Fenshaw went to Sudak to arrange for the necessary horses; this duty, strictly speaking, belonged to me, but I allowed him to have the pleasure of acting for a time as *aide-de-camp* to the Duc de Richelieu, as it gave me the opportunity of visiting Karassu-Bazar. Fenshaw was to provide sixty saddlehorses at every stage for the governor-general, his staff, the persons invited to accompany him, and the servants; also, twenty pack-horses to carry our luggage, tents, cooking utensils, dinner service, plate, linen, wines, etc. From the number of horses, the reader may judge of the importance of our caravan, and the singular spectacle it presented.

Between Kaffa and Karassu-Bazar, the road passes through Eski-Krim, or Old Krim, the ancient Cimmerium, formerly the chief town of the Khans, later given up in favour of Batchi-Serai. This town, formerly of considerable importance, gave its name to the Cimmerian Gulf, marked on modem maps as the Gulf of Kaffa; the palace, part of which is still standing, must have been magnificent, but it now contained only one habitable apartment, then occupied by the colonel of a regiment of Cossacks, who were distributed along the coast of the Crimea to prevent smuggling.

The Armenians had just settled at Eski-Krim, having fled from Persia with all their possessions, on account of the religious persecution to which they were subjected. They found at Eski-Krim a place of refuge, protection, safety, and liberty of conscience, and, thanks to them, the little town, once the residence of a prince, had revived within the last few years.

The Bulgarians had built a village a short distance from Eski-Krim, and this colony was flourishing. M. de Richelieu, who arrived early, went to inspect it the same evening. The next day he went to the Armenians, visited the ruins of Eski-Krim, and left at eleven o'clock for Karassu-Bazar.

This pretty town, important on account of its commerce, has a large population; the Greeks called it Mauron-Castrim; Colga-Sultan, one of the first *Khans* of the Crimea, took up his residence there. Situated in a fertile valley, surrounded by high hills, with the River Kara-su (Blackwater) running through it, the heavy rains and melting of the snow causes the town to be flooded; and the slight inclination of the ground prevents the waters receding rapidly, and their stagnation leads to severe cases of fever in the autumn; two hundred dragoons were in the hospital when we passed through the town, and only a quarter of them recovered. Karassu-Bazar contains eighteen mosques, a synagogue, a Greek, an Armenian, and a Roman Catholic church, the latter of great architectural beauty, numerous Turkish baths, shop or bazaars kept by Tatars, Greeks, Armenians and Jews from Poland.

The life given to the town by this motley crowd of merchants and a considerable garrison, rendered our visit very entertaining. Karassu-Bazar is surrounded by pretty villas, with gardens full of fruit-trees and rare flowers; the contrast between them and the old Tatar houses, the variety of costume, the Eastern manners side by side with those of Europe, is very interesting.

I was present at the sequel to a curious story. Towards the close of the reign of Louis XV, an Alsatian soldier named Schultz, deserted his regiment (then in winter quarters on the Rhine) and went to Russia. He was appointed in turn instructor, officer, colonel, major-general, and finally commander-in-chief, and distinguished himself in all the wars of those times. After Field-Marshal Suwaroff's campaign in Italy and Switzerland, Schultz retired, covered with wounds, and decorated with all the Russian orders, to Karassu-Bazar, where he had been in garrison. Thanks to the kindness of the Empress Catherine and of the Emperor Paul, he enjoyed a magnificent estate and a pension earned by his loyal services.

He had married, while still a captain, a German lady, but had no children. He often spoke of relations in France in poor circumstances, and especially of a younger brother, of whom he had heard nothing, though he had written to him several times, telling him of his high position and begging him to come out to him. He learned from Alsatian colonists, who had come to Russia, that his father and mother were dead, his brother had gone to the Antilles, and nothing more was known of him; his sister had married a first cousin of the same name, who was cook to the Cardinal Duc de Rohan, Bishop of Strasburg. All tidings had ended with the Revolution of 1789. The brave general had begun to suffer from age and infirmities, and was much distressed that there was no one to whom he could leave his fortune and his title of Baron; his wife also had no relations.

Now Cardinal de Rohan's cook had died, ruined by the Revolution, leaving to his only son, in default of money, his talent for cooking; he had exhausted his last resources in tending his wife, the sister of the old general, who had died after a long and painful illness. The times were little favourable to a disciple of Vatel, and whilst waiting for happier days, young Schultz was taken as a conscript, and sent to the frontier. Following the example of his uncle, of whom he had often heard, he took the first opportunity to escape into a foreign land, and support himself by his talent. He wished to go to Russia, as he knew his uncle had joined the Russian Army, though he did not know what had become of him.

After several vain attempts, he found himself at Vienna, and out of a situation, owing to the death of his master. Here he learned that the Duc de Richelieu was passing through Vienna on the way to St. Petersburg, having been recalled by the Emperor Alexander, who wished to confer upon him the government of Odessa. The duke was really seeking a cook, as it would probably be difficult to find one in his new government. He engaged Schultz on the recommendation of a family in Vienna, and took up his position as Governor-General of New Russia, in place of Baron Rosemberg, who had lately died.

Soon afterwards he made a tour through the vast regions under his rule, and, of course, the cook went with him. Imagine the man's delight when he discovered the uncle he was seeking at Karassu-Bazar, in General Schultz. The worthy fellow had plenty of good sense and good feeling. He saw, at once, that without wounding the pride of his uncle and, still more, that of the baroness, he could not abruptly announce himself as their nephew, while wearing the white cap and garb of a cook, and wielding the knife in place of a sword. He said nothing at the time, but, on his return to Odessa, he told everything to the Duc de Richelieu. The duke praised his discretion, and wrote to the old general as follows:

My Dear General,
I am writing to tell you of the arrival of your nephew in Odessa. I can certify to his identity. I knew him in Vienna, where he was employed by a business house. He was highly recommended to me, especially for his integrity. The Revolutionary storm and his limited means have interfered with his education, but I assure you, you will never regret acknowledging him as your nephew. This letter will be delivered to you by young Schultz. On my next visit to the Crimea, I will confirm what I write, and give you further details.
        Believe me, my dear general, etc.,
                                Richelieu.

It will be seen, this letter stated nothing but the exact truth. M. de Richelieu was incapable of acting otherwise; only he did not mention the kind of employment in which Schultz had been engaged. When handing him this letter, M. de Richelieu advised him to be reserved in his manners, and wished him success.

Provided with this letter and all his papers, Schultz went to his uncle, who received him with open arms, delighted to find a relative bearing his name. The baroness, less enthusiastic, was cautious about adopting this nephew; she wrote to friends in Odessa, and some rather uncharitable ladies told her that her nephew was no other than the cook that M. de Richelieu had brought with him from Vienna. Hence a coldness on the part of the general, humiliated at the thought of the humble position of his new heir, forgetting his own early career. Schultz wrote for advice, and the Duc de Richelieu in reply told him to wait until his next visit to the Crimea, and, above all, to seem to be quite unaware of the little intrigue.

As soon as he arrived at Karassu-Bazar, the kind duke did not hesitate to embrace his former cook, calling him, "My dear Schultz." This demonstration of friendship put an end to the gossip and dispelled the anxiety of the old baron. He said to his wife:

You see, someone has evidently had a spite against our nephew; if he had been really the Duc de Richelieu's cook, the great noble would never have embraced him before everybody.

A few months later, Baron Schultz and his wife both died, leaving a nice little fortune to their nephew, who married not long after.

Every time M. de Richelieu came to Karassu-Bazar, Schultz superintended the cooking of his meals; he used to say, he "knew his tastes."

CHAPTER 5

A Holiday in the Crimea

The inspection over, and the reconciliation between General Schultz and his nephew complete, we left Karassu-Bazar for Soudagh, as it is pronounced by the Tatars, Soudak according to Russian spelling. For a few weeks, we laid aside our important affairs, and gave ourselves up to the enjoyment of our tour.

Our cavalcade was formed as follows: The duke and his military suite; M. de Borodzin, Civil Governor of the Taurida, who wished to do the honours of the province; two doctors; three colonels; six *mourzas* (Tatar nobles); two merchants, one French and the other Genoese; a German draughtsman (a great friend of the Fenshaws); lastly, the cook with his utensils and provisions, and all our servants. At every halting-place, Christian and Mussulman landowners joined our party, to show their respect for the governor-general.

Our first stage was Soudak, the *Soldaga* of the Genoese—twelve old towers, some round, some square, old walls, an old fort, a very curious old church, such was the scene before us; the whole delightfully situated by the sea and near a fertile valley. The walls are covered with inscriptions in Gothic characters.

★★★★★★

A Genoese, Oderico, has published a work in which he gives the key to these inscriptions, and very interesting particulars with regard to the Genoese possessions in the Crimea and along the coast of the Black Sea.

★★★★★★

The Empress Catherine II had given a large estate in the Crimea to Prince Potemkin; he planted the whole valley of Soudak with vines, brought from the Bordelais, Burgundy, Spain, and even Madeira.

He built immense cellars for the wine on his plantation; the nature of the soil and the warmth of the sunshine rendered the vines very fruitful. Prince Potemkin died without children or direct heirs, and the property reverted to the Crown. The Emperors Paul and Alexander continued the work, and sent for vine-dressers from the different countries that had provided the vines; thanks to their help, excellent wine was obtained.

We remained at Soudak two days in order to make arrangements for our journey on horseback along this southern coast; orders had to be given in advance for lodgings and relays of horses.

The first day's journey was not long. After breakfast, we set out in correct marching order. We were to sleep at Kutchuk-Uzen, a little village, half Greek, half Tatar. The Duc de Richelieu was hospitably received by a learned Greek doctor, who had travelled much and was of good family. He was married to a pretty and entertaining Rumanian lady, and, thanks to her conversation, we spent a delightful evening. We did not expect such luck in a place so far removed from civilisation.

The next day's journey would have been too long: we divided it. Leaving Kutchuk-Uzen very early in the morning, we reached Irskut at dinnertime, after a very hot journey. It is a Tatar village, delightfully situated. The mountain-chain running from east to west shelters it from the north wind, leaving it exposed to the heat of the sun, tempered by the sea-breeze which rises at sunset. The nights are delicious, but the days are tiring.

The fig, orange, olive and pomegranate flourish on this coast, although usually they are only met with ten degrees farther south. Many streams come down from the mountains, and cause a luxuriant vegetation. Irskut is situated at the end of a little bay. As I was the first to arrive, I had the pleasure of watching our cavalcade following the windings of a zigzag path, too narrow for anything but single file. Hospitality worthy of ancient times awaited us in the village, and the duke decided to prolong our stay there, and make an excursion to the top of Chatyr-Dagh, the highest mountain in the Crimea, eleven *versts* on our right.

Batyraga-Murza, a rich landowner whose whole life had been devoted to Russia, came to Irskut with his three sons, charming young Tatars, to beg M. de Richelieu to do him the honour of having luncheon with him on our descent from Chatyr-Dagh. His house was two *versts* away, on the northern slope of the mountain, on the side of Simferopol, in a village, Mahmoud-Sultan, that was entirely his property. The duke thanked him, and explained why he could not accept the invitation. It was impossible to alter his plan without serious difficulties, as all the preparations had been made a week ago; he promised on his return to Simferopol, not only to have luncheon, but to pass the whole day with him. This promise consoled the aged *Murza*, but as he made a point of offering us luncheon, he told one of his sons to prepare a repast in the open air on our return.

The horses could only go about half-way up this little Mont Blanc, the rest of the ascent must be made on foot. After climbing for an hour, we thought we had gained the summit; it was only the first stage; another great effort was needed to reach the top and enjoy the view, which takes in the whole of the Crimea. Sebastopol seemed to lie at our feet, and it was twenty leagues away. The Chatyr-Dagh, or Mountain of the Tent, seen from the sea, has the appearance of one of those immense tents formerly used in the East. It is 1,200 feet above the Black Sea; the base from north to south measures ten *versts*.

Although we had a good appetite after our exertions, we dreaded the Tatar cooking, for fowls and eels à *la Tatare* are unknown in those parts; it is a happy fiction on the part of our chefs. A more solid luncheon awaited us. Two very fat sheep had been killed on the spot, prepared, and roasted whole in front of a hot fire. A long pole, supported by stakes driven into the ground, was passed through the sheep; four Tatars took it in shifts, two at a time, to turn this primitive spit and at the same time sprinkled the meat with sea-salt to render it succulent.

The Tatars had timed the roasting so that the mutton should be done to a turn when we arrived. The dish was worthy of Homer or Rabelais; with one consent, we pronounced it perfect. The *Murza* had brought fresh bread, and, as a retired Major of Hussars, he forgot the Prophet's prohibition and drank some excellent wine, of which he gave us a sample. After luncheon, and a delightful *siesta* under the shade of the trees, we mounted our horses to go on to Alushta, a charming village, where we spent the night.

Very early next day we took the road to Urzuff, where we were to remain forty-eight hours. Kutschuk-Lambat, M. de Borodzin's estate, was midway on our journey. As the house he was building, was not finished, he had prepared luncheon for us in a beautifully furnished tent; his clever cook had brought together the most *recherché* French dishes, and iced champagne of the best brand. A strange contrast to the mutton à *la Tatare* we had eaten the day before!

The reason why we were to remain so long at Urzuff was as follows: the Duc de Richelieu, delighted with this southern coast, and resolved to return every year to rest after his arduous duties, wished to have a house there. A small estate between Urzuff and Kisiltache was for sale; it had belonged to a rich Tatar who had died without heirs. The Mussulmans do not allow Christians to settle among them; when an estate is for sale, they club together, buy it, and divide it among themselves. The small property of which I have spoken was put up for sale at Akmetcheff, the chief town of the province; the Mussulmans were making arrangements for the purchase, when they heard that the Duc de Richelieu was inclined to buy it. Out of respect and affection for him they, with one accord, withdrew, and allowed a large garden, a ruined house, and a few bits of land to fall to him for 4,000 paper *roubles*, about 8,000 *francs*.

The view from this house was wonderful: the Black Sea in front, on the left the village of Urzuff, with its Genoese port, built on a rock that juts out into the sea, and bears the name of Aju-Dagh (Mountain of the Bear), on account of its shape and its almost black colour. We were to lay the foundation-stone of the house that was to take the place of the ruin; a clever architect from Odessa had prepared the design. The ceremony, which was carried out with great solemnity, astonished the good Tatars. The house, designed in the Greek style, seemed to them a palace, only to be compared to those of their ancient *khans* at Batche-Serai. A German landscape gardener who superintended the greenhouses and gardens of M. de Borodzin, laid out the garden.

Two days later we left this charming spot with much regret. The duke resolved to come there often. At the same time, we seemed to be permanently settled in Russia. M. de Richelieu, who was growing more and more attached to me, said, "I will leave Urzuff to you at my death; you will be able to spend your old age there." So, he often called me Urzuff-Aga. The events of 1814 altered these arrangements; he gave this delightful retreat to Colonel Stempkowski, his Russian *aide-de-camp*, who sold it, later, to Prince Michael Woronzoff.

From Urzuff we went on to Déré-Koy, a fine large Tatar village; the heat was intolerable; leaving our beds we all slept under an immense pomegranate tree. We were expected at Alupka the nest day; at this point the road leaves the southern coast; strictly speaking, indeed, one could follow the coast as far as Foros, a village situated on Cape Kaïu-Métropon (Ram's Forehead) in Greek, or Karadji-Burum in Tatar, but no one ever goes by this difficult road, which is not interesting in any way. From Alupka, a steep narrow path winds up to the top of the mountain-chain, called. Sinab-Dagh, which separates the plain from the Black Sea, and then descends the opposite slope to the town of Kokos, where we arrived after a day's journey of twelve leagues. There our cavalcade broke up; the horsemen and servants, who had accompanied us from Soudak, returned home. The Duc de Richelieu and I, with our servants, continued our way on horseback.

Some time ago, we had been invited to stay with Admiral Mordwinoff at Baidar. This intelligent old man, disgusted with grandeur, after having been Minister of Marine for many years, had retired to Baidar, a delightful spot which he owed to the generosity of Catherine II. M. de Richelieu sent a Cossack on horseback to Akmetcheff to order his carriage to meet him at Baidar; from there he intended going to Sebastopol, passing Balaklava, called by the Greeks Cimballo, and by the Genoese Bella-Chiava. We spent four days with the admiral, looking over his fine estate, while waiting for our carriages.

Ever since the conquest of the Crimea by the Empress Catherine, Balaklava had been garrisoned by Albanian troops, who formed a regular battalion of Greek skirmishers. Later, by a *ukase*, she gave them some lands and the ownership of the port and town, which thus became at once a Greek city and colony.

The port is separated from the town by a few hundred yards. It is deep, and sheltered by high mountains; the entrance is so narrow that it is difficult for two ships to pass each other with their sails unfurled; the form is like the end of a funnel. The water being always calm, ships used to take shelter in the harbour during the heaviest storms; but as it also became a refuge for smugglers, the State forbade the entrance of any merchant vessel unless in imminent danger, or seriously damaged. To make sure that these orders were carried out, the port was closed by a heavy chain; one end of the chain was fixed into the rock, the other passed into a large ring, which again was fixed into the rock on the opposite side and fastened by a padlock; the *commandant* of the port kept the key, and he alone could use it.

An old citadel, built by the Genoese, abandoned by the Turks, and rebuilt by the present Greeks, stands on inaccessible rocks, and dominates the town; high walls, flanked with towers, unite the fortress to the port.

The day after our arrival at Balaklava, the inspection began; the battalion consisted of one thousand one hundred men under arms, their appearance was excellent, the manoeuvres were well carried out, the accounts in perfect order. The governor congratulated the officers and soldiers, and assured them that his report to the emperor would express his entire satisfaction.

This inspection took place on September 25th, the birthday of the Duc de Richelieu, who was born on September 25th, 1767. Knowing this, the *commandant* and his subordinates wished to show their gratitude to the governor-general for all his kindness to them, and their loyalty to the emperor, whom he represented. They organised a very original *fête*.

At nightfall, they invited M. de Richelieu to go on board a large boat anchored in the middle of the bay, and seat himself on a divan covered with rich Eastern stuffs in red and gold. Then we saw the battalion in full dress: red Turkish trousers, very wide down to the knee, close-fitting at the ankles, a green Mameluke jacket, the shade of the uniform of the Russian infantry, with Greek embroidery; on the head an artistic cap of waxed leather. On a signal from the boat, the battalion deployed as skirmishers along the mountain, and attacked the citadel with a well sustained fire of musketry; the veterans of the colony, entrusted with the defence, replied from the walls.

The attack was vigorously pressed by agile troops, amid loud hurrahs, and was conducted strictly according to the rules of military tactics. On reaching the Genoese citadel, the skirmishers ceased fire, and mounted scaling ladders, regardless of the fusillade of the besieged. The fort being scaled, and pronounced captured, the victory was celebrated by fireworks. Half an hour later the *commandant* invited us to supper, followed by a ball which was only ended at daybreak, when we had to think about our journey to Sebastopol. We intended to remain there a week, in order to write out the result of the inspection, draw up the reports, and make excursions in the neighbourhood; we, also, wished to see the newspapers, not a single paper having reached us since we left Kaffa.

The distance from Balaklava to Sebastopol is about sixteen *versts*. A luncheon was awaiting us at the famous monastery of St. George, belonging to monks of the Greek rite. It is built almost at the point of Cape Parthenon, on the site of the Temple of Diana, of which not a trace remains.

The situation is magnificent, so that the expression, "*As fine as the view from the monastery of St. George*," has passed into a proverb.

We were returning to Odessa by way of Batchi-Serai and Akmetcheff, when M. de Richelieu learned, while in the latter town, that an Imperial courier was awaiting him at Odessa to hand over to him a sum of six million *roubles*, to be spent in buying provisions for the army in Moldavia. The Duc de Richelieu being obliged to remain a week at Kherson in order to finish the inspection of the colonies, charged me to go to Odessa, to receive this immense sum, and to place it in the cellars of the bank until his return. I was to send the courier back to St. Petersburg and to send letters, papers and despatches to Kherson.

An hour after my arrival at Odessa, the *feldjager*, or courier, presented himself at my door, begging me to release him at once from the responsibility of his very burdensome package, the contents of which were, of course, a secret from everyone. I gave him a receipt written out by the Duc de Richelieu, after I had verified the seals of the Minister of Finance. The package measured two feet long by two feet wide by three feet high. In order to facilitate the payments, it contained only notes of one hundred, fifty, twenty-five, or ten *roubles*.

I felt little inclined to keep such a deposit. I ordered a *droschki*, and with my package beside me I went to the bank. The manager refused my deposit. He said: "I cannot receive such a large sum without a special order from the governor-general."

Argument was useless; I left at once with my wretched package, and placed it in my bedroom without seeming to regard it as of any importance. I sent a courier at once to the Duc de Richelieu to tell him of my unfortunate position. The order required by the bank manager arrived a few days later. I hastened to get rid of the treasure hidden under my bed, and at last I was able to sleep in peace.

Immediately after his return, M. de Richelieu set about buying the provisions; he was able to obtain an immense store by private treaty at a low price, which won for him the gratitude of the Emperor and of the Minister of War.

M. de Richelieu sent me to Bucharest, the depot of the main headquarters, to inform the commander-in-chief of the dispositions taken for the revictualling of his army corps during the autumn and winter, to receive his orders, and to inquire to what place the provisions should be sent. I passed the camp of the Comte de Langeron on my way. He was occupied in guarding the Danube, and I accompanied him on a reconnaissance of the fortress of Braïlov; he wanted to find out if it could be taken without a regular siege; the enemy let us know that he was there in force, and on his guard. I continued my way to Bucharest, taking advantage of the company of a regiment of *chasseurs* and a battery of artillery.

General Prosorowski seemed delighted with the news I brought him, guaranteeing provisions for five months; food was already running short. The next day, he pointed out to me the places to which the convoys should be sent, and instead of waiting a few days, and enjoying myself at Bucharest, I had to return quickly to Odessa, where I arrived seventy-two hours later with a heavy bag of dispatches.

The winter of 1808-1809 promised to be very brilliant. I was amply recompensed for all my journeys and fatigues by amusing myself to my heart's content. At the theatre, a good Italian company; at the opera, an excellent *corps de ballet*; at the Assembly Rooms, a series of enchanting balls, with Polish, Moldavian and Wallachian ladies, delightful dancers, and eager for fetes and every kind of amusement. All this helped us to bring the year 1808 to a joyous close.

In May, 1809, the Emperor Alexander sent for M. de Richelieu to St. Petersburg; political affairs called for serious consideration and the Emperor wished to have the opinion of the Governor-General of New Russia. A revolution had just broken out at Constantinople; we might hope for peace on the Danube. In Sweden, the fall of Gustavus IV and the accession of his uncle, the Duke de Sudermania, who had adopted Bernadotte; the war declared by France upon Austria; the flight of the King and Queen of Prussia to St. Petersburg—these were the main questions to be studied.

To my great delight, M. de Richelieu appointed me to accompany him; we took the road through White Russia, past Mohilev and Vitepsk. It took us ten days and nights to make the journey, with post-horses, from Odessa to St. Petersburg, a distance of one thousand eight hundred *versts* or four hundred and fifty leagues.

I left M. de Richelieu to his important political affairs, and went to see the sights of the town and neighbourhood, and above all, I went into society. As I was introduced by him, I was well received; all the Embassies and great houses opened their doors to me. . . .

Unfortunately for me, the Duc de Richelieu only remained six weeks in St. Petersburg; the conferences being ended, he turned south again, loaded with new honours. Matters of grave political and commercial importance awaited him at Odessa, and compelled him to travel very rapidly, in spite of the fatigue of the long journey.

Tsar Alexander

CHAPTER 6

Aide-de-Camp to the Tzar

Between Moscow and Odessa small outposts of Cossacks, a certain distance apart, fulfilled the duties of official couriers. A dispatch from the emperor to the Governor-General of New Russia had been lost, and numerous inquiries failed to discover the guilty outpost. I left Odessa with the order to see that all the men entrusted with the delivery of dispatches were punished. On arriving at each outpost, I assembled all the Cossacks, and said:

A dispatch of His Majesty the Emperor has been lost. Here is the order to see that the Cossacks of each detachment receive twenty-five strokes with the *knout*.

The order was carried out at once; each man, in turn, lay down, face downward, and received from his chief, without a word of protest, the number of strokes ordered; then the oldest soldier inflicted the same punishment on the chief of the outpost. Not a complaint, not a murmur, was uttered. As soon as the order had been carried out, I got into my carriage, and went on to the next outpost. It took me six days to discharge this painful duty.

As the *Sultan* was regarded by the population on the coast of the Black Sea, below Anapa, as their *suzerain*, having a right to their obedience and help in time of war, a considerable quantity of arms, munitions, and even money, had been landed at Sukkum-Kalé. The vessels conveying this contraband of war were Greek, but they sailed under the French flag, to mislead the Russian cruisers.

The Duc de Richelieu received a very laconic order from the Minister of War to place two battalions of infantry of the line, two battalions of *chausseurs*, a regiment of Cossacks, and a field battery, at the disposal of the admiral in command of the Black Sea fleet. These troops were to embark on the squadron appointed for the expedition. The choice of the commandant, a colonel, or lieutenant-colonel, was left to the governor-general. Now, the troops selected were under the immediate command of the Duc de Richelieu, moreover, he was responsible for the maintenance of order in New Russia; it was strange that an expedition should have been decided upon without his being consulted beforehand. He was never able to find out who it was that had sufficient influence thus to violate the laws of courtesy; it was the more unaccountable as the emperor continued to treat him with the greatest confidence. Probably, the blow came from officials who were jealous of the influence of a foreigner over their sovereign.

I was at Urzuff in the Crimea, looking after the workmen, when this order came to the governor-general. He appointed me to carry it out, to be present at the embarkation of the troops at Sebastopol, in short, to superintend all the details. He selected a distinguished officer, the lieutenant-colonel of the 22nd Chasseurs, to take the command.

Sometimes, things turn out very strangely in life; that which was such a source of grief to M. de Richelieu, was the making of my military career. The duke attached undue weight to the slight he had received; this sprang from his naturally irritable temperament. Wishing to ascertain if the emperor's feelings towards him remained unchanged, or if his enemies had been able to destroy his confidence, he wrote directly to His Majesty. At the close of this memorandum, he asked that I should be admitted into the regiment of the Imperial Guard, mentioning, not only my services at the embarkation of the troops, but those I had rendered to the town of Odessa—the construction of pavements, the laying out of public gardens, and other improvements.

On my return from Sebastopol, M. de Richelieu did not breathe a word to me of this letter, or of the favour he had asked for me. I found him ill, indeed greatly changed, his nerves unstrung, the result of worry. Happily, Dr. Scudéry understood his constitution very well, and was devoted to him; he said to me:

With our dear duke's nervous temperament, we must let care and affectionate attention take the place of drugs, that are powerless to cure his malady.

I was very ready to prove my filial devotion, in return for the many acts of kindness I had received from him; and the doctor and I together, were soon able to cope with this illness, which had taken the form of an obstinate nervous fever. With great difficulty, we succeeded in calming these violent, and frequently recurring, attacks, which were rendered worse by the entire absence of sleep for twelve nights, and the impossibility of inducing him to take food. The cook overcame this last difficulty by preparing a highly concentrated meat jelly, a spoonful of which was equivalent to several pounds of meat. It was more difficult to obtain sleep on account of the delicate condition of the nerves; the least sound, such as the ticking of a clock, exasperated him.

It seemed, however, to give him pleasure to hear me read. I chose the story of Gil Blas de Santillane, a favourite of his. I began reading in my ordinary tone, then gradually lowering my voice, I tried to make it as monotonous as possible, till it became a sort of hum. But this means, on the second day, I succeeded in getting half an hour's sleep, which relieved the strain on the nerves. I went on for several days, and each time sleep came more quickly and lasted longer.

The arrival of the emperor's letter completed the cure. The *Tzar* expressed his surprise to the Duc de Richelieu that an expedition should have been undertaken with the troops belonging to his division, without his knowledge, and he ended by saying that such a thing should not happen again. This letter, couched in the most gracious terms, was entirely satisfactory to M. de Richelieu. The emperor granted all his requests, so his convalescence continued, and any fear of a relapse disappeared.

My care during his illness had proved the sincerity of my attachment; and from this time M. de Richelieu showed me a truly paternal affection. It was with real pleasure that he gave me the emperor's letter to read, in which I found, to my surprise, that I was admitted lieutenant in the regiment of *chasseurs* of the Imperial Guard, a rank equivalent to that of captain in the line.

We were approaching the autumn of 1809; the season for sea-bathing was very brilliant. The recovery of the governor-general was the signal for great rejoicing. The inhabitants idolised him—this man of irreproachable conduct, just, upright, generous, always occupied with the wellbeing of others, glad to be of service to anyone.

Thus, ended the year 1809; the winter and spring of 1810 were uneventful. In May, the Duc de Richelieu, who had completely recovered, undertook once more the inspection of his provinces.

I remained at Odessa to superintend some important work on the quay, the opening of a new street, and the laying out of our private garden situated a *verst* from the Tiraspol barrier, in a sheltered valley, with a fairly large stream, a rare thing in the neighbourhood of Odessa....

Instead of remaining at Urzuff (after the inspection) as he had hoped, the Duc de Richelieu was obliged to leave hurriedly for St. Petersburg. The emperor desired to discuss important affairs with him, and "to give an explanation with regard to the annoyance the Duc de Richelieu had suffered without his knowledge," such were the concluding words of the letter. I made all the preparations, and three days after the duke's return to Odessa we left for St. Petersburg, where he was overwhelmed with marks of confidence; he received the Grand Cordon of St. Alexander Nevski and, besides this, the emperor, judging rightly that the governor's finances could not stand frequent journeys from the Black to the White Sea, gave him an order on the Treasury for fifty thousand *roubles*.

During this journey, Prince Casimir Lubomirski, an intimate friend of M. de Richelieu, presented me to the beautiful Madame Narishkin. She told the prince she would be delighted to do anything for me out of regard for M. de Richelieu. The prince did not let the opportunity slip, and asked her to obtain for me the post of *aide-de-camp* to the emperor. Four days later I received my appointment. The *Tzar*, in the most gracious manner, agreed to my remaining personal *aide-de-camp* to the Governor-General of New Russia, although I now formed part of His Majesty's Military Household.

The position of *aide-de-camp* to the emperor brought me two advantages: exceptionally pleasant duties when at St. Petersburg, and two thousand *francs* from the Emperor's privy purse, a welcome addition to the income of an officer who had only his pay to depend on. Before leaving St. Petersburg, General Ouvaroff, the senior *aide-de-camp* general, presented me to His Majesty on parade. I began my duties at the palace that day, but the emperor did not leave his apartments.

We set out on our homeward journey at the end of May, 1810. The Duc de Richelieu thought, at one time, of returning by way of Moscow, where we were expected, but urgent matters in arrear called for his presence in Odessa, and he decided to take the shortest route; we spent two days, however, at Tulchine, the residence of the Countess Felix Potocka.

(In September of this year, 1810, the Duc de Richelieu was at Urzuff, and while there, was much distressed to learn that M. Wolsey, head of the college which the duke had established at Odessa, proposed to leave. (This college, together with the University of Charkoff, was destined to educate all the youth of this part of the Empire. The following letter was received by the Count de Rochechouart:)

Urzuff,
September 20th, 1810.

I have received your letter, which has grieved me deeply. I am writing to M. Wolsey, and I wish you to give him my letter, but I have little hope of any good result, for, to all appearance, he has made up his mind. Here is a man so disinterested that after filling his pockets with ducats, he wishes, not merely to leave, but to ruin the College that ought to have been his glory. I am indignant; but I must not show it, for fear of hastening the ruin.

R.

As M. de Richelieu had foreseen, M. Wolsey left without waiting for his return. The duke applied to the Abbé Nicolle, who had every qualification for the vacant post. He belonged to the Oratorians, and was a professor in one of their colleges. Fleeing before the Revolutionary storm, he passed through Italy, Greece, and Turkey, where he directed the education of the sons of the French Ambassador at Constantinople, the Comte de Choiseul-Gouffier. Finally, he reached St. Petersburg, where he opened a school with great success; all his pupils played a distinguished part in the history of their country—the Comte Michel Orloff, the two Comtes Kisseleff, Prince Gortchakoff, Prince Mentschikoff, etc.

This good priest had now come to live at Odessa, where he had the spiritual care of the Catholic colonists around the town, preaching even among the mountains of the Caucasus. His success among these colonists of various nationalities became daily more evident; religion resumed her sway, manners became more pure, but there was still wanting the most efficacious means of moral regeneration—the education of youth. It was then that the Duc de Richelieu and the Abbé Nicolle consulted together, and drew up the plan of a college and a course of studies under the most distinguished French and Russian professors.

This college eventually rose to the first rank; the following subjects were taught there—dead and living languages, mathematics, history, drawing, music, fencing, horsemanship; no branch was neglected. The "*Lycée Richelieu*," liberally endowed by its founder, consisted of a vast building outside the town, near the citadel. When the duke was recalled to France by Louis XVIII, he obtained permission to transfer to the *Lycée* of Odessa a pension of sixteen hundred *ducats* which he received from the emperor. In 1816, the *Tzar* granted to the college the title of *Lycée Imperial*, with the privileges conceded to the universities, that is to say, that every pupil should receive his commission as an officer after his studies were completed, and he had served three months as a non-commissioned officer. These privileges were obtained by the Comte de Langeron, who succeeded M. de Richelieu as Governor-General of New Russia, by a *ukase* countersigned by Prince Galitzen; the emperor imposed only one condition:

The Abbé Nicolle shall retain the direction of studies.

In 1819 the *abbé* was recalled to Paris by the Duc de Richelieu and placed at the head of the College Rollin. He left the *lycée* at Odessa in the most flourishing state, thanks to the generosity of the *Tzar*, and the impetus given to it by its founder.

CHAPTER 7

Madame Narishkin in New Russia

In May, 1811, we learned that Madame Narishkin, on the advice of her physicians, was leaving St. Petersburg to seek a warmer climate for her daughter Sophie. The emperor was the father of the little girl, and was the more attached to her as she was the only one left to him; her elder sister had died, as also his two daughters by the Empress Elizabeth. All his affections as a father were centred on this charming child of six years old. He could only be persuaded to part with her by the assurance that the climate of Odessa, and the sea-bathing, could alone restore her to health. She returned home perfectly cured; later she was betrothed to Count Schouvaloff, but died suddenly when very young.

It would have been difficult to entertain Madame Narishkin suitably at the governor-general's residence, a simple, unpretending middle-class house. M. de Richelieu told me to look for one suitable to receive this numerous and distinguished company.

The Countess Potocka had a fine large house, with a beautiful garden running down to the sea. I left for Tulchine to beg as a favour the use of this house for Madame Narishkin. Three days later, I brought back the required permission. I had not hesitated to tell Madame Potocka how much I was indebted to Madame Narishkin, and this most kind lady appreciated my feelings of gratitude, and granted me the favour I asked.

We expected eighteen persons—Madame Narishkin and her daughter, Sophie, three ladies in waiting, a Russian, a Pole, and an Englishwoman; a German doctor; M. Vicomte, a Frenchman who acted as secretary; M. Pauloff, the chief huntsman, under M. Dimitri Narishkin, the Master of the Hounds, who fulfilled the duties of Chamberlain, Mlle. Sophie's governess; three lady's-maids, a cook, a butler, a courier, and three footmen.

Madame Narishkin, born in 1780, was the daughter of Prince Chetwertinski, who was killed during the Polish wars. She was married when only fifteen to M. Narishkin, the brother of the Grand Chamberlain, and a descendant of the former favourite of the Empress Catherine. The Emperor Alexander was attracted by her beauty and wit, and after she became a widow she was generally regarded as his mistress.

Madame Narishkin's visit took up all our time. I sought every means of making it pleasant to her. For two months, balls, concerts, boating excursions on the sea, rides and drives, followed one another without interruption.

The warm climate and cloudless sky of Odessa like the skies of the East, and the sea-baths, soon had a marvellous effect on the little Sophie's health, which had often been a source of anxiety to her father and mother. In order to complete the cure so well begun, the physician at Odessa, advised a tour in the Crimea, where the climate was even warmer. Everyone welcomed the idea with enthusiasm, but it was necessary to obtain the emperor's consent. The reply was not long delayed. The emperor approved, and allowed every latitude, only stipulating that they should avoid fatigue.

I am writing these lines thirty years after the expedition, but the most trifling details connected with it are engraven on my memory; it seems as if it were but yesterday, for it would be impossible to dream of a more delightful tour.

We set out on Tuesday, September 5th, 1811; certainly, never since the journey of the Empress Catherine II had such a numerous and brilliant company appeared in those parts. The loading of the luggage, and other arrangements, prevented our leaving Odessa till noon; the first stage of our journey was, however, only eleven leagues; we were to pass the night at General Cobley's.

The advance-guard was composed as follows: a van with all Madame Narishkin's cooking utensils, a wagon-load of provisions, a britzka with the dinner-service, plate, and trunks; my carriage followed. I had for companion M. Doulais del Castillo (our friend the Spanish Consul); behind us, alone in his carriage, was M. Perrawski, a natural son of Count Rasumovski, who had recommended him to M. de Richelieu; he acted as Civil Secretary. This journey was most fortunate for him, as it resulted in his marriage with Mlle. Charlotte de Sally, one of Madame Narishkin's maids of honour. A travelling-carriage followed for the ladies-maids; the carriage of M. Vicomte, the secretary, with M. Müller, the German doctor; the carriage of M. Pavloff with the Countess Artzen, and Mlle. Charlotte de Sally, both ladies-in-waiting, and the governess of the little Sophie.

Then, in the last carriage, Madame Narishkin and her daughter, and the Comte de Venanson, chief of staff of the Duc de Richelieu's division. The poor fellow, who was very handsome, is said to have been too attentive, in short to have paid a little court, to the great lady. Did she jest about it later, with her august lover, or did someone in malice tell the emperor? Certain it is, that the Comte de Venanson distinguished himself greatly in the campaigns of 1812, 1813 and 1814, without receiving any promotion or decoration; he left the Russian Army, and entered that of Sardinia, his native country, and quickly rose to the rank of lieutenant-general. The Duc de Richelieu, who wished personally to make arrangements for the relays of horses for our carriages, had left two days before, with his cousin, Count Charles de Rastignac, a colonel in the Russian Army. Our party comprised twenty-eight persons.

Our itinerary took in Kherson, Perekop, Akmetcheff, Batchi-Serai and Sebastopol, where the most brilliant reception awaited us. Embarking on a light vessel, we passed in front of the entire fleet dressed with flags, which greeted us with cheers and broadsides. Dinners and *fêtes* in the drawing-rooms of the Admiralty, decorated with naval emblems, were followed by an excursion to the monastery of St. George. We took it into our heads to act the *Tragedy of Iphigenia* on the very scene of the play.

At Balaklava, the *commandant* of the battalion and of the Greek Colony, repeated, at our request, the representation of the capture of the fort which he had given on the 25th September, 1808, in honour of the birthday of the governor-general. There being no carriage-road along the southern coast, eighty saddle horses, and fifty pack-horses for the luggage, provisions, kitchen utensils, etc., were awaiting us at Balaklava. We were everywhere received with the greatest honour, original fetes were organised, as if by magic, by our hosts of 1808, concerts, dances, picnics, plays, fireworks, illuminations. At Batchi-Serai, hidden in a gallery of the Mosque, we saw the *dervishes* dancing and singing, till they fell to the ground, half dead from exhaustion; another time, Madame Narishkin visited the *harem* of a Mussulman chief; this visit very nearly turned out badly.

I was fair, and clean shaven; my skin was fine and white. Madame Narishkin took it into her head to make me put on the dress of one of her ladies, and a hat with a large veil; thus disguised, she insisted on my going with her. The ladies of the *seraglio*, much interested in the details of the dress of European ladies, came around us, touched us, and looked at us; the corset especially puzzled them. One of them came to me to make a thorough examination; fearing a grave scandal, I pretended to be in a very bad temper, and went aside to a *divan*, seeming to sulk. It was a dangerous position for me too, among so many beautiful women, very scantily clothed. However, I came away without further molestation; the sullen lady was left to herself.

We remained five days at Urzuff, which was then quite finished; the ladies took sea-baths, and were never tired of looking at the view of the Black Sea from the garden.

Madame Narishkin everywhere gave presents with royal munificence, so delighted was she with the fetes, in which everyone sought to outdo the other in originality and luxury. We were all young and merry, and it was one continual burst of laughter for four weeks. Little Sophie had taken a great fancy to me. She called herself my little wife, and as such showed me all her father's letters, masterpieces of simplicity and tenderness within the capacity of a child of six.

As I have said, we left Odessa on September 5th, and on the 30th we slept at Sudak; carriages were waiting to take us on to Kaffa, where the whole party were to meet. We arrived by three different routes, as there were not enough horses in the relays for all our carriages. Forty-eight hours were given up to showing the sights of Kaffa to our travellers. On the evening of the second day, M. de Richelieu announced that *fêtes* must end, and serious work begin; he had just received dispatches, ordering us to begin a campaign to capture Sudjuk-Kalé, a port on the Black Sea, south of Anapa; it was an old fort built by the Genoese. It had lately been used by the Turks for sending arms and munitions to the Circassians. In accordance with the orders given, troops were awaiting us at Anapa. General Rondzewitch, second in command of the expedition, was at Taman with a regiment of Cossacks.

Thus, we were to separate at Kaffa, some returning to St. Petersburg and to Odessa, the others crossing the Straits of Kertch to join the Expeditionary Force. Madame Narishkin was bent on accompanying us as far as Anapa, to be able to say she had been in Asia. In order to free himself from responsibility, M. de Richelieu insisted that Mlle. Sophie should not take part in the expedition, but should remain at Kaffa with her governess, the doctor, M. Vicomte, the cook, and half of the servants. When this was settled we went to Kertch, where we were to find transports provided by the Imperial Navy to convey us to Taman. The transports had not arrived, and we waited for them two days; we employed our mornings in exploring the ruins of the ancient capital of Mithridates, and the evenings in playing at proverbs in the presence of a curious assembly of spectators—Cossacks, Mussulmans, colonists of all nationalities, Russian soldiers, etc., and this on the very site of Monima's tomb.

The delay on the part of the Admiralty seemed the more unaccountable, as everything had been fixed and arranged beforehand between the Duc de Richelieu and the Marquis de Traverset, recently appointed to the Ministry of Marine. According to the emperor's orders, the expedition to Sudjuk-Kalé was to be undertaken by the army, a squadron at Sebastopol was to supply the provisions, munitions, and artillery required for the occupation and garrisoning of the town.

The transports having arrived, we crossed the Straits of Yeni-Kalé, slept at Taman, and set off very early next morning, leaving two splendid sloops for Madame Narishkin on her return from Anapa. Our four ladies, surrounded by a brilliant staff, and with an escort of Cossacks, both in advance and in the rear, were in a carriage drawn by six horses; small detachments were stationed along the route to avoid the danger of ambush.

It may easily be imagined what a charm this military display had for our travellers; they greatly enjoyed this beginning of the campaign. The distance to be covered was fifteen leagues; we halted midway to take food and to allow the horses and servants to rest. Anapa has no inn, so when night came the accommodation was very primitive; mattresses laid on the ground, with shawls for covering, took the place of beds. The ladies, delighted with this semblance of a bivouac, made no complaint; the encampment only formed a new subject for merriment.

The nest morning our Amazons mounted their horses and accompanied M. de Richelieu to the camp to review the troops. In the evening, we improvised a ball; a regiment of infantry in garrison in the town sent their band. During the ball, M. de Richelieu presented to Madame Narishkin one of our most loyal and devoted friends, Haslam-Gheraï, and told her his story.

Haslam-Gheraï, born in 1786, belonged to an old Tatar family that had given several *khans*, or sovereigns, to the Crimea; our hero was very tall, with a fine figure, and beautiful face. When he was only four years old his father was killed by Khalabat-Aglu, the powerful chief of the Abbazes, who, at the same time, seized all the herds and other possessions of his victim. Left an orphan, Haslam was received by a distant relative, Mouradin-Bey, a declared enemy of Khalabat.

Accustomed to bear arms from his childhood, in consequence of the wars Mouradin was continually waging, either with the neighbouring princes or with the Cossacks of the Black Sea, Haslam soon became an accomplished soldier. Of heroic courage, and with a true genius for war, in another country he would have become a great general. He fell in love with Mouradin's daughter, Mira, justly considered the most beautiful girl of that country, where all the women are beautiful, and much sought after for the *harems* at Constantinople. He asked for her hand. Mouradin replied:

Understand that my daughter is worth thirty thoroughbred mares, and as many sacks of salt, how can you ask me to sacrifice such advantages?

Haslam had nothing to give. His whole fortune consisted in his arms, his horse, his bravery and noble birth. Driven to despair, the lovers resolved to fly; Mira, revolted at the thought of being exchanged for so many mares, was quite ready to follow the man who preferred her to all the treasures of the world, and whose love she returned.

Haslam thought of seeking refuge for the beautiful Mira and himself with the Cossacks against whom he had fought so often; but first he must cross the Kuban. This was done in the most romantic way. Fully armed, and in his coat of mail, he with some difficulty reached the rendezvous agreed upon with Mira. He placed her behind him on his faithful charger, and went like the wind. Mouradin had kept a watchful eye on the movements of his young relative, and as soon as he saw that he had fled, he sent fifteen servants in pursuit.

Notwithstanding the swiftness of their horses, they only overtook the fugitives on the banks of the Kuban, just as Haslam, clad in mail, plunged into the river, dragging his horse with one hand, swimming with the other, and holding his sword between his teeth. Mira held the horse's mane with one hand while with the other, armed with her lover's pistol, she showed him the opposite bank, as a harbour of refuge where they would be safe from her father's vengeance. A few minutes sufficed to cross the Kuban.

The Cossacks questioned them at length, and in order not to involve themselves in a quarrel with Mouradin, they, as a first step, put the lovers in quarantine, and then sent word to the *Attaman*. Haslam, fearing lest he should be given up to Mouradin, begged that his arms might not be tied as he wished to die fighting rather than be assassinated in cold blood.

A few days after these events, the Duc de Richelieu, in the course of an inspection, arrived very opportunely. The Attaman Boursak related Haslam's adventure, and asked his orders. Boursak was inclined to give up the fugitives to avoid Mouradin's anger.

M. de Richelieu, touched with so much affection, asked to see the hero of this romance. Haslam was brought into the presence of the governor-general the next day, and received with sympathy. M. de Richelieu promised him an allowance from the emperor if he would live in Russia and enter the army. He gave orders that the fugitives should be received, and that no notice be taken of Mouradin's claims or recriminations. Haslam could not find words to express his joy and gratitude, when the duke told him he would be treated as a Russian field officer. He became an invaluable ally on account of his bravery, his knowledge of the country, and his experience in mountain warfare.

These events happened in 1806. Haslam, admitted into the Russian Army, obtained permission to settle in the Crimea, where his family had reigned for so many years; then a *mollah*, delegated by the *mufti* of the Crimea, united him lawfully to the beautiful Mira, whom, up to this time, he had respected, notwithstanding his passionate love and the customs of the Mussulmans.

At the time of the expedition of 1807, he hastened to offer his services to M. de Richelieu, wishing to show his gratitude to one who had received him so kindly, and to whom he owed his happiness, by fighting the chiefs who had taken part with Mouradin, and were therefore his bitter enemies. After the capture of Anapa, he aided our column in General Ganguebloff's expedition, going in front of the skirmishers armed with his pistol, full of ardour, courage and skill.

After this campaign, on the recommendation of General Ganguebloff, M. de Richelieu obtained for Haslam a gold medal with the riband of St. George, as Mussulmans cannot receive the Cross. The riband of this purely military decoration is yellow and black. From 1807 to 1811 he never ceased to give proof of his devotion to Russia. In 1810 his brilliant exploit in being the first to go up to the assault of Sukum Kalé won for him a gold sabre, with the inscription "For bravery."

Madame Narishkin received the hero most graciously. The next day she proffered a request to him, and only realised its levity by his reply. After having asked him to arm himself as if for the combat, which he did with remarkable ease, she urged him to rush forward, sword in hand, as if he were in the presence of the enemy. He replied:

What *Madame* asks of me cannot be acted. If she would see me fight, let her come with us on our next expedition; then, out of regard for her, I will show her how I fight against the enemies of the emperor, my master and hers.

The next day we made a kind of reconnaissance, or rather, we advanced a league within the territory of the Abbazes, without firing a shot, to the great disappointment of our companions.

After three days of sham-fighting, Madame Narishkin returned with the same precautions along the road to Taman, bidding us a touching farewell, with many wishes and prayers for the success of our expedition. In the evening, we received a note announcing that she had safely arrived at Kertch; and later we heard that she had left for Kaffa, and then for St. Petersburg.

CHAPTER 8

Expedition to Circassia: Plague in Odessa

Although it was beautiful weather and there was a light breeze, the squadron did not appear at Taman. We waited a week. Then M. de Richelieu, at the end of his patience, sent my colleague Stempkovski to Sebastopol; the duke could not take the responsibility for such a delay, which, apart from the complications that might arise, entailed great expense for the troops in campaign. Urged by my comrade, the admiral set sail, and promised to be before Sudjuk-Kalé within forty-eight hours. Assured of the departure of the fleet, M. de Richelieu returned to Anapa, and we set off at eleven o'clock the next night.

The Expeditionary Force began the march in good order, and in silence. According to the guides, the distance was only eight leagues, and there was a good road. We had, in fact, no difficulty in transporting our artillery, two complete batteries. The troops only took rations for two days, as the fleet was to furnish supplies. It was necessary to act very quickly and we did not know the nature of the ground, or the difficulties to be overcome; but Haslam, in whom we had every confidence, kept a watchful eye on our Circassian guides, self-styled friends.

We were halting on a table-land at three o'clock in the morning, having found no trace of habitation or cultivation along our route, when we heard a shrill cry on our left. It was continued till it was answered by another, equally shrill, in the distance. This signal of alarm showed clearly that we were observed, and might expect an attack at daybreak. The Circassians, our allies, however, renewed their assurances that there were no preparations whatever for an attack.

After resting for an hour, we resumed our march, the officers keeping a watch over their soldiers to prevent their stopping, for the Circassians do not take prisoners, and any soldier captured by surprise is killed; thanks to these precautions, the descent from the plateau was effected without difficulty, following the valley which grows wider till it reaches Sudjuk-Kalé. Towards six o'clock, the rising sun showed us a magnificent view: in the centre of the plain was a small fort, built in the days of old by the Genoese to command the bay, but now in ruins; the open sea stretched out two leagues away on our right; the squadron at anchor lay at the entrance to the bay, which on the land side was about half a league in width, and grew wider towards the open sea; on the left there was no trace of habitation or cultivation of the ground, only grass and brushwood. We went down a gentle slope.

On reaching the plain the column deployed, having the artillery in the centre, protected by a strong line of skirmishers. What useless precautions! The fort consisted of four walls without a roof, with not a man to defend the ruins; the troops bivouacked at the foot of the walls. We were much disconcerted; the Duc de Richelieu was perplexed. How could the War Office at St. Petersburg have ordered such an expedition! Why send out 6,000 soldiers and a considerable force of artillery? Why bring out a fleet of ten vessels or corvettes? Why this expense? To seize four walls! A splendid port, it is true, but of what use would it be? We were all seeking the solution of the enigma.

The Cossacks of the division set out on a reconnaissance, searched all the woods around and returned, having found neither inhabitants nor dwellings; the only thing they discovered on the other side of the bay was a well-beaten, much-frequented road, and the fresh print of horses' feet. This road led into the woods; they had followed it for some time without meeting anyone; but they had noticed a vessel at anchor. We could not see it from our position, a slight elevation of the ground hiding it from our view. This report put us on the alert; we must place the main guards and take precautions against an ambush.

As the evening fell, M. de Richelieu ordered three cannon-shots to be fired as a signal to the fleet of our arrival. The signal and the fires of our bivouac should have been sufficient; we were the more convinced of this, as we distinctly heard the cannon which gave the order to strike the flag, a manoeuvre that we were able to follow perfectly with our glasses. The next day, at sunrise, a cloudless sky enabled us to see the fleet motionless in the same place; not a movement could be discerned on board the ships. M. de Richelieu, anxious to explore the road reconnoitred the evening before, ordered a regiment of Cossacks to mount and take with, them half a mountain battery. Protected by

103

them, he advanced about half a league nearer the squadron, and ordered three cannon shots to be fired to attract their attention. There was no signal in reply. Eight other shots had the same result.

The position was becoming serious. The country did not offer the slightest resources, and the troops would be short of provisions the next day. M. de Richelieu begged me to go on board the vessel discovered by the Cossacks, in the hope that they might be able to supply us with some provisions. On my approach, the large merchant brig hoisted the French flag. I hailed the captain in French, and was answered in Italian: "The *commandant* is not on board." Continuing my questions, I learned that the vessel was Greek. All this seemed to me rather underhand. I threatened to order my escort to fire. Then the captain, who was said to be absent, appeared. He offered to show me his papers, signed by the French consul at Constantinople.

I went on board with a few men. The papers seemed to be in order; however, I insisted on searching the ship to make sure that it contained nothing contraband of war. The captain threw himself on his knees and confessed that he had a cargo of young girls; he was employed in supplying the *harems*, and had just made his purchases, and was returning to Constantinople when the Russian fleet anchored at the entrance to the bay. Curious to see this new kind of cargo, of which I could form no idea, I went down to the cabin; I saw forty little girls, the eldest might be seven. It is impossible to describe the terror of these children, the embarrassment of the captain, and consternation of his crew at my inquisitive act, and, above all, the astonishment of the men who accompanied me. I found a few provisions, but only enough for our own table. I paid for them liberally, and a sloop was to convey them to the camp.

On my return, I suggested to M. de Richelieu that I should take the long boat and be conveyed to the fleet to speak to the admiral; he gladly consented. The Greek captain was steering the boat himself, and there were two oarsmen. I suggested that he should take me to the fleet, but, probably fearing treachery, he said it was impossible; he consented, however, to my taking his boat and his oarsmen on condition of allowing him to rejoin his vessel. I showed the sailors, on the one hand, ten *ducats* and a bottle of rum, on the other a brace of pistols. In face of such arguments they did not hesitate. M. de Richelieu rapidly wrote a letter to the admiral; he begged him to land the provisions at once, as he had great need of them. Beyond this, he did not express the least annoyance or surprise at his remaining stationary.

After an hour and a half at sea, I reached the *Ingoul*, a three-decked vessel flying the admiral's flag. My oarsmen, who were quite exhausted, could not have made the voyage with a contrary wind, but for the bottle of rum. As the emperor's *aide-de-camp*, I was wearing a uniform of dark green with scarlet collar and facings, silver epaulets and lace, the epaulets embroidered with an A, surmounted by the Imperial crown. This uniform caused me to be received with great alacrity. The commandant of the vessel, Stouli, happened to be a great friend of mine; he embraced me, and led me to the admiral, who seemed much embarrassed. Without a word, I handed him the governor-general's letter.

He said: "How is this? The governor-general arrived two days ago! I had no idea of it."

"Your excellency must, however, have heard our cannon."

"They certainly told me there were cannon-shots, but I thought the firing was much further off; I thought it was from an advance-guard."

I made no reply, and seemed to accept the stupid excuse. The admiral at once gave orders to weigh anchor, enter the bay, and approach as near as possible to the fort. I begged him to fire three cannon-shots, the signal agreed upon with M. de Richelieu, to announce the success of my mission. The duke afterwards said to me: "The sound of cannon never gave me such pleasure before." His happiness was complete when he saw the fleet enter the bay.

I heard piercing cries from my two rowers; they were being deprived of the tow-lines. I begged Stouli to allow them to be towed, though contrary to the rules. Pitying their fatigue, he consented. I threw them the ten *ducats* agreed upon, and let them have the rest of the bottle of rum.

Taking advantage of a moment when I was alone with Stouli, I asked him if he had really not heard our cannon. "Perfectly well," he replied, "but as we count for nothing in this expedition—it brings neither honour nor profit to the navy—the admiral would not move without being asked. From what he said to me just now, when giving orders to sail, he regrets his fit of sulks. He said: 'I did not know one of the emperor's *aides-de-camp* was attached to the expedition.' I put the finishing stroke to his embarrassment by saying that you were the nephew of M. de Richelieu."

"We will forget these vagaries," I replied. "The main point is that our men should have something to eat and drink in the morning."

As night fell, the squadron cast anchor as near the shore as possible, and they began to disembark the provisions into large boats. Wishing to make us forget his misdeeds, the admiral suggested that I should go on shore with him, so that he might pay his respects to the commander-in-chief and receive his instructions with regard to the unlading on the morrow. Thus, my little expedition ended happily. M. de Richelieu was very grateful to me for having thought of the sloop. The rivalry between the two services was often a source of grave difficulty. In this case, the admiral, in a fit of temper, was simply leaving 6,000 men to die of hunger.

The following evening the squadron left us; one frigate only remained behind, according to the orders from St. Petersburg, until we should have repaired and garrisoned the fort. Our engineers caused a moat to be dug around the old fort, restored the roof and built a strong palisade in front of the moat. The fort, armed with four guns of large calibre, was garrisoned by a company of grenadiers, as well as the artillery. Thus, without striking a blow, Russia came into possession of another magnificent port. During this week, the men on fatigue duty cut down trees in the neighbouring woods to make the roof and palisade for the fort. There was no sign of the presence of the enemy, but two Circassian princes came to see Haslam-Gheraï, to try to persuade us to make an expedition into the neighbourhood. They said the inhabitants were demoralised by the capture of Sudjuk-Kalé, which cut them off from communication with Turkey and from receiving munitions, etc.

If you go a very short distance out of your way you will come to the *aoul* of a powerful chief, who, at this very time, is planning with other chiefs an attack on the territory of the Zaporogue Cossacks.

The Duc de Richelieu fell in with the idea at once; it seemed to him a contemptible thing to do to enter upon a campaign with the fleet and a considerable number of troops, and then return home without firing a shot.

Leaving Sudjuk-Kalé two hours before daybreak, we arrived towards noon at a well-cultivated valley, in the centre of which was a fairly large group of houses. While the infantry rested and partook of food, Haslam set off with the Cossacks to reconnoitre. He returned to M. de Richelieu in great distress, saying:

I am indignant at the treachery of the two chiefs who have

drawn us here; above all, at the arguments they used to deceive me and which led me to induce you to undertake this enterprise. I will severely punish the wretches; I swear it, or I will die in the attempt. I will be avenged, and show that I am incapable of treachery! The chiefs mentioned are, indeed, here, but they are accompanied by at least 10,000 warriors, hidden in the woods. From the preparations I have seen, you will soon be attacked. Try to get possession of the pass at the end of the valley before the Circassians seize it.

The Duc de Richelieu at once declared that he had no doubt of Haslam's loyalty and devotion, and gave the order to advance. Haslam, with gleaming eyes, then threw his grey cloak to the horseman who attended him, and appeared in complete armour; he drew his sabre, which hung from his wrist by a richly-embroidered sword-knot, bent his bow, took an arrow from the quiver, and was off like the wind at the head of two regiments of Cossacks to seize the pass. It was splendid to see him. Two battalions of *chasseurs* and four cannon galloped after the Cossacks. They met with no resistance; but scarcely had the centre begun to move, endeavouring to follow the Cossacks as closely as possible, when shrill cries, on all sides, gave the signal for a general attack. Several volleys of grape-shot failed to check these valiant warriors. We had to charge with the bayonet. A fierce hand-to-hand struggle followed, which ended in a frightful slaughter.

In the heat of the combat the Circassians did not notice that they were between the fire of the advance-guard and that of the centre. To complete their rout, the possession of the defile having been assured, Haslam-Gheraï led his two regiments of Cossacks in another direction. Alone, and in advance of the line, he encouraged them by word and gesture, and had reached the verge of the wood to cut off all retreat from the enemy, when he was wounded by a bullet. He called his friend Sultan-Ali and said: "Hold me up so that our enemies may not have the triumph of seeing Haslam fall." At the same moment, a second bullet broke his jaw. The Circassians rushed forward to pick him up, but the Cossacks, who loved him, would not let them have the body.

Our victory was complete; the Circassians left about 2,000 dead on the field. The Cossacks went everywhere, setting fire to the houses, and carrying off the herds dazed by the flames and the sound of the gunfire. The ambush that had been laid for us cost its authors dearly!

I have heard it said that, twenty years later, the Circassians still spoke of this battle in which they lost their most renowned chiefs. With the exception of Haslam, our losses were inconsiderable.

Haslam, when dying, his eyes already dim, commended his wife and children to M. de Richelieu, who had hastened to him. All his friends escorted his remains to the village in the Crimea where he lived. In accordance with the government orders, he was accorded the honours due to a colonel, the rank the *Tzar* had conferred upon him the previous year.

★★★★★★

A Scottish artist, Mr. Allen, professor of drawing to the Countess Potocka's children, painted a picture of Haslam and Mira crossing the Kuban. The likeness was good and the details very exact; the picture was much admired. The Grand Duke Michael bought it, and had it engraved. The Cossacks who idolised Haslam adorned their tents with the engraving.

★★★★★★

Mira married Sultan-Ali a few months after Haslam's death.

The close of the year 1811 passed quietly. I had returned to my ordinary way of life. The visit of Mme. Narishkin, our journey and military expedition had thrown my work into arrears. In the house that she had occupied I found a chain that had been forgotten when we left for the Crimea. I sent it to her, and she replied:

Peterhof, Dec. 24, 1811.

Was there ever a package more unexpected than the one I have just received from you, dear M. de Rochechouart! But what gave me most pleasure was the kind letter you sent with it. As for the chain, I am sorry you did not keep it as a memento of your 'little wife,' and of her whom you called your mother-in-law, at least for that summer. I hope—oh! yes, I hope—that we shall all be united by a chain of flowers, extending from your Principality of Urzuff to my new estate.

I long to see my little *château* furnished, and, still more, to stay in it; so, more than ever, I am determined, next summer, to fly to the promised land. Rejoice, then, my dear good son, that your mother-in-law is disposed to come nearer you, and may all your little society, among whom I should be so glad to find myself again, rejoice too! Be sure and tell them so, in order that, at least, my letter may not make them jealous, for this time I am

108

writing to you alone. It is quite allowable to have a preference for one's son.

I have given your letter to your dear little wife, but the poor child is not in a fit state to reply, for she has not quite recovered from an attack of scarlatina, which seemed to be lying in wait for her here. How this confirms me in my wish to seek a milder climate for her, and to take her back to the part of the country where she had such good health! You too, try your best to improve and adorn the retreat for your little wife, and while waiting for me to bring her to you, think sometimes of your mother-in-law.

Sally is inconsolable because you have forgotten her. She says: 'He mentions me, indeed, in his letter to Sophie, but cannot he write me a separate letter?' Make haste to atone for your fault, and I will obtain your pardon.

The winter boded ill for amusements, and the political horizon was very dark. There were mysterious rumours and vague anxieties; the stagnation of commerce, and the famous comet of 1811, all presaged a catastrophe.

In March, 1812, the governor-general received orders from the emperor to dispatch all available troops at his disposal to Volhynia, and to go himself to St. Petersburg to take part in the conferences to be held there. The old general, Prince Kutusoff, Commander-in-Chief of the Russian forces in the provinces on the Danube, was entering into negotiations for peace with Turkey. The council was to study the conditions of this peace, to examine the situation in the Caucasus, and, above all, to prepare for the struggle that was opening between those colossal powers—Napoleon and Russia. Napoleon was marching on Russia, not only with the entire military force of France, but with that of all the powers of Europe, except Sweden, who remained neutral.

Russia had no ally but England, with whom she was negotiating a treaty, which, however, was only signed in 1813. The Duc de Richelieu passed his whole time in the emperor's cabinet. I took my turn as *aide-de-camp* at the Winter Palace without seeing the *Tzar*. Once only I came to tell him the password. Many and grave affairs occupied every moment of the sovereign and his ministers and advisers. A fortnight later, we hurried back to Odessa to hasten the dispatch of the troops, arrange for their concentration, superintend the supplies, and take all measures necessary to secure the tranquillity of the frontiers of the Caucasus. The complete success of our last expedition guaranteed us, at least, a truce on that side.

When the Duc de Richelieu took leave of the emperor, he told him he was leaving on April 11th. The evening before that day, he received a letter from His Majesty, written at Tsarskoe Selo, the Russian Versailles. I give this letter in full; the original is in my possession; it establishes an historical fact that has been much disputed by certain historians who have not known all the details; the idea of retiring into the interior of Russia, in order to draw on the French, in the event of a defeat of the Russian Army, had already been decided upon by the Emperor Alexander. Here is the proof:

> I had been hoping, General, to have the opportunity of saying a word to you about the lady who has been my companion for twelve years, and about my child. They will again place themselves under your care, but this time they will need care of another kind, to guide them, in the event—which God forbid!—of our being compelled by some catastrophe to retire so far as to place your provinces in danger; in that case, conduct them into the interior, to Penza or Saratoff for instance; in a word, counsel and direct them. I look for this service from your friendship for me and for her; I need not tell you how dear these two are to me.
>
> *Adieu*, my dear General, the truest friendship is yours for ever.
>
> Tsarskoe Selo, April 9th, 1812.

This letter shows that the emperor was resolved to resist with all his power the unjust aggression which threatened his country, and to draw the French, as far as possible, into the interior of his vast empire, rather than conclude a peace which would be shameful for Russia. Perhaps, he already foresaw that the winter would aid him against his enemy. It also shows the deep and sincere attachment of the sovereign for those whom he commended so particularly to the care of M. de Richelieu, at a time when many grave events claimed his attention; and lastly, it shows his great confidence in the duke.

Madame Narishkin refused, however, to leave the emperor at this crisis. It was well she did so, for the plague broke out in Odessa, and Southern Russia became as dangerous a place to stay in as it had been delightful the year before.

Immediately after his return to Odessa, the Duc de Richelieu took in hand the various matters that had been arranged with the emperor.

He began by assembling the troops of his division, scattered over his three provinces, leaving only depots in the interior, and only as many troops on the Caucasian frontier as were actually needed to guard against a surprise; this reserve consisted of convalescents and recent recruits.

Volhynia was a long way off, and, in spite of forced marches, some of the regiments were unable to get there before the end of July. While waiting for them the government was occupied with negotiations with Turkey. The military incapacity of the *grand vizier* facilitated the conclusion of peace. He had allowed himself with his whole army, to be surrounded in a most unfavourable position by Prince Kutusoff. Sweden offered her mediation, which was accepted. The peace that was signed is called the Treaty of Bukarest...We were living tranquilly, while, far away, terrible battles were being fought, from the crossing of the Niemen on June 24th by 500,000 men, under the greatest leader of modern times, to the capture of Moscow two months later. The sacrifices of every kind made by the nobles, the clergy, the merchants, and the entire Russian people, in this supreme crisis, will remain for ever a monument of the patriotism of the Russian nation, who forgot all their personal interests in the effort to serve their country.

The assembling of the troops of our division, which was to form part of the army corps under the command of General Tormasoff, was at length completed; we were about to leave for Volhynia, when, at the end of August, the plague broke out in Odessa. It had been raging for some time without our suspecting it; the mortality had become frightful; after the medical reports, the town council, under the presidency of the Duc de Richelieu, decided to declare the town plague-stricken.

Before proceeding to this extremity, the governor-general had to struggle against all the interests that would suffer from the regulations—rigorous, it is true, but necessary—ruinous to the immense commerce of the town, reducing the large industrial population to despair.

In the midst of these terrible surroundings the character of the governor-general stands forth in all its greatness. He sacrificed his dearest interests, his strongest inclinations, his noble and lawful ambitions, to the duties of his position, and the interests of the town entrusted to him. Instead of leaving Odessa, as he had intended, to take up the military command conferred upon him, he devoted himself to the safety of the inhabitants and the town he had created, and of the

111

three provinces under his government. He allowed the military command to be temporarily transferred to another, convinced that by his presence, and example, and energy, he could render greater service to the country of his adoption than on the battlefield.

He announced his firm resolve to remain in the midst of the scourge, and to devote his every care, even at the risk of his life, to conquer the malady. He assured the inhabitants that the best way to attain this end was to conform to his regulations, and to submit to all the sacrifices involved.

Odessa was declared in quarantine; everyone was forbidden to leave his house; special commissioners went from house to house to supply each family with the necessary food. Like protecting angels, the duke, the Abbé Nicolle, our friend the Spanish Consul, and other devoted men hastened to all parts where the plague raged most fiercely. No sleep or rest for them; scarcely a moment snatched for food, or for the most urgent business. Day and night, they were to be seen visiting the hospitals, tending the sick, or succouring the poor. Spade in hand, the noble duke himself assisted at the burying of the dead, after having received the orphan from the hands of the dying.

One poor mother, with a child in her arms, was about to fall a victim to the scourge, when the governor, with the Abbé Nicolle, happened to pass the house; she dragged herself to the door, and held out the child, begging them to care for it. The duke took it, and comforted her, and the Abbé Nicolle blessed her, and gave her absolution; her last words breathed only gratitude and resignation: "God be praised. I die in peace."

The Comte de Maistre, Sardinian Minister at St. Petersburg, wrote to the Abbé Nicolle, on April 17th, 1813:

Deeply anxious about you in this terrible trial, I am no less anxious about the Duc de Richelieu, who, during the plague, has shown himself, not only better than others, but, if it be possible, better than himself. At last, thank God! it is all over.

On the other hand, the Abbé Nicolle wrote:

M. de Richelieu had not escaped the influence of the prevailing unbelief of his day; but if the religious convictions in which he had been brought up had grown somewhat weak, they had never been effaced from his heart. When the plague struck with such terrible force the people to whom he had become a father, religion came back to him; his noble soul felt the need of it.

After having laid before me certain doubts, which happily I was able to dispel, I found him calm and resolute; I heard his General Confession, and had the consolation of giving him Holy Communion in the Catholic Church at Odessa.

I might cite other letters, but these will suffice to show the courage and devotion of M. de Richelieu.

As soon as he had made up his mind to remain, he ordered his chief of staff, the Comte de Venanson, to join the troops of the division and lead them to their destination. At the same time, he ordered me to leave Odessa and take his dispatches to General Tormassoff, explaining the overwhelming necessity which compelled him to remain at Odessa until the plague should have disappeared. As he embraced me he added:

As your uncle, I beg you to make no objection; as your general, I order you to obey without a word. Go, my dear Leo, may God protect you. My blessing goes with you; let me often hear from you; think sometimes of him whom you have left here amid dangers without glory!

I threw myself into his arms, mingling my tears with his.

The next day I left this abode of sorrow, heartbroken to part from my second father, while he was in the midst of such dangers. I entrusted the charge of the house to Stempkovski. The devotion of this kind young fellow never slackened for a moment. He remained with the Duc de Richelieu until his death.

My equipage, though hastily made, was complete. A *britzka*, drawn by two good horses, a coachman, two soldier servants, lastly, two good and beautiful saddle-horses. My carriage contained all kinds of provisions: wines from Bordeaux and Madeira, tea, rum. I had in my dressing-case 200 gold *ducats* (2,400 *francs*).

I left Odessa on October 5th, accompanied by the Comte de Venanson and another staff officer, who had been detached to hasten the march of an infantry regiment from Ekaterinoslaff that was late.

THE RETREATING FRENCH CROSSING THE BERESINA

CHAPTER 1

The Crossing off the Beresina

Prince Casimir Lubomirski received us at Dubno, a town within the government of Volhynia. The reader will remember that I was indebted to the prince for my appointment as *aide-de-camp* to the Emperor. He was an intimate friend of M. de Richelieu, and I found him greatly distressed that the duke should have remained in the plague-stricken town, exposed every moment to such a sad death for a soldier.

The post no longer ran; only the Cossacks went to and fro. Whilst we were at Dubno, one of them brought us news of the evacuation and burning of Moscow.

The peace with Turkey permitted the so-called Army of Moldavia, commanded by Admiral Tchitchagoff, to leave the Danube. It effected a junction with the army corps under General Tormassoff, which included the Richelieu Division that we were leading. These two army corps formed together an effective force of 75,000 men, of whom 20,000 were excellent cavalry.

They were divided anew into two corps: the first, under the admiral, consisted of veterans returned from the provinces on the Danube, and the 22nd Regiment of Chasseurs, who had accompanied us in all our expeditions to Circassia; it was to oppose the Austrian Army of Prince Schwarzenberg; the second corps, consisting of less seasoned troops under General Tormassoff, was to remain in Volhynia, awaiting events.

The Comte de Langeron was occupying Lutsk with his division; I went to see him, and he suggested that I should remain with him; he undertook to present me to the admiral, and to obtain his permission to keep me on his staff until I could rejoin the emperor. Strictly speaking, as *aide-de-camp* to the emperor, I ought to be on the admiral's staff; M. de Langeron easily obtained permission to keep me with him.

As soon as I was installed at Lutsk, I wrote to M. de Richelieu, telling him what had been done, and asking his approval. Owing to the disorganisation of the post, his letter, which accorded with my wish, only reached me a fortnight later.

Then began a series of marches and counter-marches, following the supposed movements of the Austrian Army, crossing and recrossing the Bug, now in the duchy of Warsaw, now in the government of Grodno, now in Volhynia. Evidently, on both sides, there was a desire to avoid an engagement, for, apart from some skirmishes of the advance-guard, the armies never came in contact. In the following incident, I saw a proof of this tacit understanding.

The Château of Nesvige, the residence of the eldest of the Radzivill princes—the hereditary estate and chief place of their principality—contained a unique collection of armour, rare manuscripts, medals, jewels and ancient bronzes. All these treasures were endangered by our comings and goings, for the Austrians and Russians were alternately in possession of the town. To preserve this precious collection, which, thanks to this measure, remained intact, the admiral sequestrated all the furniture and fixtures.

Towards the end of October, General Tormassoff, having been ordered to join the main army under Marshal Kutusotf, our organisation was modified; the admiral, with 40,000 men, proceeded to White Russia, with orders to occupy Minsk and Vilna, in the hope that Napoleon might be taken between two fires, and his retreat cut off. Count Sacken, at the head of 30,000 men, was to continue the game of prison-bars with the Austrian, Saxon and German Army, forming a corps of 55,000 men.

Up to this time I have followed the Russian calendar; henceforth I will follow the Gregorian, calling attention to the fact that it is twelve days in advance of the Russian. On November 4th, then, we seized Minsk, containing immense stores of clothing, equipment, munitions, and supplies. The Polish general, Bronikowski, to whom Napoleon had entrusted the defence of the town, was surprised by our advance-guard, under the Comte de Lambert, an emigre in the service of Russia. Besides, 2,000 men could not resist 40,000. General Bronikowski withdrew to Borissoff, joining forces with General Dombrowski; together they repaired the bridge-head, constructed to protect the passage of the Beresina.

It is impossible to understand how the Governor of Minsk came to be taken by surprise. Why was he not forewarned of the march of our army corps? How did he come not to have scouts, if only to keep in touch with Prince Sohwarzenberg? No doubt this feeling of security arose from the inaccurate reports given by the *Grande Armée*, which announced victories everywhere, and the annihilation of the Russian Armies. Lastly, how came it that Napoleon left only 2,000 men to defend such important military stores? This confidence cost him dear.

We ourselves were in complete ignorance of the events following the evacuation of Moscow, after the burning of the Kremlin. We did not know where Napoleon, or his army, might be; we did not know what army corps we might be called upon to fight, or its numerical strength. We did not know the deplorable condition of the French army. Our constant marches had deprived us of all regular communications; we went on at a venture, but very cautiously.

The slowness of the admiral's operations, and his conduct at the passage of the Beresina, have been severely criticised; it has not been taken into account how much he was surprised to find himself suddenly, and without warning, face to face with Napoleon. He could not go at a break-neck pace, still less could he endanger his army corps, composed of excellent troops, capable of rendering eminent services to their country if opportunity offered. It will be seen in what position he found himself on receiving positive orders from Prince Kutusoff. The admiral could not, therefore, have acted otherwise than he did; it is easy to criticise after the event and to say:

If he had manoeuvred in such a way this would not have happened.

I am going to relate what I have seen; I will not depart from the strictest truth. I shall speak of events that happened under my own eyes, and in which I bore a part.

The two days following our entry into Minsk were occupied in resting the troops, tired out with the incessant marching, and in supplying them plentifully with everything they needed; then we consulted together as to what should be done. After having collected all the information we could obtain as to the position of the Russian and French Armies, which did not help us much, as nothing was known with any certainty, we hesitated whether to march on Vilna, in order to seize the immense stores that were there, or to go to Vitebsk, by way of Orcha, in order to destroy the bridge over the Dnieper.

We decided to march on Vilna, but first to seize Borissoff (French historians write Boris-ow) with its bridge-head over the Beresina. The operation was entrusted to Lieut.-General the Comte de Lambert, who had been in command of our advance-guard since we separated from the corps of General Count Sacken. The effectives under his orders were 10,000 men, more than half of whom were cavalry, with a few heavy guns. M. de Langeron allowed me to accompany M. de Lambert, so I joined the advance-guard, and presented myself to the general. He said:

> You come most opportunely, my dear Rochechouart, my *aide-de-camp* is ill, and has remained behind at Minsk. I require an officer to take the command of the infantry; it is not my branch of the service.

Delighted with such a reception, I promised to do everything in my power.

Thus, on November 19th we marched on Borissoff, covering on that day twenty-two *versts*. On the evening of the 20th we bivouacked opposite the French outposts. M. de Lambert put off the attack on the entrenchments till the next day.

At dawn, the attacking forces drew up in formation. The general sent me, at the head of the skirmishers, to reconnoitre the position and the strength of the enemy. Soon, the outposts retired. I gathered at once, from the weak and uncertain defence, that our foes were not Frenchmen, but troops of various corps and nationalities. The outposts having withdrawn, a fire of artillery began, which killed some of our men and several horses. Colonel Michaud, a distinguished Piedmontese officer, chief of the staff of the division, lost his right arm at the first volley; it was amputated on the battlefield.

The road we were taking led to the extreme left of the bridge-head. I quitted it with my skirmishers and made for the opposite side, where I imagined the defence would be weaker. The division continued to follow the Minsk road. I succeeded, in fact, without difficulty, on the extreme right of the entrenchments, near the river, the banks of which are very steep at this point. Not having enough troops with me to attempt anything serious, I placed my men in cover, behind some rising ground, telling them to wait for me without moving. I set off at a gallop, greeted with a violent fusillade, and joined M. de Lambert in the midst of his troops. I asked to be reinforced by another battalion, telling him that the entrenchments on the extreme right were in a very bad state and might easily be taken.

We had very few infantry and plenty of cavalry, as is usual with an advance-guard, but it is not an arrangement favourable to the capture of trenches. The general had with him the fine regiment of hussars of which he was the commander, its five squadrons in full strength. He made 300 hussars dismount, and said to them:

Mes enfants, I am giving you a grand opportunity to distinguish yourselves; you are going to take those entrenchments in company with the grenadiers, who are not strong enough. Forward! *A la Carabine!*

This address was received with cheers. The general added four companies of infantry to this dismounted cavalry, and promised to delay the attack of the centre and right wing to give me time to carry out the operation on our left.

In order to calm the impatience of the troops. General de Lambert ordered some cannon-shots to be fired on the guns posted on the top of the fortifications of Borissoff; a frantic cheer from the whole line replied, gave the signal for assault, and drew the enemy troops to the left of the bridge-head; it was then easy for me to penetrate the almost undefended line with my original skirmishers and the hussars, who were able to keep up with me. Thus, we brought about the immediate abandonment of the bridge-head, for seeing themselves unexpectedly attacked almost within their entrenchments, the enemy fled down the long wooden bridge leading to Borissoff, hoping to have time to cut it or burn it. But conquerors and conquered entering the town together pell-mell, prevented the destruction of the bridge.

I learned that the Comte de Lambert had just been wounded in the shoulder by a bullet as he was accompanying his troops to the assault. I hastened to him to inquire how he was and to make my report. He said: "It is nothing, I hope. It is rather painful. Do not be uneasy, I shall not forget you." M. de Lambert did indeed mention me in his despatches, saying that I was the first to enter the bridge-head; soon after I received the Cross of Chevalier de St. Vladimir.

I followed M. de Lambert into Borissoff, which had been hastily evacuated by the Saxons. Order having been restored in the little town, the wounded general was placed in a beautiful house, the residence of the ex-*commandant* of Minsk. I noticed there was a fireplace in the drawing-room, a rare luxury in those parts. I mention this detail as it led to important results. In this fireplace, a large fire had nearly burnt up some papers. I guessed they were important, and ran forward to save some scraps. I was fortunate in finding among them a letter from the Maréchal Duc de Bellune, addressed to General Bronikowski, Governor of Minsk.

> Monsieur le Gouverneur,
> My *aide-de-camp*, Prince Sulkowski, who will deliver this letter to you, is ordered at the same time, to superintend the carrying out of the following orders. His Majesty Napoleon should arrive the day after tomorrow, the 23rd, at Borissoff, and will be at Minsk on the 25th. The long marches which the army has had to make, and the many and glorious battles it has fought, necessitate rest and food; take steps that all should be ready; above all, a great many new boots will be required.
> Maréchal Duc de Bellune.

It is easy to imagine our surprise on learning that the next day we should have the whole of the *Grande Armée* upon us. M. de Lambert said:

> Take this letter at once to Admiral Tchitchagoff. You will add that I am only keeping a small detachment here; all the rest of the advance-guard will at once take the road to Orcha. As I am obliged to keep my bed on account of the serious nature of my wound, I give the command to General Count Pahlen. If I had been able to mount my horse, I would never have ceded to anyone the honour of commanding such brave soldiers.

I set out at once, leaving my servants and equipage at Borissoff. I told my servant to find somewhere for me to sleep on my return.

I met the admiral on the way; having heard of the capture of the bridge-head, he had at once mounted his horse and gone with his whole staff, to examine the position. I handed him the Duc de Bellune's letter, and gave him M. de Lambert's message. After listening to me very attentively, he said:

> I did not know General de Lambert was wounded, I will go and talk with him, and see what is to be done.

Although we were riding so fast I finished the narrative of the capture of Borissoff. Returning to the town, worn out with fatigue, I went to my lodgings, supped hastily, and went to bed.

The next day, the 22nd, I went to see M. de Langeron, who was stationed with his division in advance of the bridge-head, where the whole of the army corps joined him in the evening, and bivouacked on the right bank of the Beresina, connected with the town by a bridge of immense length on account of the marshes on the left bank. I returned to pass the night in the town.

On the 23rd, the admiral assembled all his generals to a Council of War. He was impatiently awaiting news of the advance-guard, which had passed the night at Lochmitza, six *versts* from us, and ought then to go to Bohr. In the evening, I was dining with the Madame Rochman-off, the wife of the Chief Commissary of Stores of our army. I knew him very well, as he had lived a long time at Odessa, before he was appointed Civil Governor of Kherson. In the middle of dinner, we saw some Russian hussars, who had formed part of the advance-guard, galloping up. They were shouting *"Frantzouzi, Frantzouzi,"* and mak-ing for the bridge. Madame Rochmanoff, seized with panic, insisted, happily for her, in at once crossing the river to go to Minsk, in spite of all my efforts to reassure her. I pressed her, at least, to wait for coffee.

"Come and take it at Minsk," she replied.

The number of fugitives increased every moment; yet these same soldiers had fought bravely the day before. Instead of hastening to my rooms and ordering my servant to cross to the other side, I tried to check the fugitives,—in vain. A prey to terror, drunk with fear, if I may use the expression, they shouted *"Frantzouzi, Frantzouzi,"* inca-pable of saying anything else. Some guns, followed by their caissons, galloped through the town, knocking down, or crushing everything in their way. I was obliged to go with the torrent, and took my way towards the bridge; there I found Madame de Lambert, bare-headed. She had succeeded in stopping some of her husband's hussars, and was saying in Russian: "Children, will you forsake your wounded general!" They dismounted and carried their leader on their shoulders; four mounted hussars leading the horses of their comrades, went first to clear the way and protect the wounded officer, till they reached the other end of that interminable bridge.

I took advantage of the escort to cross the Beresina in the midst of the *mêlée*, and having a score of times run the risk of being crushed, or forced into the river, I reached the bivouac of M. de Langeron, and there I waited in vain for my horses and carriage. I had not even my cloak.

The admiral was sitting down to dinner with his officers. He had to leave his dinner, and, like me, to pass that wretched bridge on foot. Within the space of half an hour all was over; that is to say, out of

12,000 men and twelve guns, forming the division of the advance-guard, only 1,000 men and two guns crossed, the rest were taken prisoners or scattered. Fifty French *chasseurs* of the Legrand Division, under the influence of a strong ration of brandy, had surprised the outposts of our advance-guard before Lochmitza, charging them with fury; French and Russians reached the square of the little town together, and caused the panic which led to the rout of the whole corps.

Poor Pahlen was never able to rally even a hundred men to charge the French *chasseurs*; having only been placed in command the evening before, and being unknown to the troops, he was carried along, in spite of himself, by the mass of fugitives; he arrived at our bivouac in a state of despair impossible to describe.

★★★★★★

This event had very grave consequences. The authors who have written upon this celebrated retreat, M. de La Beaume, the Comte de Ségur, Baron Fain, M. de Norwins, even M. Bout-ourlin, *aide-de-camp* to the Emperor of Russia, not knowing the motives and details of our rout, have ascribed it to extraordinary causes, whereas they were quite natural. I have just shown it by the simple and accurate account of what happened. I have carefully read all the works by French officers who have related the strange evacuation of the town of Borissoff at the very moment when the Russians ought to have done their utmost to defend it; I have also read the narrative of M. Boutourlin on the campaign of 1812. Not one of these writers gives a correct explanation of this fray, through not having drawn their information from a reliable source. Only one, little known, work gives a full account of the attack on the bridge-head and the rout of the Russian advance-guard, under Count Paul Pahlen. This work is entitled, "*Mémoires pour servir à l'histoire de la guerre entre la France et la Russie en 1812,*" *avec un atlas militaire par un officier d'état major de l'armée française.* 2 vols. London. 1815. Inserted in the text in the French original.

★★★★★

As soon as the admiral reached the other bank, fearing every moment the arrival of the *Grande Armée*, the strength of which he did not know, he ordered the bridge to be cut in two places, which rendered all communication with the opposite bank impossible.

Evening was drawing near, and I had received no news of my servants. I despaired of ever seeing my belongings again, when my

Cossack suddenly appeared before me; he brought what was of inestimable value at the moment—my cloak; and was leading my best horse ready saddled. This intelligent and devoted man told me that, on the first alarm, he had run to my servants and found them at dinner. In vain he said to them: "Put the horses in at once and escape"; they would not believe him. Then he took my cloak, which was on the box of the *britzka*, and hastily saddled a horse. Setting off at a gallop he found the bridge cut. Such difficulties do not stop a Cossack, accustomed as he is to continually meeting with obstacles; he said to himself: "We cannot cross this way now, we must try somewhere else."

Going down the river, he found a ford a league farther on, and came to look for me "where I ought to be." I embraced him, so delighted was I with this mark of devotion. Provided with my precious cloak, I went to sleep at the bivouac of the Comte de Langeron's *aides-de-camp;* the cold was intense that night, so the happiness of possessing my fur-lined cloak made me forget my other losses.

In the morning of the 24th my soldier servant appeared; he threw himself at my feet, begging my pardon. Everything I had in the world was in the hands of the French; he only brought a little bag containing what I required for the night. The French had reached my rooms at the very moment when he was trying to take away my dressing-case, containing my jewellery, money and papers—the dressing-case made of rosewood from the palisades of Anapa. The entire fortune left to me consisted of a night-shirt, comb, slippers, the shirt I had on, three handkerchiefs, a hundred paper *roubles* in my pocket-book, a horse, and above all—my cloak.

Early in the morning we rallied the scattered troops; very few hussars failed to answer the roll-call; the greater part, following the left bank of the river as far as Beresino, had found a bridge, and were able to reach headquarters; six guns never reappeared.

In the evening. Colonel Michel Orloff, at the head of a reconnaissance, met a detachment of Cossacks, bringing a letter from the *generalissimo*, Prince Kutusoff, to the admiral. These Cossacks belonged to the Hetman Platoff, commanding the Don Cossacks.

The letter announced that the *Grande Armée* was approaching in disorder; and that to save as many troops as possible. Napoleon would be certain to hasten to cross the Beresina; the admiral ought, therefore, at all hazards, to delay this crossing, in order to give time for the *generalissimo* to effect a junction with Prince Wittgenstein's army corps, and with the Hetman Platoff. Prince Kutusoff ended his letter as follows:

You have to do with Napoleon, a general of the greatest genius; he is sure to make a demonstration of crossing at one point, in order to attract your attention, while he crosses at another; therefore, prudence and vigilance.

Having received information, directions and advice from his commander-in-chief, the admiral was bound to follow the counsel of his superior. While carrying out their mission, the Cossacks had kept their eyes open, and gave Colonel Orloff much information as to the position of the French Army.

The admiral sent a detachment of light horse along the right bank of the Beresina, to try to get into communication with Prince Wittgenstein; the *commandant* of this detachment warned the admiral that the French seemed to be trying to throw a bridge over the river at Studianska, twenty-five *versts* up the river from Borissoff, a very marshy spot, and consequently very unfavourable for the building of a bridge. Believing that the enemy wished to draw attention to this point, while he crossed somewhere else, at Beresino, for example, where there was a good road and a solid bridge, the admiral ordered his entire army corps to proceed to Beresino. Only the Comte de Langeron, with 4,000 men, waited before Studianska to observe the enemy's manoeuvres.

Beresino was twenty-five *versts* down the river from Borissoff; we marched all night, in terrible cold and along very bad roads. Arriving, on the 25th, at Beresino, we saw no trace of the French Army. The admiral began to fear he had made a wrong manoeuvre. In the evening, he learned with certainty that this fatiguing march had been greatly to the advantage of Napoleon. An *aide-de-camp* of the Comte de Langeron came to inform him that the French engineers were constructing a bridge opposite to him; the work being protected by a battery of forty heavy guns. M. de Langeron had only eight guns; fearing to be annihilated by such superior forces, he withdrew to Borissoff, to join the detachment at the bridgehead, and await further orders.

In spite of the terrible roads, we returned to the bridge-head, but with men and horses tired out, leaving many stragglers, occupied for the most part in dragging the cannon and wagons out of the mud where they had stuck. We spent the day of the 27th in rallying all the troops.

On the 28th, at daybreak, we advanced on Studianska. I was with the 22nd Regiment of Chasseurs. Happily, for me, I met M. de Langeron. He said:

Rochechouart, leave the *chasseurs*, they are taking the high road;
come with me. I am going to occupy a wood with two battalions of grenadiers and a regiment of Don Cossacks.

When we reached the verge of the wood, three squadrons of General Oudinot's *cuirassiers* charged us; they sabred, and put to route our
grenadiers, but our Cossacks stood their ground, and enabled us to
rally the main body of the army. As for the 22nd Chasseurs, overwhelmed on this fatal day, charged by a regiment of *cuirassiers*, and
taken in flank by a battery of artillery, they returned to the camp
with one hundred and fifty men, three officers, and the flag. They had
numbered 2,000 men when they set out in the morning. Three days
later, 1,200 men of this regiment who had been made prisoners, took
advantage of the general confusion of the French Army to escape.

Thanks to our false manoeuvre on Beresino, the French Army was
able to cross the Beresina, the last river wide enough to check its
progress; the Parthouneaux Division alone, about 4,000 strong, forming the rear-guard, was cut off, compelled to lay down arms, and made
prisoners of war.

The blinding snow-storm during the day was followed during the
night of the 28th-29th November by 26° (*Réaumur*) of cold, and during the following days it reached 30° (*Réaumur*).

CHAPTER 2

The Pursuit of the "Grande Armée"

I have now to relate great sufferings, fearful disasters, in a word, to try to give an idea of that catastrophe, an image of the anger of God bringing down the weight of His arm upon men.

On the morning of November 29th, the admiral organised his advance-guard, composed entirely of Cossacks; these were to move on the left flank of the French Army, and prevent it from turning to that side, where there were better roads and, above all, abundant provisions; while our main army corps pursued them closely. In spite of the total devastation of the country (we found all the houses burnt) we were fortunately not short of supplies, and our horses received regularly their ration of oats and fodder; moreover, they were rough-shod, according to the custom in cold countries.

On the 30th, I found myself at the place where the French Army had effected a crossing. Nothing could be more sad, more heartbreaking. We saw heaped up the dead bodies of men, women, and even children, soldiers of all arms, and of all nationalities, frozen, suffocated by the crush of fugitives, or mown down by the Russian grapeshot; horses, carriages, cannon, caissons, wagons, abandoned. It is impossible to imagine a more appalling scene than the two broken bridges with the river, frozen to its lowest depth. Immense treasures lay scattered over this region of death; peasants and Cossacks prowled around these fragments of bodies, carrying off whatever was most precious. I found my servant ransacking a carriage; he said he was looking for shirts, handkerchiefs, stockings, etc., to replenish my wardrobe, since, through his fault, everything had been taken. . . . (A few of the more painful details have been omitted from the translation.—Tr.)

Both sides of the road were strewn with dead, frozen in every attitude, or with men dying of cold, hunger, and fatigue, with their clothing in rags; they begged us to take them prisoners, and enumerated all the things they could do. "We were assailed with cries: "*Monsieur*, take me with you, I can cook," or "I am a valet," or "a hairdresser," "for the love of God give me a morsel of bread, and any rags to cover me." In spite of our great wish to do so, we could not help them.

The Langeron division pursued the French Army so closely that our quartermasters arrived at Studianska before the officers of Napoleon's staff had left the only house remaining intact; we had, therefore, every interest in keeping it from destruction, and by a mutual agreement the Russian General Staff was allowed to make it their headquarters. All the other houses were pillaged and burnt; the French burned the villages that had sheltered them for the night, in order to check our pursuit. The room occupied by Napoleon was assigned to the Comte de Langeron; the *aides-de-camp*, and officers of the staff, divided the other rooms among them.

We usually found written in chalk over the door the names of the orderly officers who had occupied the room before us. My comrades pointed out to me the name "Baron de Mortemart" over a door. It was evidently Casimir Duc de Mortemart, (the playfellow of de Rochechouart when they were little boys together in England.—Tr.); the emperor, only recognising titles that he himself had given, had created him a baron. The room was assigned to me; thus, it had been occupied by a Rochechouart, *aide-de-camp* to the Emperor of the French, and then by a Rochechouart, *aide-de-camp* to the Emperor of Russia. This curious coincidence was continued until we reached Smorghoni.

After December 1st, there was no more thought of fighting, but only of marching as quickly as possible to Vilna, where the French counted upon finding provisions, boots, and clothing. The Russians pursued them, to drive them out of their territory. As long as I live, I shall never forget the misery we saw, the cries of pain we heard, without being able to render succour. This distressing scene was renewed every day, every moment, yet it was impossible to hear these despairing cries without deep emotion.

At Smorghoni I met three *aides-de-camp* to the Emperor Alexander: Count Stanislas Potocki, Count Braniki, and Lamsdorf, son of the tutor of the Grand Dukes Nicholas and Michael, the younger brothers of the emperor. The first two, who were very rich, had brought with them abundant provisions— wines, liqueurs, sugar, tea, etc. They very kindly suggested to Lamsdorf and me that we four should mess together, an offer we gratefully accepted. M. de Langeron gave me a horse, I bought a little sledge from a Jew, and put my servant and my modest baggage in it; my faithful Cossack led my saddle-horse, and, overcome with the cold, I shut myself into Lamsdorf's carriage, which was fixed on a sledge.

At Osumiana we were joined by M. de Vlodeck, also an *aide-de-camp* to the emperor. He came from the General Headquarters, which could not follow the French as quickly as we could, for it was impossible to take the troops along a route which had been so completely ravaged, burned and devastated. M. de Vlodeck obtained permission to join the advance-guard, and came to us. Kutusoff's army, leaving the road, threw itself to the right and left; it thus found some provisions, but, like us, it suffered from the intense cold.

At Osumiana I witnessed several incidents which complete the picture of the sufferings endured by the remnant of the finest and bravest army in the world. I went into a *kartchma*, a tavern kept by a Jew. I wanted a sheepskin coat for my servant. I saw two men, unaccountably thin, whose clothing consisted of drawers, torn stockings, no shoes, a wretched vest, no shirt, and on their heads a black silk stocking with the foot hanging down negligently behind.

They were talking Portuguese, and, as I entered, one of them said to the other: "Here is an officer; let us beseech him."

I went up to them and said, also in Portuguese: "What do you wish, gentlemen?"

They seemed greatly astonished that a Russian officer should speak their language.

If you are a Christian, in the name of all the Saints, come to our help. I am the Vicomte d'Asséca, I belong to the Souza family; my comrade and I were in the corps commanded by the Marquis d'Alorna, which was serving with the French Army. A company of Cossacks surprised us yesterday, at this tavern, where we were trying to warm ourselves; they carried away our uniforms and our boots; we have had nothing to eat or drink for twenty-four hours; this rascal of a Jew pretends he has nothing for himself. While the Cossacks were stripping us, I hid a well-filled purse in the stove; it would enable us to buy food, if we could get out of this wretched inn; our only hope is in you; we appeal to you as a Christian and an officer; in mercy, save us!

I answered:

I will do what I can; it is very difficult, but I will try my utmost,

128

in memory of the welcome I received in Portugal in 1801-1802.

I had first of all to find two sheepskin coats for these gentlemen, then they could alternately get up into my sledge. I called the tavern-keeper, and drawing from my purse a hundred-*rouble* note: "This is for three *schouhi*." The sheepskin coat worn by Russian peasants is called a *schouha*, in the plural, *schouhi*.

"If you gave me three times as much, I could not get you a single one."

"Ah! That is what you say!" I exclaimed, seizing him by the beard. "First, you are going to give me the one on your back, and I swear you shall find me two more, or I will not leave a hair in your beard!" And I shook his beard so vigorously, that he began to howl frightfully. His family came running with three sheepskin coats; two of them were women's coats that had been hidden in the loft.

I gave one to each of my Portuguese, and the other to my servant, who was waiting to know the result of my bargaining. A new sheepskin coat costs ten *roubles*, and I was paying a hundred *roubles* for three old ones. This generous, but, under the circumstances, just act, caused my Jew to forget my somewhat Cossack manners. He showed his gratitude by giving us each a glass of brandy, begging us not to tell anyone he had it, or he would be plundered by every passer-by. The matter being thus happily settled, I took my officers away; my servant gave them a pair of boots, taken at the Beresina; they would do for the one that went on foot; when they reached Vilna, they would be able to get out of their difficulties by means of the money in their purse.

I had forgotten this incident, when, two months later, the Vicomte d'Asséca called on me at St. Petersburg. I could scarcely recognise in the handsome and elegantly dressed nobleman, the half-naked wretch I had rescued. He overwhelmed me with thanks and blessings, and told me that, when at Vilna, a Russian general whom he knew had given him leave to go to St. Petersburg, while awaiting his release as a prisoner of war. I met him again in 1816. He was settled in Brazil, as Minister of the Interior, and was a very important personage.

After my expedition to the Jewish tavern, I went back to my comrades, and made them laugh till the tears came into their eyes by the story of my adventures. Of course, my Portuguese were invited to dine with us. After dinner, we left Osumiana to spend the night at a *château* belonging to a friend of the Count Potocki. . . . As we were passing through this unhappy town we saw a hundred or so officer prisoners, crowded into the gaol of the place, behind iron bars; they were in their shirt sleeves, having been robbed by the Cossacks of their coats, etc. When they saw us, they called to us through their bars, asking for food and fire, and besides their heartbreaking cries they made certain signs.

Such scenes were met at every step, so I was much surprised to see my comrades go up to them and give them the remainder of our provisions and some clothing, and then go on to the *starotz*, the Slav name for the *mayor*, or *chief*, of the village. They insisted upon his having the stove lighted in the prison, and they left some money to be spent on clothing, bread, and meat, threatening severe penalties if their orders were not attended to. I asked Vlodeck the reason of this extraordinary sympathy; he said:

> These are Freemasons; they made us the sign of distress; as we are Freemasons ourselves, we are bound to succour our brothers if we are able.

On December 11th, when the cold was 29° Réaumur, I entered Vilna, crouching, with Lamsdorf, at the bottom of his carriage; it went forward amid human remains, frozen on the road, and hundreds of horses that had died of hunger and cold, or had broken their legs, for they were not rough-shod; our servants walked in front thrusting to the right, or left, the obstacles in the way.

We were assigned rooms in a suitable house, but they were already occupied by French or Polish officers, wounded or sick; the proprietor preferring to house four of the *Tzar's aides-de-camp*, rather than dying enemies, had them carried to a convent, and gave us their rooms, well *warmed*, an inestimable luxury in that temperature.

It is impossible to imagine the state of Vilna during the four days after our arrival; we found sick or wounded prisoners—Frenchmen, Poles, Germans, Spaniards, Italians and Portuguese, crowded into the various convents and monasteries. It was necessary to house everybody. Happily, the French Government had accumulated immense stores of provisions, which they had not been able to use, being so closely pursued by the Russians. These were distributed among all.

The frozen snow which covered the streets deadened the sound of the vehicles that were constantly passing, but did not prevent our hearing the cries of the wounded asking for food, or the drivers urging on their horses; in short, we did not know where to hide to get an hour's sleep. My first care had been to find out if Casimir de Mortemart were lying sick, or wounded, in one of the houses of the town. During my wanderings, I met Charles de Saint-Priest, *aide-de-camp* to the Emperor Alexander; he too was looking about to see if he could not find some friend or relative. We were animated by the same desire to succour our unhappy fellow-countrymen, deprived of food, clothing and medical care.

Thanks to our position as *aides-de-camp* to the emperor, we hoped to be able to obtain for them all the help possible, well knowing that he would be pleased with what we were doing. We were waiting for the *Tzar*, but these unhappy people could not wait. A dreadful scene met our eyes at a monastery that had formerly belonged to monks of St. Basil; not only the dead, but the living, were being thrown out of the windows on every storey, to make room for the sick and wounded Russians, who were arriving in crowds.

"Be it so, as regards the dead," I exclaimed, "but we cannot allow it to be done to those who are crying for mercy as they fall."

The sufferings of the unhappy men who were still living were increased by the terror of such a barbarous act. Saint-Priest stopped this inhuman execution in the name of the *Tzar*, and I ran to find a detachment of the Imperial Russian Guard. Thus reinforced, it was easy for us to restore order in this hospital, and to arrange for those who were still alive to be placed again in the rooms, rather close together, it is true, but it was necessary to shelter both friends and enemies. Finally, two government officials were ordered, in the name of the *Tzar*, to have blankets, provisions and medical stores distributed to the wounded foreigners, who overwhelmed us with thanks.

As we were going away, a young officer said:

You must be French nobles, come with me, and I will take you to a hole where hundreds of officers are crowded together; several of them have died since yesterday, others are still breathing, but they will die of hunger; most of them have their feet frostbitten; they cannot drag themselves about, like me.

I answered:

We are certainly French; show us the way; we shall be happy if we can lighten the lot of our fellow-countrymen.

He took us to a little tavern, some few feet square, where about eighty men lay dead, or dying; one of them, dragging himself along on his knees, spoke to me, and I recognised the Comte de Durfort. I had him removed to another house with M. de Montigny, the officer who had been our guide. The dead were removed to make a little more room for the living, who received the care necessary to their health. Charles de Saint-Priest and I spent all our time in alleviating the sufferings of these unhappy men. I could give other details, but the recital would become monotonous, for everywhere we found the same privations and sufferings.

The Emperor Alexander arrived at Vilna on December 22nd; the severity of the winter compelled a suspension of all military operations.

Knowing nothing of the sanitary conditions of Odessa, I asked Prince Wolkonski, the Chief of Staff of the emperor's Military Household, for leave to go to St. Petersburg, to replenish my equipage, and to recover my health, which had suffered greatly from this terrible campaign; my lungs especially needed care, a little warmth, and complete rest. I was called into Prince Wolkonski's office, and he said:

His Majesty gives you a holiday; you will convey an important dispatch to Prince Gortschakoff, Minister of War, and you will escort a distinguished prisoner, the grandson of the Maréchal de Castries, *aide-de-camp* to Maréchal Davoust. His Imperial Majesty will allow him to winter at St. Petersburg; I have informed him of this favour; you will be his guard. You will start tomorrow morning; here is the dispatch, the money for the journey, and the *podoroge* giving you the right to horses as the emperor's courier. Considering the severity of the weather His Majesty places a covered sledge at your disposal. When you reach St. Petersburg, you will at once give the dispatch to the Minister of War. You will stay at the Hôtel Desmoute, or elsewhere, if you prefer it, only you must inform Prince Gortschakoff where you decide to stay.

The Maréchal de Castries, driven away from France by the Revolution, had taken refuge in Russia. The Empress Catherine offered him a command. He replied: "I need nothing more. I beg your Majesty to transfer your sympathy to my grandson, Edmond de Castries; he is six years old."

The empress ordered that the name of this little child should be enrolled as a cadet in the Regiment of the Semenowski Guards, of which the hereditary grand duke was colonel. Edmond de Castries returned to France in 1803. The grand duke, now the Emperor Alexander, having recognised the protege of the empress among the prisoners at Vilna, very graciously assigned him St. Petersburg as his place of residence.

I found Edmond de Castries when I returned to my rooms, and we soon became friends. Thanks to the mission entrusted to me, I should travel quickly, with a delightful companion, and at no expense to myself. Our preparations were soon made; they consisted in lining the bottom of the sledge with hay, and providing a mattress, with good blankets, our fur coats and two sheepskin overcoats. We left at midnight, with 28° (*Réaumur*) of cold, a glorious moon, and snow in excellent condition for a sledge. A strange circumstance was that, as we went farther north, the cold became more bearable; we alighted every time we changed horses for a cup of very hot tea, with rum; during the winter every post-house keeps boiling water always ready in a *samovar*, a large copper kettle.

We entered St. Petersburg on December 28th, and I went to the Ministry of War; a courier, who had left Vilna six hours before us, had announced our approaching arrival. Prince Gortschakoff received de Castries kindly, and advised him to share my rooms as long as I stayed. Thus, ended for me the terrible year 1812, which witnessed the end of the dreams and fortune of Napoleon.

Baron Fain, private secretary to Napoleon, and confidant of his most intimate thoughts, says in his *Manuscrit de 1812*:

> The Continental Blockade is his dominant idea; he is occupied with it more than ever—too much, perhaps. But how can he help being carried away by hopes so near realisation.

The blockade, which Napoleon had devised in hatred of England, and which had become with him a fixed idea, could only become effective in co-operation with Russia. The Treaty of Tilsit and the interview at Erfurt gave hopes of this co-operation; but Alexander had promised more than he could perform. No sooner had ships been forbidden to enter the ports than cries of distress arose in all parts of the Empire; the ruin of commerce was imminent; it was necessary, at all costs, to avert it. The Emperor Alexander had recourse to the neutral flag of the United States, and commerce went on as before. Napoleon, seeing his plan fail, remonstrated vigorously. Baron Fain, in his *Manuscrit de 1812*, reproduces the *Tzar's* reply:

> I have contracted no obligations which can prevent my subjects

trading with neutrals; Russian commerce is restricted, it .suffers; it has rights which I ought to respect; the first is its existence; after so many sacrifices it is impossible to deprive it of its remnant of trade with neutrals."

Napoleon resolved to compel Russia to submit to his will, like all the other Continental Powers. The so-called breach of the Continental Blockade by Russia and Sweden led to the campaign in Russia.

Napoleon's plan was worthy of his genius; first, he re-established the Kingdom of Poland, thus making reparation for that shameful crime of modern times, the annihilation of a great nation; then he entered Russia, crossing the Niemen at the head of 500,000 men, divided into four armies; the first at the extreme left, commanded by the Maréchal Duc de Tarente, was to march on St. Petersburg; the second, under the Duc de Reggio (Oudinot), was to operate between MacDonald's army corps and the *Grande Armée* commanded directly by Napoleon, which was to march on Moscow; lastly, the fourth army, under Prince Schwarzenberg, was to operate in Russian Poland, Podolia, Volhynia and the Ukraine.

The Russian Army, attacked in a semicircle, was compelled to retire. After the sanguinary Battle of Moskowa, and Napoleon's entry into Moscow, he thought Russia was crushed; but Napoleon's generals had not carried out his orders. The Duc de Tarente, instead of marching on St. Petersburg, remained for three months besieging Riga; the Maréchal Oudinot, having been wounded, yielded the command to General Gouvion St.-Cyr who was afraid to advance; Prince Schwartzenberg tried to baffle General Tormassoff, and was himself baffled by Admiral Tchitchagoff, who, leaving General Sacken with 35,000 men facing Prince Schwarzenberg, marched on Minsk, destroyed the military stores, and tried to cut off the retreat of the French Army.

Thus abandoned, and badly served. Napoleon, believing that his orders had been executed, remained at Moscow awaiting the result of his strategy; could he have acted otherwise? The expressed determination of the Emperor Alexander not to enter upon any negotiations as long as the French Army was on Russian soil, and the burning of Moscow, at length opened the eyes of the great general. He thought of retreating. We have seen how cold and hunger annihilated this splendid army, and all these military plans.

If Napoleon had remained forty-eight hours longer at Moscow, or on the way to the Beresina, he would have found the river frozen to its depths, and could have crossed wherever he chose, and saved his artillery, wagons and baggage; he did not do this.

Napoleon's plan was admirable, and its success certain according to all human probability; it was the decree of Providence alone, baffling all human foresight, that brought about this great disaster, and rendered it irreparable.

CHAPTER 3

The Battles of Lutzen and Bautzen

The weeks passed quickly at St. Petersburg. I presented De Castries to Mme. Narishkin and the Countess Potocka, both of whom welcomed me as a friend. De Castries and I enjoyed ourselves very much, and did not miss a single *fête*, all doors being open to us. The end of my two months' leave was drawing near, but the weather remained as cold as ever, and there was no talk of resuming hostilities. All the same, I went to the Minister of War, he said:

> There is no hurry, stay where you are; I will let you know when I am in a position to send you to Headquarters; you will be entrusted with a mission that will call for the utmost discretion, and it can only be confided to you when you are on the point of leaving. Enjoy yourself while waiting. I will let you know six hours before the time for starting.

March passed thus, and on April 3rd Prince Gortschakoff said to me:

> On returning to your rooms you will receive a visit from Baron de Marschal; he was formerly *Attaché* to the Austrian Embassy at St. Petersburg, and has been *Charge d'Affaires* since the ambassador, the Count St. Julien, left. He will ask to be allowed to offer you a seat in his carriage as far as General Headquarters, which have just been removed from Kalisch, nearer the front. Here is your passport; you are accompanied by your secretary; you know who that secretary is; in order that no one may recognise him you will leave tonight; maintain absolute secrecy as to what I have told you—this is essential. Here is a dispatch for His Majesty, and another for Count Nesselrode; also, a thousand

roubles for your travelling expenses, for you must show great hospitality to your Secretary. Goodbye. A pleasant journey!

In accordance with these orders we left St. Petersburg at one o'clock in the morning. I did not lose a moment in covering those 450 leagues, yet it was not till April 18th that I reached the Grand Headquarters at Lauban, a little town in Saxony. In order to conceal the baron's arrival from the officers of the emperor's staff, who nearly all knew him, I left him hidden in the carriage, and went to receive Count Nesselrode's instructions, and to give him my dispatches. He was evidently pleased with the news of the secret arrival of the diplomatist and congratulated me warmly on the discretion with which I had carried out my mission. He advised me to let no one see me till the next day, adding that, at dusk, he would send a staff officer for my Secretary. I returned to the hotel, had supper, and went to bed, being very tired. The baron was no longer any concern of mine; I slept quietly, delighted to be once more with the army, for the campaign was about to begin.

On April 16th, two days before my arrival, the old field-marshal, Prince Kutusoff, had died, at Bunzlau, in Silesia; the fatigues of the campaign of 1812, the marches and counter-marches on the flanks of Napoleon, after the Battle of Moskowa, had sapped the strength of the great general, who was sixty-eight years old.

On April 19th, the emperor received me most kindly. His Majesty remained some days at Lauban. Before leaving he made a very handsome present to the proprietor of the house where he had stayed. All the same, his host sent in his account to Count Tolstoï, the Controller of the Household—fifty *thalers* for plants to decorate the staircase, three *thalers* for a bottle of Burgundy offered to the emperor on his arrival, sixteen *thalers* for sheets for the beds of the emperor's footmen, etc.; the bill was paid without a thought; the Germans do nothing for honour.

On April 20th, we marched from Lauban to Reichenbach—five German miles; the 21st was devoted to visiting the Moravian Brethren, or Anabaptists. The emperor went in a *droski*, accompanied by his whole staff, to the village where they lived. Alighting at the inn, he asked for a guide to show him everything.

"Who are you?" he was asked.

"I am Alexander."

The news quickly spread, and the whole village came to do hon-

BATTLE OF BAUTZEN

our to the sovereign whose kindness was proverbial.

On the 22nd His Majesty arrived at Bautzen, the capital of Upper Lusatia; the headquarters of the King of Prussia were also in this town; thenceforth, unless the difficulty of finding billets prevented it, the two headquarters were always together. The whole town was illuminated with the arms of Russia, or the monogram of the Emperor Alexander.

On the 23rd the army passed the night at Radeberg, and, on the 24th, made a triumphal entry into Dresden. The handsome young Emperor, at the head of his Guards and the Prussian Guards, had the King of Prussia and his sons on his left hand; the most brilliant staff in the world followed the two sovereigns; all the inhabitants lined the streets, and. young girls strewed flowers before their Majesties as they passed; the day ended with a magnificent illumination. The reception was so cordial that when Napoleon re-entered Dresden, after the Battle of Lutzen, he answered the deputation of the Municipality as follows:

> You deserve to be treated as a conquered country. I know all you did when the Allies were living in your town. I have a list of the volunteers you have clothed, equipped, and armed against me. I know what insults you have lavished on France. How many contemptible libels you have to hide, or burn; your houses still show faded garlands, and we still see on the pavement the flowers strewn by your young girls beneath the feet of the Allied Sovereigns. (Baron Fain, *Manuscrit de 1813*, chap. 1).

The 24th April was Holy Saturday, according to the Greek rite. High Mass (called in the Greek rite the "Mass of the Resurrection") was celebrated at midnight in the Emperor's Chapel. The next day, the 25th, the Festival of Easter, there was High Mass, parade, and a dinner with the Emperor; and in the evening a gala representation at the Opera. We only remained six days in this delightful town.

On April 29th, we were to have slept at Geringswalde, but the distance (nine German miles) was too great; we bivouacked in the open fields, in splendid weather, so as to allow the troops to rest.

On the 30th we left the heavy baggage at Geringswalde in order to march more quickly; at night, the headquarters were at Frohburg, and the next day, May 1st, at Borna. The order was given to be ready to mount at two in the morning. It was the eve of that memorable day, Sunday, May 2nd, which was to decide the fate of Europe if we

BATTLE OF LUTZEN

were conquerors.

At four in the morning the Emperor of Russia and the King of Prussia, with their staffs, arrived at Pegau; the new Commander-in-Chief of the Russian Army, the Count de Wittgenstein, was waiting at the rendezvous. General de Wittgenstein had acquired a great military reputation in the campaign of 1812; he was able to maintain his positions and manoeuvre so skilfully, that he withstood the attacks of Oudinot and of Gouvion St.-Cyr. On the 2nd May, however, he showed grave want of foresight in making the entire Prussian Army, infantry, cavalry, and artillery, pass in front of the Russian Army in order to take their place in the battle.

This manoeuvre, which might easily have been carried out the evening before, paralysed all his efforts, by delaying the commencement of the battle for three hours. His second fault was in keeping his reserves, which numbered 20,000 men, under General Miloradowitch, at so great a distance; they could not take part in the battle, and only arrived on the field when night was closing in, and the retreat had begun.

An officer attached to headquarters knows all the details of a battle from the reports which come in every moment; I am therefore about to relate what I saw and heard.

All historians admit that Napoleon was surprised; he had been deceived by an attack of the Prussians in the direction of Leipsic, and did not believe the Russian Army was so near; moreover, he expected the attack would begin on his left, whereas it was his right that sustained the first shock.

The Allied Army consisted of 55,000 Russians, 30,000 Prussians, and a reserve of 20,000 Russians. The French Army, under Maréchal Ney, was of about the same strength, but had very little cavalry. If, instead of beginning the attack at eleven o'clock, on account of the passing of the Prussian Army, it had begun at 6 a.m., there would not have been time for Prince Eugene, Viceroy of Italy, to come to the help of the French, engaged in an unequal struggle; according to all probabilities they would have succumbed, especially if the Russian reserve, composed of the Imperial Guards, and consequently of picked troops, had not remained three leagues behind the field of battle.

The Russians attacked the villages of Goerschen and Kaya in the centre; these two villages having been taken and retaken several times, with equal bravery on either side, the position remained undecided. On the right, the Prussians were completely crushed; the Royal

Guards sustained enormous losses, 12,000 killed, wounded or taken prisoner. The attack of the left wing had been pressed vigorously; at 4 p.m. there was still hope of a great victory, in spite of the Prussian losses, but at a quarter past four all was changed. The Viceroy of Italy, encamped near Leipsic with 22,000 men, hearing the cannonade, came in all haste; the Allies' left was obliged to give way before these new forces. It, however, made a brave defence while awaiting the reserves. Unlike Prince Eugéne, the Russian Imperial Guard had not hastened forward at the sound of the cannonade, but awaited the order to advance; leaving at five in the evening, it arrived at nine. It was too late. The villages of Goerschen and Kaya remained definitely in the hands of the French; the cannon were silent, each side prepared to bivouac on their positions.

Reports kept coming in from all sides. They spoke only of Prussian losses, those of the Russians were comparatively unimportant. With the help of the reserves, they could well have resumed the battle, next day, on the field; but the King of Prussia, disconsolate at the losses sustained by his Royal Guards, brought about a decision, in a great council of war held in the open air, that he should withdraw beyond the Elbe in order to take up a strong position, and wait for the numerous reinforcements that were on their way. Reports showed that the French had suffered considerable losses, eleven cannon and numerous prisoners remained in our hands.

It was impossible to turn the King of Prussia from his idea; and the retreat took place during the night. We had been on our horses since two o'clock in the morning, when we alighted at midnight at Geitch, a village three miles from the battlefield, having had nothing to eat or drink. The moral effect of this hasty retreat was immense; Napoleon derived great benefit from it; his reports of a victory, spread over Europe, prevented the defection of wavering allies and revived the courage of his troops. The opposite effect was produced in the Prusso-Russian Army; the soldiers were brave and numerous, but they had not a general capable of triumphing over the genius of Napoleon. It needed a strange intervention of Providence, a few months later, to equalise the chances of success, and even to weigh down the balance on the side of the Allies.

The day after the Battle of Lutzen, the Russian headquarters remained at Poenig; the Emperor Alexander posted to Dresden with his chancellor, in order to study the situation at leisure. The staff took two days in making the same journey. The emperor remained at Dresden till May 8th.

On the 9th we joined the Russian Army at Bischoffswerda, on the other side of the Elbe. The Allies took up an excellent position between the Spree and the Neiss, fortified it, and awaited an attack.

On May 11th, the headquarters of the Russian and Prussian Armies were established at Bautzen, where we had been so well received a few weeks before. The aspect of the town was greatly changed; sadness had taken the place of joy and enthusiasm; everything, even the temperature, was changed. The heavens were veiled with dark clouds, as if on the eve of a tempest.

On May 12th, our headquarters were moved to Hochkirch, a name of evil omen, recalling a defeat of Frederick the Great in 1752; on the 19th two important items of news were privately discussed by the staff; an engagement had taken place on our extreme right, near Koenigswartha; General Barclay de Tolly had defeated an Italian division under General Péry; seven guns and two thousand prisoners, among whom was General Balathier, remained in the hands of the Allies. Secondly, a request for an armistice had reached our outposts, but it had been refused in the hope of a complete victory over the French army, and perhaps, in the hope of the success of the negotiations secretly opened with Austria, through Baron Marschal, to induce her to join the Allies; this treaty would have been signed, but for the fatal retreat from Lutzen.

On Thursday, May 20th, began the great battle, called by the French the Battle of Bautzen, and by the Russians the Battle of Würschen. In order to follow all the movements, the Emperor Alexander exposed himself recklessly; wherever he went with his staff, our brilliant uniforms drew on us the enemy's fire; several officers were killed or wounded; a ball passed between the legs of my horse, and he shied so that I was unseated, and fell on a heap of stones. I was injured, and lame for some days. After a desperate struggle, and prodigies of valour on both sides, the firing ceased towards ten o'clock at night. Our troops, not having sustained great losses, bivouacked in their positions, with the exception of our left, which, reinforced by the Imperial Guard, advanced a German mile. The emperor and the King of Prussia both passed the night from two to three miles from the battlefield.

The next day, the 21st, the cannon began to rumble about four o'clock in the morning. Towards two in the afternoon Napoleon made a feint on our extreme left, protected by the mountains that separate Bohemia from Saxony. At the same time, he ordered Maréchal Ney

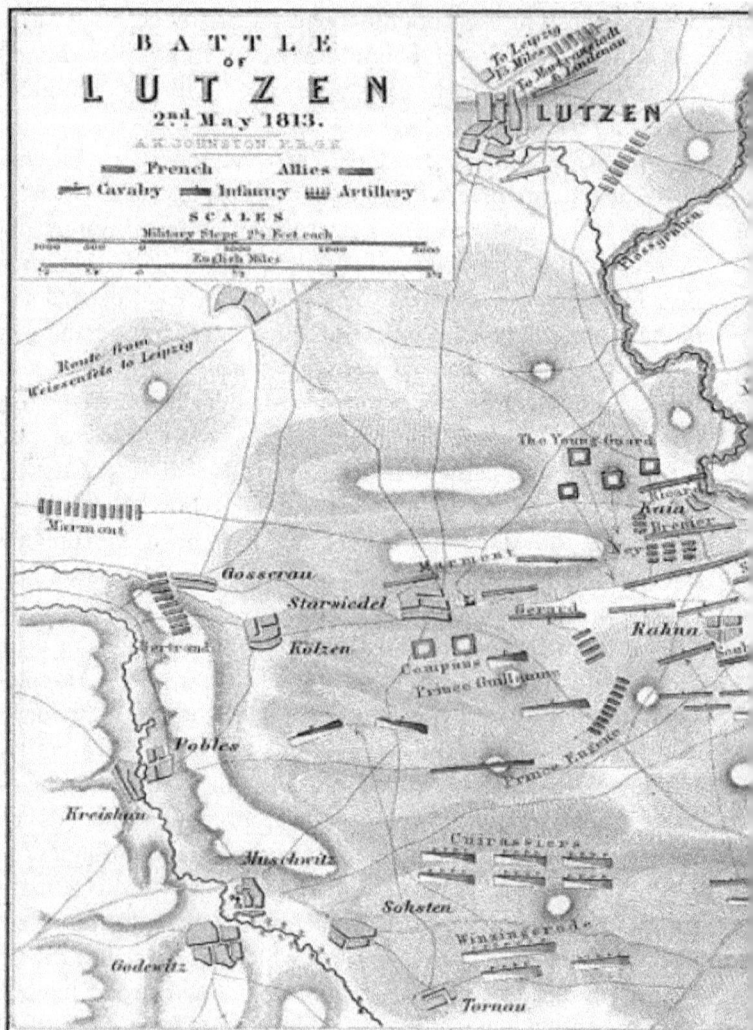

BATTLE
OF
LUTZEN
2ⁿᵈ May 1813.

A. K. JOHNSTON, F.R.G.S.

━━ French   Allies ━━
━━ Cavalry   ━━ Infantry   ━━ Artillery

SCALES

Military Steps 2½ Feet each

English Miles

Route from
Weissenfels to Leipzig

Marmont

LUTZEN

To Leipzig
13 Miles
To Markranstadt
To Landsmen

Flosergraben

The Young Guard

Ricard
Raia
Brenier
Ney

Gosserau

Starsiedel

Bertrand

Kolzen

Gerard

Rahna

Compans
Prince Guillaume

Pobles

Prince Eugene

Kreishau

Muschwitz

CUIRASSIERS

Sohsten

Godewitz

Winzingerode

Tornau

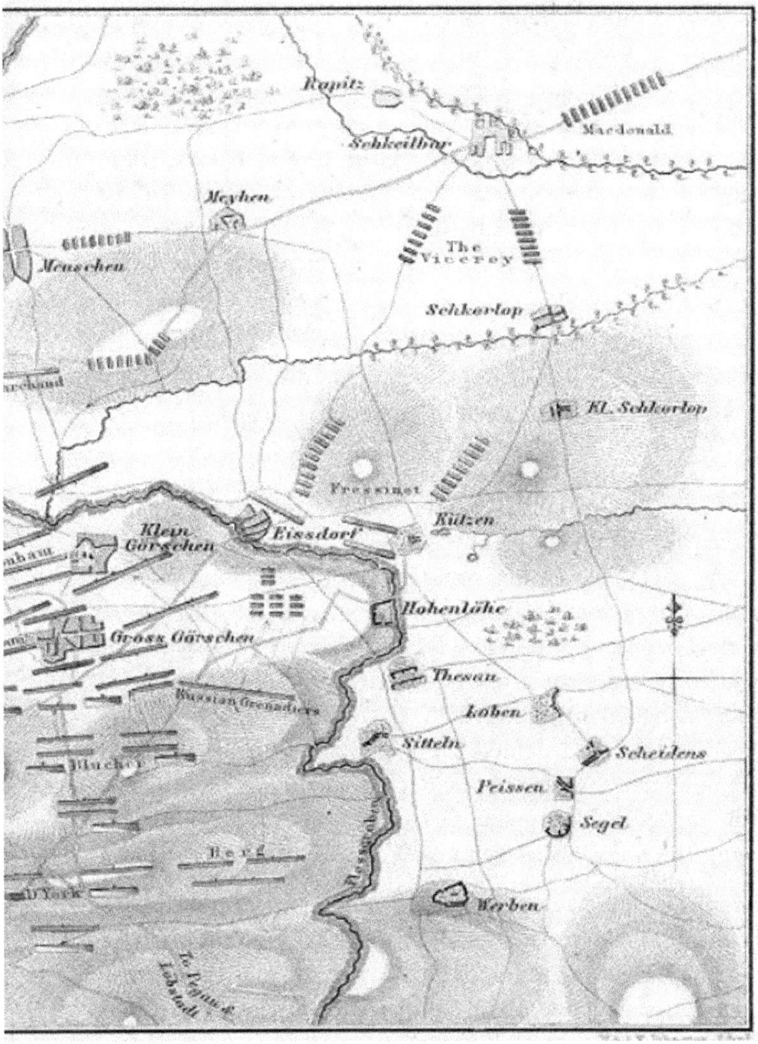

Rapitz

Schkeilbur

Macdonald

Meyhen

Menschen

The
Viceroy

Schkorlop

Kl. Schkorlop

Fressinet

Kitzen

Klein
Görschen

Eissdorf

Grösz Görschen

Hohenlöhe

Russian Grenadiers

Thesau

Sitteln

Löben

Scheidens

Peissen

Segel

Blucher

Werben

Berd

York

to reinforce his army corps with the Reynier and Lauriston divisions, and with his entire force of 60,000, to fall upon two detached corps of our extreme right, commanded, the one by the Russian general, Barclay de Tolly, the other by the Prussian Blücher. These two divisions, being in danger of being separated from the army, recrossed the Spree. The Emperor Alexander, fearing to be driven into a corner against the mountains of Bohemia, resolved to retreat while there was yet time.

At six in the evening, the Imperial Guard was ordered to take the head of the column, and proceed at once to Hochkirch, the other troops to follow as quickly as possible. This memorable retreat covered the Russian Army with glory, by the admirable regularity with which it was executed, without haste or confusion. Count Paul Pahlen commanded that brave rear-guard that the finest troops in the world were unable to break through, though they pursued it relentlessly; nor could they even capture a single gun. This drew from Napoleon, who himself commanded the advance-guard, the exclamation:

> What! After such slaughter, no result! No prisoners! These fellows will not leave me a nail! (Baron Fain, *Manuscrit de 1813*, chap. 1.)

The Baron de Croissard, Colonel of the Staff of the Russian Army, an officer who combined dauntless bravery with great military experience, and incredible enthusiasm, had a conversation with the King of Prussia in my presence. This conversation, which took place on the battlefield, a few moments before the order to retreat was given, might have caused such a change of events that I will give an extract. I can remember almost the very words.

Baron de Croissard denied the importance of the check to our right wing which was falling back, declaring that it did not matter, and might be turned to a complete victory for the Allies. Pointing to the left wing, which was no longer attacked, he exclaimed:

> *There* is the victory; we have a great united force; let us take advantage of it to throw down whatever is before us; let us fall upon the right wing of the French Army, which is depleted just now, it is certain; by so doing we shall overturn all the plans, and render unavailing the skilful manoeuvres of the great general; he will not have time to ward off the destruction of his right wing; the movement assures us of complete victory.

The King of Prussia, much struck by the idea, went to the Em-

BATTLE OF LUTZEN

peror Alexander, and suggested the manoeuvre advised by the Baron de Croissard. It was clear that there was still time to carry it out, and if it had succeeded, what a change in the events following the Battle of Bautzen! The Emperor Alexander, after reflecting a moment on this strange suggestion, replied:

> It is too late. I cannot make such a decision without a few moments' reflection. I am going to give the order to retreat.

I have often called to mind this conversation, and the more I reflect, the more it seems to me that the manoeuvre could have been executed, and might have changed defeat into victory.

On the evening of this memorable day, the Emperor Alexander and his staff slept at Reichenbach, four German miles from the battlefield; we arrived there at midnight, half dead with hunger and fatigue. The next morning, at seven o'clock, Prince Wolkonski gave me the order to go to Bunzlau, on the Bobre: (1) to give fresh orders to the French garrison at Thorn, who, according to the terms of capitulation, were to return to France; (2) to give orders to the reserves, under the command of General Kertel, where he would arrive on the 23rd, or 24th, at the latest.

I was obliged to go as far as Lowenberg, five *meilen* from Bunzlau, to find the Russian staff officer charged to escort the garrison from Thorn. Happily, I met him just as he was taking a road that would have brought him directly into the midst of our retreating army. He turned towards the left, and I accompanied him as far as Werdan, a *château* belonging to Count de Frankenstein. I spent a delightful evening with the family; the disastrous results for the Allies of the Battle of Bautzen were not yet known in this town, and I took good care not to mention them. My two missions being fulfilled, I found the emperor at headquarters at Godeberg, on the 24th; as His Majesty was presiding at a council, I made my report to the Chief of Staff.

On the 4th of June, we learned, in the little village of Schneidnitz, that an armistice had been signed at Pleiwitz by Count Schouwaloff for Russia, General Kleist for Prussia, and M. de Caulaincourt, Duc de Vicence, for France.

Everybody, soldiers and civilians, welcomed the news. In my opinion, the suspension of hostilities was to the disadvantage of Napoleon—it gave his enemies time to collect more troops, and allowed the Emperor of Russia and the King of Prussia to press on the negotiations with Austria, and, eventually, to induce her to join them with an army of 200,000 men. Napoleon also had great need of rest, in order to receive reinforcements and supplies—but he ought to have yielded to the pressure of circumstances and hastened to make peace, and so break the coalition that threatened him. But the decree of Providence had been pronounced, against which human effort and science are nothing.

CHAPTER 4

The Battle of Dresden

On June 5th the Russian headquarters were removed to Peter-swalden, a village in Silesia, chosen for the emperor's residence on account of a magnificent *château* belonging to Count Stolberg. General Barclay de Tolly, Commander-in-Chief of the Prusso-Russian Army, remained at Reichenbach, a little village in Silesia five *meilen* from Peterswalden; he had with him his staff and all the diplomats who accompanied the Russian Army. The armistice permitted us to make many excursions in this beautiful province; the diplomats worked, and exchanged notes and protocols, and the army rested.

Early in July, Count Nesselrode, Chief of the Cabinet of the *Tzar*, sent for me, and said:

> Two Bourbon princes, Mgr. the Comte d'Artois and Mgr. the Duc d'Angoulême, have just arrived at Colberg, a little port in Pomerania, on the Baltic; they have remained on board the English frigate that brought them, and are awaiting a reply to a letter they have written to the Emperor Alexander. This letter places us in a somewhat embarrassing position, for if, on the one hand, the emperor has a strong desire to see the King of France re-established on his rightful throne, on the other, he must exercise great tact with regard to the Emperor of Austria, who is ready to join the Coalition.
>
> Let these confidential words suffice to explain the exceptional position of our sovereign; I am not at liberty to enter into fuller details, as they are connected with important diplomatic secrets. You know enough, from what I have said, to be able to add whatever you think suitable to the letter that you are to take from the Emperor to these august personages. The letter is not

so clear as His Majesty could have wished. You should therefore try to persuade these princes to be patient, and to wait, either at Colberg or elsewhere, for a time more favourable to their interests—-after a victory, for instance. As for the results of the negotiations at Prague—I cannot tell. Speak to the princes of the emperor's good intentions, that he never ceases to pray that they may return to their country, but make them understand clearly that the present moment is not opportune for an open declaration in their favour.

Such were the instructions I received; it was necessary to grasp them thoroughly in order to deserve the confidence the minister had placed in me; though I did not disguise from myself that the choice had fallen on me because I was a French noble, and not on account of any merit of my own. Together with the emperor's letter. Count Nesselrode gave me a Prussian passport, and a dispatch from Count de Hardenberg, to the *commandant* of the fort at Colberg. He gave me a sum of three hundred *ducats*, in order that I might make this long journey, and stay an indefinite time at Colberg, in a manner befitting an *aide-de-camp* of the Emperor of Russia on an official mission. I went to Berlin, by way of Breslau, and as I arrived, too late for the *visé* of my passport, and of the order for relays of horses as a courier, I spent the night in Berlin.

Stettin being occupied by the French, I had to go a long way round by Stargard; it took me three days and four nights to cover a hundred and eighty leagues. No sooner had I alighted from my post-chaise, than I went to Colonel Dumoulin, the *commandant* of the fort. After reading the dispatch from Count de Hardenberg, the colonel said to me in very good French:

Mon Dieu! I am distressed at what has happened. The French princes left this morning at day break; the English frigate that brought them, could not wait any longer, having important business at a Swedish port. The princes certainly told me they were expecting an answer from the General Headquarters of the Allies, but I had received no orders on the subject, and my fortress being in a state of siege, I did not consider that I ought to allow them to land and remain here until the arrival of this reply, for fear of compromising myself by a diplomatic intrigue that was out of my province.

I was annoyed by these singular words, and said:

151

I am sure, colonel, you will be blamed by your government for refusing hospitality to princes who are certainly not enemies of your sovereign. They had frankly told you why they wished to remain at Colberg; and besides, you knew their reason quite well, having signed the passport of the courier that the princes sent to Reichenbach. I have brought a letter to them from His Majesty the Emperor of Russia. I must carry out my mission. Is there not a boat of some kind that I can take at once, and try to overtake the English frigate?

A little disconcerted at what he had done, the *commandant* answered:

There is no boat in the port, or the roadstead, on account of the state of siege. I have two fishing boats at my disposal, but they are not fit to put out to the open sea; as you may see for yourself if you will go with me to the quay.

On walking down to the quay, I found it only too certain that I must abandon all hope of delivering the emperor's letter.

The next day, on looking over the fortifications, the major of the garrison informed me that Colonel Dumoulin was a descendant of the Protestants who had taken refuge in Prussia after the Evocations of the Edict of Nantes. The major added:

The colonel was very disagreeable, not to say rude, to the princes; he was glad to make the descendants of the Great King feel his inveterate hatred on account of the exile of his ancestors.

Since then, I have noticed that the bitterest enemies of France are the descendants of the Protestant exiles after the Revocation of the Edict of Nantes.

I remained twenty-four hours at Colberg. Colonel Dumoulin insisted that I should stay with him; in spite of his efforts to keep me longer, I made my way back to Berlin, much annoyed at having missed such a good opportunity of being of service and being presented to princes of the Royal Family of France, my natural lords.

As there was no hurry about my return, I spent three days in Berlin, occupied in seeing the town, and making some necessary purchases; among other things, I bought a very light carriage, which was most useful to me during the rest of the campaign.

On returning to Peterswalden, I gave an account of my unsuccessful mission to Count Nesselrode, and returned him the emperor's letter. I easily saw that he was pleased with my non-success. Thus, the matter ended to the satisfaction of Prince Metternich, who was well known to hate the Bourbons in general, and Louis XVIII in particular. During my absence, the alliance with Austria had been concluded. No further events happened at our headquarters till August 10th, the eve of the expiration of the armistice; the negotiations entered upon at Prague having been broken off, hostilities would be resumed on August 17th.

The offensive and defensive alliance between Austria, Prussia and Russia necessitated a new plan of campaign; it was decided upon in a grand council of war. A Russian and Prussian army corps were to join the Austrian Army in Bohemia to harass the French Army in flank and rear, while the rest of the Russian and Prussian forces attacked in front. The emperor gave us our choice, either to accompany the Imperial Guard by short stages to Prague, the general rendezvous, or to post there at our own expense; this permission only applied to the emperor's *aides-de-camp*; we all chose to post there. So, on August 10th, my comrade Lamsdorf got into my carriage, drawn not by post-horses but by our own horses, and followed by our servants with our saddle-horses; we travelled quickly, by short stages, on a good road, through charming scenery.

The first night we slept at Frankenstein, the second at Machod, the first town within the frontier of Bohemia; we stayed there for a time in order to visit the magnificent *château* of the Duchesse de Sagan, the daughter of the last Duc de Courlande, the two fortresses of Josephstadt, Königgratz, the battlefield, and last of all, the town of Kolen. We reached Prague on August 15th, at the same time as the Emperor Alexander.

The Emperor of Austria, who had come to receive his new ally, offered him the magnificent palace of the Kings of Bohemia as a place of residence, and assigned several palaces to the staff.

On August 17th, the Emperor of Russia presented his military household to the Emperor of Austria. On several occasions, I had been charged by Prince Wolkonski, Chief of the Emperor's Staff, or by Count Nesselrode, head of the Cabinet, with different missions and ordered to report directly to the emperor on my return; but various circumstances had prevented my reporting to him. So, the Emperor Alexander did not know me; I had never had the honour of speaking to him. When it was my turn to be presented, the *Tzar* could not remember my name; he said to me, colouring: "Give your name yourself."

Much distressed, I stammered my name, making a low bow, and passed on, feeling grieved to have caused such embarrassment to the emperor. This little annoyance remained long in his memory; I was uneasy as to the consequences it might have on my military career, but quite wrongly, as will be seen later.

In the evening of this, to me, disagreeable day, my comrade, Rapatel, *aide-de-camp* to the Emperor of Russia, said to me:

My dear friend, I want to present you to a distinguished fellow-countryman, my former general. I remained faithful to him after his fall, and shared his exile. I mean General Moreau, lately come from America, in order to take advantage of any events that may arise, to return to our dear country, and there live under a legitimate government; above all, a more paternal government that the one that is now ruling.

I gladly agreed, and went with Rapatel to see the great general, who had given proof of his military capacity in the earliest wars of the Revolution, and was the only general in Europe capable of contending with Napoleon. As soon as Rapatel had presented me. General Moreau said:

I am delighted, M. de Rochechouart, to see you here; it is where one of your name should be, and not with that usurper. However, he will soon receive the just chastisement he deserves.

I confess I was much astonished to hear these words from one whom I believed to be a sincere Republican.

I shall have to refer to Maréchal Moreau several times. I say *maréchal* because the Emperor Alexander had just conferred the title of field-marshal upon him in attaching him to his service. This illustrious man had retained an almost brutal frankness. The day after my visit the *Tzar* gave a great dinner in his honour; his military household and several Austrian and Prussian generals were present. During the dinner the emperor, who had the Prince de Schwarzenberg on his right and General Moreau on his left, took up a decanter to pour out some wine. The new *maréchal* abruptly seized his arm.

Sire, do not drink that; it is poison, for either what I have just tasted is scandalously adulterated, and so cannot be offered to you, or it contains some deleterious substance, shown by its execrable taste.

The emperor burst out laughing, and turning to the grand marshal of his household, said:

Count Tolstoï, do you hear that? But it is the wine you have been giving me for several days.

Later I shall cite a second outburst of the *maréchal* during the Battle of Dresden.

Moreau had just left America at the urgent entreaties of his wife, by whom he had been brought into communication with Louis XVIII at Hartwell. Louis had promised him the greatest honours if he would consent to place himself at the head of an army that he alone—the rival of Bonaparte—could hope to command with success. Rapatel, and later François d'Escars, told me that Madame Moreau and the French princes in England carried on a very active correspondence.

The Emperor Alexander, when negotiating with regard to the entry of Austria into the coalition, proposed Moreau for *generalissimo*; thus, the *amour-propre* of all would have been satisfied. He had spoken of the indisputable talents of the great general; but Prince Metternich insisted, under threat of breaking off the negotiations, that the title should be conferred on Prince Schwarzenberg. The emperor expressed his regret to Moreau, who replied:

Sire, I understand the reluctance of Austria; if your Majesty had done me the honour to consult me sooner, I should have advised you to claim the supreme command for yourself. All opposition would have disappeared before such a leader. I should have been your major-general, and the operations would have been under a single direction. Now I can only offer your Majesty the advice dictated by my long experience. May God be our helper!

General Jomini came to offer his services at the same time as Moreau. Born on March 6th, 1779, at Payerne, in the canton of Vaud, he rose to the rank of brigadier-general in the French army; he assisted General Eblé in constructing the bridge over the Beresina, and later became chief of staff to Maréchal Ney. Napoleon not having appointed him general of a division, a rank to which he considered he was entitled, Jomini came to our headquarters. The *Tzar* made him *aide-de-camp* general, and by his experience and military knowledge he rendered great services to the Allies.

On August 20th, we left Prague to renew the campaign, and we slept at Schlau; the march was uneventful till the 24th. On the 25th the Emperor Alexander and his whole staff made a reconnaissance of the environs of Dresden; a few cannon-shots were exchanged without result.

On the 26th, the first day of the Battle of Dresden, the attack began too late, and was not pressed vigorously; the allied army, however, took several redoubts situated between the gates of Freyberg, Dippotiswald and Pirna. Their forces surrounding Dresden exceeded 200,000 men, and on that day, were only opposed by the corps of Maréchal Gouvion St.-Cyr. It must soon have fallen if (1) the attack had been begun two hours earlier, and there was nothing to prevent it; (2) if, after the first success, the attack had been pressed vigorously instead of the Allies being content with sending reinforcements from time to time, which only kept up the combat without carrying it to victory. We ought to have attacked only the whole line at once with all the troops at our disposal. Field-Marshal Moreau said to Alexander:

> But what are we doing? Why do we not advance? From the weakness of the defence, it is evident that Napoleon is not there; we have only to do with one of his army corps.

The emperor, struck with the force of this remark, took Moreau to the *generalissimo* that he might repeat it to him. The Austrian general gave very insufficient reasons to justify the slowness of his action, which he called prudence. At last, driven into a corner, he added "We do not want to destroy the town of Dresden."

"Oh! that is the reason," replied the victor of Hohenlinden. "But we do not make war, prince, to spare our enemies; rather to do them all the harm we can. In that case, why attack this town? You should have chosen another battle-ground."

Then, exasperated at the indifference with which his advice was received, he flung his hat on the ground, exclaiming:

> Oh! *sacré bleu, monsieur,* I do not wonder that you have always been defeated in the last seventeen years!

These were the words we all heard. The effect may be imagined. The emperor tried to calm him and to draw him aside. As he was going away Moreau added this prediction:

> Sire, that man will ruin everything.

A few moments later we saw issuing from the three gates of Dresden, of which I have spoken, three columns in close formation, each consisting of at least 15,000 men. These masses thrust the Allies well beyond the lines they had just occupied. Napoleon, having heard the cannonade, had hastened forward with all his forces, crossed the Elbe, and entered Dresden, just when least expected. The fusillade and cannonade continued until eight o'clock in the evening.

The next day torrents of rain, which will always be remembered by those who took part in the battle, began to fall, and lasted without intermission for three days. I do not give the strategical details of this second day, so unfortunate for the allied armies. Instead of the victory they had every reason to expect, they experienced a crushing defeat. (See *Manuscrit* of Baron Fain or the *Campagne de Saxe*, 1813, *par* M. d'Odeleben.)

We began that famous retreat which soon became a rout. The Emperor Alexander, with a far too numerous staff, attracted the enemy's attention. Towards one o'clock a French battery sent several volleys into the midst of us, which caused great disorder. Maréchal Moreau said to the *Tzar*:

Sire, they are firing at you. Your person is too valuable to risk, especially as we are obliged to beat a retreat in consequence of the mistakes of yesterday, last night, even this morning. I entreat your Majesty to avoid a danger, which there is no glory in facing, and which might throw your subjects and the Allies into despair.

The emperor understood that there was nothing more to be done. He turned his horse, saying: "Go first, Field-Marshal." At the same moment, a ball from a French battery that was very near struck Moreau on the right knee, passed through his horse, and carried away the calf of the general's left leg. Rapatel, who was talking to me, rushed forward to raise Moreau. I, too, went forward, and heard him say, "Dead! Dead!" Then he lost consciousness. The emperor remained on the spot, a prey to the most violent grief. Five or six balls fell around us. They dragged the emperor and the wounded man a few steps away, behind a hillock.

The *Tzar's* surgeon declared that a double amputation would be necessary. A stretcher was hastily made of the branches of trees; blankets and cloaks formed a protection from the rain which was falling heavily. Forty grenadiers, Russian, Prussian and Austrian, took it in turn to carry the wounded general to the town of Lahn, where

Trachau

Pieschen

Scheunen

Kaditz

Neudorf

Prem. Maxen

Uebigau

RIVER

Ostra Gehege

Kaiser A.

DRESDEN

Neu
stad

Friedrich
Stadt

Priesnitz

Lausa Neudorf

Schuster
hauser

Cotta

Dresch.berg

Rhein
v. Hamburg

Bürgstädel

Löbda

Ockerwitz

Wolnitz

Compitz

Gorbitz

Roeck

Plauen

Nausselitz

Gen. Freiberg

Bobritz

Rosthal

General
Gulay

Altfranken

Tütschen

CLASSE

St. Pesterwitz

Potschappel

Gittersee

Zauckerode

Burg

Döhlen

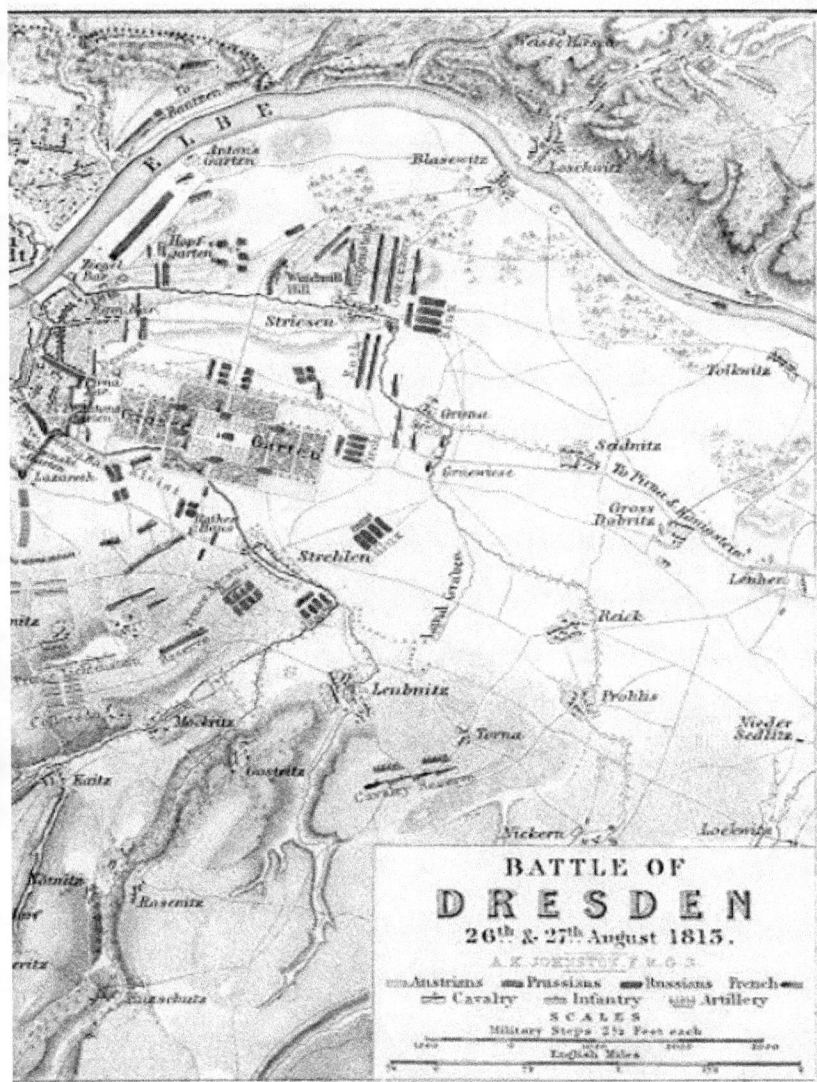

BATTLE OF
DRESDEN
26th & 27th August 1813.

A.K. JOHNSTON F.R.G.S.

Austrians Prussians Russians French
Cavalry Infantry Artillery

SCALES
Military Steps 2½ Feet each

English Miles

BATAILLE DE DRESDE, LIVRÉE LE 26 AOUT 1813.

the operation was performed the following day. Having amputated the right leg, the surgeon told Moreau that it was necessary also to amputate the left. Moreau merely asked permission to smoke a cigar between the two operations. He bore them with admirable courage, resignation and fortitude. They were unavailing; he died the next day, the 28th, after having dictated to Rapatel a farewell letter to his wife and daughter. His body was embalmed and taken to St. Petersburg, where he was buried with the honours due to a *field-maréchal*. (His daughter, Isabella Moreau, was appointed Maid of Honour to the Empress of Russia, and later married the Comte de Courval.)

The Emperor Napoleon received the news of Moreau's death at the same time that he learned he had joined the Russian Army. The only tribute he paid to him was to call him the "New Coriolanus."

On the evening of the disastrous day, the 27th, Prince Wolkonski sent me to Freyberg to find out how our retreat was being conducted, and the position of the Austrian corps that was covering our left. I found myself in the midst of such disorder, such a *sauve-qui-peut,* that it was impossible to make any observations or receive any exact information. I went to Dippotiswald; the same confusion. Not knowing the position of the belligerents, seeing the day closing in, the roads broken up and inundated, realising the imprudence of going forward, I asked hospitality from a bivouac of Don Cossacks; and having had nothing to eat since six o'clock in the morning, I enjoyed my share of a frugal repast.

On the 28th I rejoined the headquarters at Reichstaut, just as the emperor was about to leave. I told Prince Wolkonski what I had seen, the day before, and even that morning. The emperor, coming up, said to me:

All your comrades are absent on duty. Take another horse and two Cossacks of the Guard, and try to find General Barclay de Tolly. You will tell him that we are returning to Bohemia, and that he should go there too. At the same time, you will find out everything you can as to the position of our troops and those of the enemy. Start at once. You will rejoin me at Altenberg. General Barclay de Tolly ought to be near Gieshübel.

My two intelligent Cossacks helped me immensely to carry out this difficult task. One of them rode in front to make sure that we did not fall in with, or even come within range of, some French outpost. Happily, for me, I spoke German readily. I questioned the peasants, and

NAPOLEON'S RETREAT FROM MOSCOW

they told me the French were occupying Gieshübel, that their out-posts were ten minutes away from us, and they gave me a rough idea of the route taken by the Russians. I hastened on the whole day, only coming across isolated groups; they did not know where their corps was, or which way they were going themselves. I showed them the route they ought to take to reach Bohemia, the general rendezvous.

At nightfall, noticing fires down in a valley, I sent one of my Cos-sacks to ascertain, with all the precautions of these marvellous scouts, if they were the fires of friends or of enemies. At the end of five min-utes my Cossack returned with a Cossack of Barclay de Tolly's corps; his horse had been killed, and he had remained behind. This Cossack assured me that the fires in question belonged to a large Prussian army corps, under General Kleist. I then advanced without fear, made my-self known to the outpost, and was conducted to the general.

After we had exchanged many questions, he told me we were in the Telnitz Valley; as he was not being pursued, he intended to remain all the next day, in order to collect the fugitives and the scattered guns. "For, besides the artillery of our division," he added, "I have already received Austrian, Russian and Prussian guns." I asked if he could give me news of General Barclay de Tolly. He replied: "I was in com-munication with him this morning. He is going to the left to succour General Osterman's brigade, which is composed of two regiments of Russian Guards—the *chasseurs* and the regiment of Semenowski. It has been vigorously attacked, I think, by General Vandamme, and is retiring on Töplitz."

I shared the fire and the *soupe-au-lard* of the Prussian general; and at daybreak next day, the 29th, I set off to rejoin the emperor at Alten-berg. He had just left for Duks, a magnificent *château* belonging to the Wallenstein family. Although exhausted with fatigue, not having taken off my boots since four o'clock in the morning, and having spent all my time on horseback, I went on to Duks. I went at once to Prince Wolkonski to give an account of my mission. He said: "Your report is very important. Come, and repeat it to the emperor."

He took me to the drawing-room, where I found the emperor, the King of Prussia and Prince Schwarzenberg. I began my narrative over again; they made me relate in the greatest detail everything concern-ing General Kleist, the name and position of the valley where I had left him in the morning. The King of Prussia called one of his *aides-de-camp*, Colonel Schoeller, and said:

"Set off at once and find Kleist. Give him the order to march with

RUSSIAN COSSACKS

all the forces he has collected and attack the French corps to-morrow morning in flank and rear; it will debouch at Kulm. We will attack him at the same time in front and turn his left flank."

We were then dismissed. I gave Colonel Schoeller exact directions as to the route to follow, and hastened to my rooms. My friend Lamsdorf told me what had happened during my absence. The army was retiring into Bohemia in the greatest disorder; nations and even regiments were mixed up. The Emperor, the King of Prussia, and Prince Schwarzenberg had passed the day on the high road, sorting out the fugitives and showing them the road they should take. The *Tzar* directed the Russians in the centre; the King of Prussia sent his soldiers to the left; Prince Schwarzenberg pointed out to his soldiers the road to the right.

During the day they had succeeded, with great effort, in rallying 100,000 men.

General Osterman, who had rallied to his two regiments of the Russian Guard, a regiment of grenadiers commanded by Prince Eugéne of Würtemberg, and some scattered soldiers, in all 15,000 men, was attacked by General Vandamme with a corps of 30,000. General Vandamme had been ordered by Napoleon to bear down all resistance and reach Töplitz before the routed army of the Allies, and complete its destruction. General Osterman, at great cost, defended the ground inch by inch. This determined resistance covered with honour the general and the troops under his command, and saved the allied army, by giving time to reorganise the masses coming from Dresden.

★★★★★★

To commemorate the fine conduct of the Russian Guards on this day, the Emperor of Austria caused a monument to be erected on the battlefield with this inscription: "To the honour of the Russian Guards, August 29th, 1813," The Allies call this the Battle of Kulm.

★★★★★★

General Osterman, who had lost one arm in battle, remained on foot in the midst of his grenadiers to encourage them. Twenty-two officers of the regiment of Chasseurs of the Guard, to which I belonged, were killed.

Early in the morning of August 30th, General Vandamme was attacked in the centre by the main army corps, 80,000 strong; on the right by 20,000 Prussians; on the left by 25,000 Austrians. Not being able to stand against such forces, he began to retreat along the way he had come the day before, when he was attacked in the rear by General Kleist with his artillery. Surrounded on all sides, Vandamme vainly tried to break through, but, in spite of the valour of his troops, was forced to surrender. The French lost 4,000 men killed or wounded, and left in the hands of the Allies General Vandamme and three other generals, 22,000 prisoners, 40 guns and 3 eagles.

On the 31st we took up our quarters at Töplitz, a charming watering-place, where many visitors come every year for the baths. While there we heard that General Bülow had defeated Maréchal Oudinot at Gross-Beeren, and General Blücher had defeated Macdonald at Katzbach. These victories restored the courage of the allied soldiers.

A few days later we learned the reason of the sudden check in the pursuit of our disorganised army. A violent attack of fever, brought on by a chill, had compelled Napoleon to return to Dresden instead of going on to Pirna. The absence of orders from the French headquarters had prevented the advance, which might have been decisive. Vandamme alone went forward, believing he was supported, and he was crushed. Napoleon accustomed his generals too much to receive all their orders from headquarters, and to have no initiative. . . .

CHAPTER 5

Bernadotte

I had forgotten to say that, during my last visit to St. Petersburg, I had been promoted, by seniority, to the rank of "second captain" in the regiment of Chasseurs of the Guard, a rank corresponding to that of major or chief of a battalion of the line. After the enormous losses suffered by my regiment on the eve of the Battle of Kulm, I found myself, still by seniority, "first captain," or lieutenant-colonel of the line. I began to feel a decided taste for a career that appeared under such favourable auspices—lieutenant-colonel at twenty-five! Up to this time I had owed my promotion to seniority, and not to my personal merit, having done nothing remarkable; but an opportunity was about to occur, in the most unexpected way, to bring me to the notice of the Emperor Alexander, and from this time he loaded me with favours.

On September 7th, we learned at Töplitz that Bernadotte, Prince Royal of Sweden, with an army corps composed of 25,000 Swedes, 30,000 Russians, and 25,000 Prussians had completely defeated Maréchal Ney at Jütterbach, the Battle of Dennewitz according to French historians. In spite of his success and of the superhot forces at his disposal, Bernadotte had not followed up his victory. To stimulate his zeal and induce him attack more vigorously, the Allied Sovereigns resolved that they would each give him a signal mark of satisfaction. The *Tzar* sent him the Grand Cordon of St. George, the Emperor of Austria, that of Maria Theresa; the Grand Crosses of these two purely military orders are only bestowed on commanders-in-chief who have gained a decisive victory. The King of Prussia sent the Grand Iron Cross, an order recently created for military valour; no one but the king had hitherto worn this cross.

The sovereigns resolved to send each decoration by one of their

BATTLE OF KULM

aides-de-camp. The Emperor Alexander sent for the *aide-de-camp* on duty to carry a dispatch, and ordered that he should start at once. Happily, for me, I was on duty that day. Count Nesselrode explained the mission I was to undertake, and added:

Come back in a quarter of an hour with post-horses. The emperor lays great stress on his *aide-de-camp* being the first to reach the Prince of Sweden."

I ran to my rooms, took a little portmanteau, and went to the post-house to ask for the regulation carriage with two couriers' horses. But the governor of the province had just sent orders that no post-horses should be given to anyone before four o'clock, and it had just struck twelve. In vain I said, "For the service of the Emperor of Russia." The posting-master could not infringe a positive order. While I was discussing the matter, I noticed a very handsome carriage and pair being got ready; I was told it was for Lieut.-General Baron de Hardeck, *aide-de-camp* to the Emperor of Austria; so, this sovereign, also, wanted his courier to be the first to arrive. then it occurred to me to travel two stages on horseback, and so get the start of my formidable competitor.

I went back for my dispatches, and told Count Nesselrode of the impossibility of obtaining post-horses. I added: "All the same, I shall go, and I shall arrive first even if I kill my horse, and that of the Cossack who goes with me."

The chancellor replied:

Excellent, my dear fellow, the emperor will be pleased with your zeal. Here is your dispatch, your passport, and travelling expenses. You will find the Swedish Headquarters in the neighbourhood of Zerbst, so you have seventy-five leagues to cover. You will alight at Colonel Pozzo di Borgo's rooms, he is our Plenipotentiary to the Prince Royal. He will present you, and give you an outline of what you are to say. Start at once, and try not to fall into some French outpost—rather take a longer route.

Five minutes later, I was galloping along, on a good horse, escorted by a Cossack. I stopped at Zittau and gave my horse to the Cossack; I had gone ten leagues. Once in Saxony, I no longer feared the order of the Governor of Bohemia. No courier had appeared as yet; I set off at once, delighted to have outdistanced, and outwitted, the Austrian general. Every time we changed horses, I inquired about the position

of the armies; once only, I passed very near a French outpost; I gave a gold piece to the postilion, and he took me over the dangerous place at full gallop. I reached Zerbst, safe and sound, twelve hours before the Austrian general.

I alighted from the carriage at Colonel Pozzo's quarters, and gave him the dispatches addressed to him. He expressed his satisfaction that I should be the first to reach the goal; and while I adjusted my toilet, somewhat disarranged by my hard race, he put me through my lesson.

I think the Prince Royal will be gratified that a Frenchman should have been chosen for this mission. Listen carefully to everything he says, so that you may repeat it to me, word for word. Let us go to him at once; you are the first to arrive; draw his attention to your eagerness to outstrip the couriers who were bringing decorations from the Emperor of Austria and the King of Prussia.

We made our way immediately to the *château* where the prince was staying. He received me with extraordinary demonstrations of satisfaction; he especially thanked the Emperor of Russia for having chosen one of his former compatriots to bring this high token of favour. All this was said with a charm, and choice of language, that impressed me greatly. His clever words were spoken with the strongest Gascon accent.

As soon as he had read the *Tzar's* letter, he asked for news from the Grand Headquarters. I answered his various questions. Then he turned to Colonel Pozzo: "You will come back to dinner, will you not? Meanwhile, I will keep M. de la Rochechouart; I want to talk to him up to the time when we sit down to table."

As he withdrew, the diplomatic Pozzo threw me an expressive glance, as though he would say: "Do not forget my advice." So, I remained alone with this remarkable man. Bernadotte, Prince Royal of Sweden, born in 1794, was then forty-nine years old. He was tall and slight; his eagle-face greatly resembled that of the Great Condé; his thick black hair harmonised with the pale complexion common among the inhabitants of Béarn, his native place. His appearance on horseback was very martial, perhaps a little theatrical, but his bravery, his coolness in the midst of the most bloody battles, made one forget this trivial fault. He had the most winning manners and speech imaginable; he captivated me completely, and if I had been attached to this person, I should have been sincerely devoted to him. It has been said that, in order to gain people to his side, he made use of Gascon promises that he did not always keep. In all this, there was no intentional deception but great kindness of heart, and a most amiable disposition.

My first interview led me to hope for a more intimate conversation; as he rose from table, he said: "Be sure and come tomorrow, at noon; there are a great many things I want to ask you."

In the evening, I rendered an exact account of my long conversation to Colonel Pozzo. The fact that I was a Frenchman, and that I had been the first to arrive at Zerbst, gave me a great advantage. Bernadotte frankly said so. Besides, the ambassador of the Emperor Francis Joseph, the Baron de Bender, a diplomat of the school of Metternich, was uncongenial to his honourable, frank and confiding disposition, and the relations between them remained very cold. Bernadotte had a marked dislike to Prussia, which General Krüsemarck had not been able to overcome; the Prince Royal expressed himself to me in a way that left no doubt on this point. He spoke disparagingly of Field-Marshal Blücher, and said: "I beat him utterly at Lubeck."

He did not like the English minister any better. "He is my moneylender," he said, laughing. He showed a great affection for the Emperor Alexander, and admired his noble character. He did not much like Colonel Pozzo; and always spoke of him as "that crafty Corsican." I saw at once that Colonel Pozzo's intriguing disposition was not congenial to him; my youth and frankness won his confidence. I hoped, therefore, to learn his ulterior projects during my audience on the morrow. I begged Colonel Pozzo di Borgo to give me an idea of what I ought to say, and to show me how far I might go in my questions without awakening the suspicion of the prince, who seemed to be on his guard. The skilful diplomatist summarised his instructions, thus:

> Try to find out the reason for this inaction, which he seems unwilling to abandon, in spite of his military genius, and his undoubted victory over Maréchal Ney; use every argument to persuade him to come out of this inactivity, at which everybody marvels; listen, and remember what he says about this.

Punctual to the rendezvous, as may be imagined, I was announced after the reception of the Austrian and Prussian generals. The first had arrived twelve hours, and the second fourteen hours after me. The welcome given to them was purely diplomatic, with the customary gravity and ceremonial. My reception was quite different, and the conversation very intimate. In order to preserve all the shades of meaning, I will give it in the form of a dialogue.

Prince: "Are you quite rested? Well, M. de *la* Rochechouart, there are the two officers bearing the favours of their Majesties the Emperor of Austria and the King of Prussia arrived last, as usual; these gentlemen do not know how to move quickly. You have outstripped them; that is as it should be; you are a Frenchman, they are Germans. Just think, my friend, who would have said to poor Sergeant Bernadotte twenty years ago: 'You will be treated as my friend and brother by the Emperor of Russia, the Emperor of Austria, and the King of Prussia?' For their Majesties are all very amiable and polite to me. I know what an honour the Grand Cross of Maria Theresa is considered; tell me, what is the Order of St. George? As for the Grand Cross of the Prussian Order, I care little for it, it is too heavy to wear."

Rochechouart: "*Mouseigueur*, in order to obtain the Grand Cross of St. George, it is necessary to have gained a decisive battle, as commander-in-chief; no one possesses it just now; the last to receive it was Field-Marshal Kutusoff."

Prince: "Then it is an immense honour to me. I shall always wear it; I am attached to the Emperor Alexander for life and death."

Rochechouart: "I will tell him, *Monseigneur*. May I be the bearer of another proof of his esteem for Your Royal Highness, when you shall have followed up your last victory without giving the enemy time to look round."

Prince: "Ah! Listen, my friend; great prudence is necessary in my position; it is so difficult, so delicate; apart from my natural repugnance to shed the blood of Frenchmen, I have my reputation to keep up. I do not deceive myself; my fate hangs on a battle; if I lose it, I may beg six *francs* all over Europe, and no one will lend them to me."

Rochechouart: "Such an idea cannot enter the mind of Your Royal Highness, it is impossible. Besides, *Monseigneur* has already taken a step from which there is no going back."

Prince: "If it were only Napoleon that I had to fight, it would soon be done. Bonaparte is a knave; he must be killed; as long as he lives, he will be the scourge of the world; there must be no emperor in future, it is not a French title; France must have a king, but a soldier king; the Bourbon line is worn out, it will never rise to the surface again. Where is the man who would suit the French better than I should?"

I felt nonplussed for the moment. I was not there to discuss such a question. Recovering my presence of mind, I replied: "No one can dispute this crown with *Monseigneur*, but before obtaining it, you must overthrow the obstacle. Napoleon is between you and that crown."

Our conversation lasted three hours; every time I urged him, the prince evaded the question very cleverly. During my audience, the Chief of the Swedish Staff came in to obtain the prince's signature to some papers, requiring immediate attention; after he had gone away, the prince said: "Do you know that officer? He is M. d'Aldecreutz, the dethroner of kings. I will manage him so well that he will be obliged to stay with me." M. d'Aldecreutz had been at the head of the Revolution that brought about the fall of Gustavus IV.

The dinner-hour came, and the prince said: "Let us go in to dinner, but come back tomorrow, at noon, and I will give you my answer to the Emperor Alexander."

As I went away from this long audience, I was an object of great curiosity; all the diplomats were wondering what I could have been doing so long in the prince's room. Colonel Pozzo seemed a little jealous, but seeing that I was not vain of it, he wrote to Count Nesselrode, praising the way in which I had carried out my mission.

I gave him an account of our long conversation, and promised to make the final charge the next day, by insisting on the necessity of crossing the Elbe, as a proof of his co-operation in the common effort.

The orderly officer who was on duty that day. Count Alexis de Noailles, came to tell the prince that the guard was relieved, and to ask the password for the soldiers, Russian grenadiers, going on guard.

"Have these brave men been given anything to drink?"

"Yes, *Monseigneur.*"

"Then let them have some more."

Bernadotte was surrounded alternately by Swedish and Russian Guards; he had excluded the Prussians from his Guard of Honour; he had completely won over the Russian soldiers by his bravery and affable manners.

The next day, at noon, I found the prince lying down with his feet very high, so that his knees formed a desk; his head which was very low, rested on a bolster.

"I always work best when I am lying down. Listen, my friend, M. de *la* Rochechouart, I am just finishing a letter to your beloved and revered emperor; let us have a talk.

Rochechouart: "I am much honoured, *Monseigneur*, by the confidence of your Royal Highness, but in order to render myself quite worthy of it, I am going to speak to you with all the frankness of youth, and the most sincere devotion."

Prince: "Speak, my friend, I am listening."

Rochechouart: "I speak from my heart, believe me; since I have been here, I have heard much, without asking, or answering any questions. All the diplomats around you are saying that you are resting too long on your laurels; they blame your inaction. From what you have done me the honour to confide to me, I understand the motive that keeps you back; but, allow me to say, it is not sufficient, and another consideration deserves to be brought before you. You have spoken in praise of the Emperor Alexander, you appear to be sincerely attached to him, and I know that he has great sympathy with you, because he counts upon your eagerness and upon your efforts to help him, by means of the great military talents that God has given you, to bring to an end the terrible struggle of which the Peace of Europe is the prize. But if he should be prejudiced by the diplomatic reports of your studied inaction—reports which will be exaggerated—his sympathy may change to indifference; his Imperial pride may awaken. Reflect, *Monseigneur*, and allow me to remind you that the son of Gustavus IV. is the nephew of the Empress Elizabeth, sister of the late Queen of Sweden."

Prince: "Say no more; I understand. I thank you for your frankness, you have put the thing before me in its true light; tomorrow, I shall cross the Elbe."

He held out his hand to me, I grasped it, and said: "Permit me to stay until tomorrow that I may tell the emperor I was present at the crossing of the Elbe."

Prince: "Be it so—Goodbye, till tomorrow. I will give you my answer as I am mounting my horse."

Rochechouart: "May I announce the news to Colonel Pozzo?"

Prince: "Yes, but without mentioning the reasons you gave me. I do not want the crafty Corsican to know them. Tell him simply: 'The prince crosses the Elbe.'"

I went away delighted. Colonel Pozzo was impatiently awaiting me. I said: "The prince will cross the Elbe tomorrow, and pass the night at Dessau."

"But what motive can have led him to this important decision?" asked the subtle diplomatist.

"*Ma foi!* I know nothing about it," I replied.

The news of the crossing of the Elbe spread rapidly. The army rejoiced at the order which was given in the evening; the advance-guard at once left for Dessau.

The next day I went early to the *château* to take leave of the prince, and receive his letter for the emperor; his horse, ready saddled, was waiting in the courtyard. As soon as the prince saw me he came forward, gave me his letter, and detached from his tunic a Cross of the Military Order of the Sword of Sweden, saying, "M. de *la* Rochechouart, this is what the Prince of Sweden gives you." Then, drawing me into the embrasure of a window, he added, "This is what your compatriot Bernadotte begs you to accept." He gave me a gold snuffbox, on which was his portrait surrounded with four fine diamonds. No one could have shown greater amiability and delicacy of feeling. I saw him mount his horse.

Pozzo also gave me his dispatch, mentioning that in it he had spoken favourably of me. He added:

It must be owned you have been well received. Just imagine! The Prince of Sweden has informed the Austrian and Russian Ambassadors that he cannot take leave of them until this evening at Dessau; having set out first, it is only fair that you should return first.

In spite of many difficulties, and having to take a circuitous route to avoid the French outposts, I arrived, two days later, at the General Headquarters in Bohemia.

I alighted from the carriage at the house occupied by Count Nesselrode, in order the more quickly to give him an account of my stay at Zerbst, and my conversations with the prince royal, omitting the few words at the end. He replied:

We have spoken prose without knowing it. Bernadotte is very grateful that a Frenchman was chosen to be the bearer of the Russian Order. I will tell the emperor how intelligently you have carried out your mission.

Next day, at parade. Prince Wolkonski informed me that the emperor wished to see me in his room. As soon as I entered, he said, laughing:

The Prince Royal is delighted with you. He thanks me for having chosen you to be the bearer of my letter and the Grand

Cordon of St. George. Tell me what he said during your long conversations. I know he is very original; it should be interesting.

Encouraged by the friendly manner of the emperor, I began my narrative, imitating Bernadotte's Gascon accent. I kept nothing back, and added:

It is due to your Majesty to tell you the whole truth. I have not told everything to Colonel Pozzo, or to Count Nesselrode.

The emperor was delighted, and laughed heartily, especially when I came to the part where the prince suggested that he himself was the only man who could replace Napoleon on the throne of France. He congratulated me on the point I had brought forward to show the importance of keeping on good terms with the Allies. "Besides you only said what is true; that is good diplomacy." As he had an audience to give, he dismissed me, saying: "Come again tomorrow evening, at seven; I have some more questions to ask you. Where is the Cross the prince gave you?"

"Sire, I was waiting for your Majesty's permission to wear it."

"I give it. I shall see you tomorrow."

In the evening, when the *Tzar* was talking to his brother, the Grand Duke Constantine, he described my mission, not forgetting Bernadotte's claim to the throne of France. He added: "Rochechouart tells it much better; he can imitate the Gascon accent to perfection."

Next day, on parade, the grand duke addressed me before all the Staff. "Rochechouart, my brother has told me about your visit to Bernadotte, and says you imitate him splendidly; relate it to me."

"*Monseigneur,*" I replied, "It is not worthwhile; I have forgotten it."

"Ah! it is another thing, Mr. Discretion." Then he turned away quickly.

In the evening, I told the emperor I was afraid I had displeased the Grand Duke Constantine, but that I could not relate everything in public. I should have felt I was ungrateful to the Prince of Sweden, who had been so kind and confiding to me, if I had lent myself to amusing everyone at his expense.

"Bravo, my dear Rochechouart," said the emperor, "I am pleased with your discretion; it is a quality I value highly. Do not be uneasy; I will speak to my brother."

Apparently, the Emperor Alexander liked me. He kept me talking for three hours, and told me things that surprised me, they were so intimate. Thus, he spoke of his sincere friendship for Napoleon, and Napoleon's efforts to win that friendship.

Imagine! In one of our interviews at Erfurt, Napoleon went so far as to say, 'I know there is a lady who possesses your entire affection. I know you keep her portrait always by you. I ask you for her portrait; I wish to wear it from love of you, to remind me always of the best friend I have in the world.' I gave it to him. I must own he gave me excellent advice. I followed it, and to this I owe the success of my campaign in Russia.

On leaving the *Tzar's* room, I found all my comrades assembled in the drawing-room, where we spent our evenings. They questioned me about my long conversation. I told them His Majesty had asked about the Swedish army and for details of the Battle of Jütterbach.

From this time, the emperor had always a pleasant word for me when he saw me; several little missions were given me by His Majesty himself, or in accordance with his orders, in which I was mentioned by name. One day, Prince Wolkonski reported that an order given to Prince Wittgenstein had not been executed.

"Then send Rochechouart to him," said the emperor, "he will know how to make him move."

I was sent forward to Komotau. I found the general, and induced him to do what was asked, for he had no good reason to give for not obeying. I relate this incident to show the change in my position, and all because by chance it had fallen to me to carry a letter from the Emperor to Bernadotte.

CHAPTER 6

The Battle of Leipsic

On October 5th, General Benningsen, who had been impatiently expected, reached the headquarters at Töplitz with reinforcements of 45,000 men. The next day the whole of the Allied forces began to advance on all sides towards the plain of Leipsic; on the 15th, they arrived before the town, and the next day began the famous battle that lasted three days.

Towards 2 p.m. a desperate charge of French cavalry broke through the line and endangered the success of the battle. The *Tzar*, who was in the centre of his army with the Cossacks of his Guard, ordered their commander, Colonel Orloff-Denissoff, to repulse the charge. The manoeuvre, bravely and successfully carried out, gave time for a division of Russian *cuirassiers*, who were about 500 metres away, to come to the support of the Cossacks. In the *mêlée*, the Emperor Alexander was for a moment within twenty feet of a squadron of French *cuirassiers*. Villages and positions taken and retaken several times, thousands of wounded, a frightful number of dead, and a country laid waste and burnt: such was the result of the first day's battle.

On the 17th the rain fell without ceasing. A general rest seemed to be imposed. The Allies brought up Benningsen's reserves, and sent a message to Bernadotte to hasten his march. Meanwhile, the French Army changed its positions and made preparations for a retreat; a few cannon-shot were all that told of the presence of the opposing forces. At nightfall, the horizon was lit up by the bivouac fires of these 500,000 men, of whom so many were to die on the morrow. On October 18th, we were all on horseback at dawn. The French line of battle had been withdrawn to a league farther back. The Allies advanced, and the battle was fought on a semicircle which was not less than four leagues in extent. I will not give the strategical details of this day of slaughter; volumes have been written on it; I will confine myself to what I saw, and did.

The Emperor Alexander, with the King of Prussia and Prince Schwarzenberg, took up their position in the centre of the battle. At two o'clock, when the combat was hottest and the 1,200 cannon were firing incessantly, fresh batteries opened fire on the extreme right of the Allied Army under General Benningsen.

"What is going on there!" the staff officers asked themselves.

The emperor called me, and said:

> Go to our extreme right, try to speak with General Benningsen, and come back without loss of time to tell me what you have seen and heard. Take two Cossacks of the Guard with you. I rely on the accuracy of your report.

There I was at full trot; the firing from our cannon guided me in this dangerous journey. I was to go the shortest way, avoiding all the villages which were in flames, or which were being taken and retaken every moment; bullets were continually whistling past me. At one moment, I thought I was lost; a strong column of infantry was before me, uttering tumultuous cries. I stopped, and was about to turn to the right, when one of my Cossacks, gifted with keen sight, said, "*Mon officier*, they have reversed their arms, they are surrendering."

Reassured by this remark, I went nearer, and saw two regiments from Baden deserting the French Army, and joining General Benningsen's corps, the very corps I was seeking. I reached the general at the very moment when he was receiving the surrender of the Baden colonels. This defection was soon after followed by that of a corps of Würtemberg infantry and cavalry, who announced that the entire Saxon Army would follow their example.

Count Benningsen gave me all the information I required: the defection of the German troops, which I had just witnessed, would enable him to make a vigorous attack. He had scarcely given me these particulars, when a Cossack was brought to him, sent by the Comte de Langeron, informing him that Bernadotte's army had just entered the line, and had got into communication with him. This news seemed to me so important that, to verify it, I went at once to the Langeron division, which formed the left wing of the army of the Prince Royal of Sweden.

After riding about a league, I found myself in the midst of a Swedish column; the officer in command told me that the Prince Royal had occupied Stuntz. Having received this precious information, I returned with all speed to the emperor. I found him where I had left him. Desperate fighting was taking place on the heights that dominate Probst-Heyda, which was captured and recaptured three several times.

I announced the defection of the German troops, pointed out the position of General Benningsen, and added, "Sire, I have another piece of good news: the army of the Prince Royal of Sweden has entered the line; his left is in communication with the Hetman Platoff, his right touches Leipsic."

"Are you quite sure?" asked the *Tzar*.

"Sire, I investigated it for myself. I spoke to the Swedish officers of that corps."

"It is indeed good news, and important news," said the emperor.

He called Prince Schwarzenberg, who appeared to doubt my report. After a short council of war, the emperor decided to send the Grand Duke Constantine to Bernadotte to strengthen him in his good resolve, and said to me, "You know the way, guide my brother to Bernadotte, and come back quickly."

I took another horse and two fresh Cossacks; the grand duke took one of his *aides-de-camp* and two hussars of the Guard, and we set off in all haste. The route was shorter; the Allies had been able to advance on account of the defection of the troops from Baden, Würtemberg and Saxony, a defection which may be called infamous treachery, a disgraceful action, unprecedented in the annals of modern warfare; for not only did these troops desert the French, but they attacked them almost at once.

The Prince of Sweden received us on a fine white charger. He was clad in a tunic of violet velvet braided with gold; on his head, a hat with white feathers, surmounted by an immense plume in the Swedish colours; he held in his hand his *batôn* covered with violet velvet, ornamented at each end with a gold crown. He was superb thus in the midst of the grape-shot, with dead and wounded all around him, encouraging by his presence a party of English artillerymen who were letting off Congreve rockets. The position was not favourable for a long conversation.

As soon as Bernadotte saw the Grand Duke Constantine, he came forward, and said, "*Monseigneur*, let us go farther away to talk."

I asked the grand duke's orders with regard to my message to the emperor. He said, "Go back; I remain here. Do not fail to tell my brother amid what terrible surroundings we found the Prince of Sweden."

As I was turning my horse, Colonel Pozzo begged me to take him to headquarters. I returned very quickly, without having had anything to eat or drink; my two rides must have totalled fifteen leagues going and returning.

Scarcely had Colonel Pozzo said a few words privately to the *Tzar*, than His Majesty gave me the following order:

> Take one of my horses, and two Cossacks, and go to the Hetman Platoff, and tell him that the enemy is in full retreat at all points; let him go with his Cossacks and light artillery and occupy the road from Wittemberg to Leipsic, near Düben on the Maulde, in order to cut off the retreat on that side. As the Hetman is under the orders of General Benningsen, you will inform the general of the instructions you are taking. I attach great importance to the prompt execution of these orders. You know the position of the different corps, and can carry out this mission more quickly than anyone else. I shall pass the night at Rötha; you will come back to me at the *château*.

I confess I was somewhat appalled at this manner of ending such a fatiguing day; the sun was going down. I had to hasten in order to get there before nightfall. I was given an excellent horse and two very intelligent Cossacks. I asked them if they had not a bit of bread.

"Here it is, *mon officier*," said one of them, and he handed me a loaf, with some bacon and a *bidon* of brandy. I swallowed a few mouthfuls from the flask, and took half of the loaf.

I said to my Cossacks, as we trotted along, "We must make haste. I have to go back to the *Tzar* at Rötha, where he slept last night."

The battle had ceased along the whole line, the bivouac fires were being lighted. After making some inquiries, I found the *hetman* in a village that was still burning; he was having tea in the ruins of a large farmhouse. Being informed of the arrival of an *aide-de-camp* of the emperor, he came forward, though he was a commander-in-chief and I only a lieutenant-colonel; he made me a low bow, and said, "What are the orders of the Tzar?"

I explained the order; he seemed to have a difficulty in understanding it, but the colonel of the staff, attached to his person, assured me that the orders I had brought should be carried out. The *hetman* added, "We will go together to inform General Benningsen. I will not go to sleep till everything is arranged; I will set out from there; meanwhile let us have tea."

I gladly drank five or six cups of excellent tea with rum, and ate a quantity of biscuits to appease my hunger. Probably the rum consumed by the chief of the Don Cossacks went to his head; he soon became more than lively. I rose, hoping to go alone to General Benningsen; this devil of a man would not have it so.

"And our visit to General Benningsen. We must go together; you will explain to him yourself the order for the departure of all my Cossacks. Bring my carriage round," he shouted in a voice of thunder, "and let them drive us to General Benningsen."

Three minutes later, the carriage was waiting for us; it was open and drawn by six horses in the Russian manner; a Cossack on the box drove the four horses abreast, and the two leaders were driven by a second Cossack mounted on the offside horse. A picked squadron, forming the *hetman* body-guard, surrounded our carriage; each of them carried a lighted torch. "Take the shortest way and do not upset us; if you do, beware of your skin." Such was the order given to the coachman.

I asked the colonel, who was sitting opposite to me, "Do you know where the general is?"

"I have no idea; but you may be sure the Cossacks will take us straight to him. Let us entrust ourselves to their intelligence and to the mercy of God."

I have never been able to understand how we reached our destination; now across fields, now over furrows, hedges and ditches, never stopping in spite of the shying of the horses and the obstacles we met with every moment; the branches of trees tore our hair and scratched our faces; our eyes were dazzled with the torches in a dark night. At last, after less than an hour of this devil's drive, we reached the village where General Benningsen was stationed. The *hetman* was in a deep sleep in spite of the jolts that threw our carriage into the air. I related to General Benningsen our singular drive to seek him, told him the orders given by the *Tzar*, and asked if he had any information to give me with regard to his army corps. He said, "I was just finishing my report of the day's results as far as relates to the troops under my orders. I will add the directions given to the *hetman's* corps, and you shall take back my report."

Ten minutes later, I rose to go, but I suddenly remembered that I had left my Cossacks and my horse at the *hetman's* encampment. Much against my will, I was resigning myself to spend the night at this bivouac, when to my surprise and joy, I saw my Cossacks, one of them leading my horse. They had followed the carriages, which I had forgotten to tell them to do, in the bewilderment of our hurried departure, worn out as I was with fatigue, dazzled by the torches, and my head, perhaps, a little excited by the tea and rum I had drunk hurriedly before taking food.

I was anxious to return to my headquarters, but I had completely lost my bearings, and did not know how to find my way. I asked the Cossacks, "Can you take me back to the *Tzar?*" "Yes, *mon officier*," and we started. The lynx eyes of my two guides, aided by their intelligence, noticed and recognised an infinity of details that I could not see, and above all, that I had not noticed as I came. I heard them say, "Ah! There is the oak we passed," or again, "Do you remember this ravine?" At last, after a good two hours' ride, to my amazement, I reached Rötha, bruised, exhausted, with, grazed skin—in short, in a pitiable plight; it was striking three in the morning.

I went up to Prince Wolkonski; he was still writing. I gave him General Benningsen's report, announcing that he had begun to carry out the emperor's orders; and I ended by describing my drive with the *hetman*. He laughed heartily. Then seeing how tired I looked, he pointed to a sofa, and said simply: "Rest there, my poor Rochechouart." I did not need asking a second time, and was asleep in a moment.

I was awakened at nine o'clock by one of my comrades shouting in my ear, "We are getting on our horses to enter Leipsic." I managed to get up, and seeing the remains of a breakfast on a table, I partook of it in moderation, to make up for my fast of the day before.

I made a wry face as I mounted my horse, so bruised was I, and I joined the staff. I saluted the emperor, who was just arriving; he signed to me to come near, and addressed the following flattering words to me before everybody, "Well, Colonel, have you recovered from the fatigues of yesterday when you discharged so well the missions I entrusted to you?"

Touched and surprised by this signal favour, for I had only been Lieutenant-Colonel for six weeks, I stammered, "Sire, such a reward is far above what I deserve, and would make me forget far greater fatigues."

Rapatel went away for a few moments, telling me to wait for him; a few minutes later, he returned bringing me epaulets of my new rank; my delight may be imagined.

The emperor set out for Leipsic. The rumbling of cannon could still be heard as we crossed the battlefield at the place where the struggle had been most desperate. The scene was terrible and heartbreaking; at last fifteen thousand dead lay on the field; we saw mutilated horses, dismounted cannon, houses burned down, more than a thousand feet of large trees cut down by the grapeshot which had been fired continuously for eight hours. I shall never forget what I felt at the sight of those fifteen thousand dead lying within so small a space; one may judge from this the number of dead and wounded during those two days of carnage. But for the infamous treachery of the troops from Baden, Würtemberg and Saxony, the victory would have been more hotly disputed, and the losses still greater.

Towards noon, when we were about half a league from Leipsic, a deputation from the Town Council came to implore the clemency of the emperor, and to give him the keys of the town, in the name of the aged king, who had remained with his family in the midst of this great disaster, in order to avert one still greater. While the emperor was talking to these worthy people, he received, at every moment, reports from the different corps who were driving the French from Leipsic. At last, a Swedish *aide-de-camp* came to announce the capture of the Faubourg of Rosenthal, and the evacuation of the town put an end to the terrible battle after four days' fighting. Bernadotte was awaiting the *Tzar* in the principal square of the town.

The emperor told me to accompany this *aide-de-camp* on his return and to announce his approach to the Prince of Sweden; I should be only a few minutes before him. So, I entered Leipsic, and found Bernadotte on the Grande Place, grasping the hand of his intimate friend. General Reynier, who had been taken prisoner by the Swedes a few moments before.

The King of Saxony, bareheaded, was humbly awaiting the victor, at the foot of the stairs of the palace, with a battalion of his Guard, lined up with their arms reversed.

The Emperor Alexander dismounted and cordially embraced the Prince of Sweden, who had already got off his horse. After exchanging many congratulations, Bernadotte said: "Sire, here is the King of Saxony, who wishes to offer you his respectful homage."

But the emperor did not seem to hear, and asked: "Where is the Queen of Saxony?"

"She is at the top of the stairs awaiting your Imperial Majesty, but here is her august husband, who wishes to be presented to you."

"Let us go and see the queen."

With such severity did the Emperor Alexander treat this aged king, the victim of his attachment and loyalty to Napoleon, a very laudable devotion, for it lasted up to the end, in spite of the defection of his troops. I was amazed at the reception—I will not say cruel, but at least ungenerous—given by the emperor to the aged sovereign, who, however, appeared rather saddened than humiliated; he followed the angry monarch into the queen's apartments, but he could not obtain a single word from the *Tzar*. The unfortunate king was treated as a prisoner of war, and sent to Berlin; one of the *Tzar's aides-de-camp* was to accompany him, and remain with him; this sad duty was assigned to my friend Lamsdorf, who, being ill, was unable to bear the fatigue of the campaign.

The Kings of Saxony and Denmark were the last sovereigns to remain faithful to Napoleon, even in his fall, but they paid dearly for their fidelity. The King of Saxony remained in Berlin till the close of 1814; the Prince de Talleyrand pleaded his cause warmly at the Congress of Vienna; he obtained for him his liberty and his kingdom, with the exception of Lusatia, which was assigned to Prussia. The King of Denmark lost Norway, which was given to the King of Sweden as a reward for his help in this campaign of 1813, and to indemnify him for the loss of Finland, which had been reunited to Russia.

The French Army, betrayed and abandoned by its allies, crushed by three days of desperate fighting, in which, indeed, it covered itself with glory but suffered enormous losses in men and military stores, was retreating in great disorder. The bridges constructed over the Elster with its tributaries the Parda and the Pleisse, had been destroyed, and the enemy was obliged to cross these rivers in order to take shelter under the protection of the fortress of Erfurt. A few of the unhappy soldiers found a ford, but many were drowned, or compelled to surrender.

In the opinion of all strategists the battlefield was badly chosen for the event of a check; it is true Napoleon never admitted the possibility of a reverse; he could not foresee the treachery of the Saxons and the troops from Baden and Würtemberg; but in war, everything must be foreseen. We shall see him later, overwhelmed and crushed, but refusing to sign the Peace Treaty; preferring to continue an impossible struggle. . . .

It is difficult to form an idea of the confusion that reigned in Leipsic, crowded with wounded, prisoners of war, and soldiers of all nations. After remaining there twenty-four hours, we left on October 21st, to pass the night at Pegau. On the 23rd, as we were entering

Weimar, the emperor said to me, imitating the accent of Bernadotte:

See here, my friend, M. de *la* Rochechouart, go and make this dreadful man listen to reason; he is marching with exasperating slowness, while a bold advance would have such good results. Tell him that I am sending you without ceremony, and without a letter, that you may persuade him to second my efforts; get him to advance. You should find him at Gotha.

I could not repeat the same arguments; I had to find new ones. Chance helped me wonderfully; my success had nothing to do with me. I met the Prince of Sweden at the head of his staff on the way to Kranichfeld, where he intended to pass the night. I addressed him in a few polite words, asking after his health. Having no letter, I began with some commonplace remarks; but Bernadotte was much too observant not to see that my visit had some other aim; he said: "My friend, come with me to Kranichfeld. I have at this very time a letter to give you for the emperor."

Dismounting from our horses, I followed him into the palace where his rooms had been prepared. He said: "I have some orders to give to the different corps of my army; after that, we will talk; you will have supper with me."

The staff-officers of each division of his army were seated around a large table, their order books before them, preparing to write the name of the cantonment of each regiment of their division. I expected to see Bernadotte consult some plans, but not a map was brought out. Placing his right hand over his eyes, as if to collect his thoughts, the prince without hesitation indicated the quarters of each regiment, mentioning the army corps, then the division, the brigade and, finally, the regiment. For instance: Russian Army Corps commanded by the Comte de Langeron. First Division, under Count Woronsoff, First Brigade, etc., etc., in such and such a village, so extraordinary was his memory and his knowledge of these localities, where he had been fighting so long.

After this geographical feat, he rose, and passed into his rooms, signing to me to follow; then he began: "Come, what have you to say to me?"

I repeated the words of the *Tzar*.

He replied: "I am going beyond His Majesty's wishes. Tomorrow you will see me continue my advance; the time for hesitation is over."

I congratulated him on his decision, and expressed my admiration of the way in which he had dictated the cantonments of his troops. He said: "Ah! Understand me, my friend, this comes from my great experience in such things." We talked on various subjects till supper-time, and also, after we had left the table.

The next morning, the Swedish staff left, and I returned to Weimar, but found the Emperor Alexander no longer there. I passed the rest of the day at Weimar, taking advantage of this short interval of leisure to write to the Duc de Richelieu, giving him details of the Battle of Leipsic, and telling him of my own appointment as colonel, dated Arnstadt, October 16th-28th, 1813.

CHAPTER 7

The Winter of 1813-1814

I rejoined the emperor at Meiningen, where he was staying at the *château* of the Dowager Duchess of Saxe-Meiningen, guardian of the young duke, her son. She had two charming daughters, one of whom married the Duke of Clarence, afterwards William IV of England, the other married her cousin, Prince Bernard of Saxe-Weimar. No troops were allowed so much as to enter this *château*, an act of courtesy on the part of the *Tzar*, whose sister had married the hereditary Prince of Saxe-Weimar.

The emperor remained two days at this little court. While there, I received a new token of his kindness which I cannot pass over in silence. Just before the dinner to which the emperor had been invited with his military household, he ought, according to court etiquette, to present us, one by one, to the princess. To my surprise, he took me by the hand:

> I should like, *Madame*, to begin with this one; he is the Comte de Rochechouart, one of my *aides-de-camp*, whom I value greatly. I present him to you the first, to make amends for an act of forgetfulness on my part. When I presented my military household to the Emperor of Austria, I could not remember his name, and he had to give it himself.

After these flattering words, I received a most gracious welcome from the princess and her ladies, who saw in me a favourite, always an important personage at a court. I mention this incident to show how the Emperor Alexander was able to win the affection of all around him.

After these *fêtes*, we continued our way to Münerstadt, Schweinfürt and Homburg. On November 3rd, while at Aschaffenburg, we learned that our Allies had gained a new victory at Hanau. The French Army had been compelled, at the cost of enormous losses, to cut its way through an Austro-Bavarian Corps. The commander of the corps, General de Wrède, had been severely wounded, and the emperor charged me to take him the Cordon of the Order of St. George of the Second Class.

The emperor entered Frankfort on November 20th, and the months of November and December, 1813, were spent there, and in visiting Baden, Carlsruhe and Darmstadt.

I went to Darmstadt on a delightful mission. Sending for me to his room, the emperor said:

> You will take this letter to the grand duke, I wish to pay him a visit. I hear the grand duchess is a charming hostess. I shall go as a relation. The wife of the hereditary prince belongs to the House of Baden, and is therefore a cousin of the empress, but I do not know in what degree; you will ascertain this clearly for me. I do not wish to be received as the Emperor of Russia, but as a cousin. I am going there to enjoy myself and divert my thoughts. A ceremonious reception would bore me dreadfully. I shall hold you to blame if there is one. I shall leave here to-morrow for Darmstadt. I shall have two *aides-de-camp* with me, Ouwaroff and Ojarowski; you will be the third. Try to arrange for a ball in the evening, and give me, beforehand, the names of the most beautiful women invited; also try to unravel for me the scandalous tales about this court. I am told there is something to glean.
>
> The grand duchess is a distinguished and very intellectual woman; she has been very beautiful. The grand duke is eccentric, and inclined to be bearish; as for the son, he must be a cipher. When he was presented to Napoleon, he remained standing without speaking. Noticing an uncommon uniform. Napoleon asked: 'Prince, what uniform is that?' 'Of my rechiment, Zire.' 'Ah! how many men are there in your regiment?' '*Che sais pas'* (I do not know), 'Who is that great fool?' said Napoleon, turning to his companion. Well, my dear Rochechouart, that big fool is my relative. I do not want to meet him, for I could not help laughing in his face when I thought of Napoleon's exclamation. Go and dress, and start at once.

Darmstadt is six leagues from Frankfort. I posted there, and after a two hours' drive, arrived at the palace, in great state, as the emperor wished. I caused myself to be announced to the grand duke as the bearer of a letter from my sovereign to His Royal Highness. I was at once shown into an immense room, more like an arsenal than a study. It was at least twenty feet high, and the walls were lined from top to bottom with weapons and armour of all kinds, from the accoutrements of the ancient Teutons, to the uniform of soldiers of our own day. This collection of helmets, shields, *cuirasses*, coats of mail, lances, swords, daggers, sabres, guns and pistols, was arranged with admirable symmetry, and furnished the room in a very curious, rare and costly manner. A magnificent cannon of the largest calibre, with its caisson, completed this rich collection of armour of all ages.

In the middle of the arsenal, in front of a splendid carved oak desk, covered with gilding and crimson velvet, stood a man of sixty-five, or seventy, years of age. One hand rested on a superb armchair, in the other he held the letter that I had just brought. He had a handsome aristocratic face, and wore a dark blue uniform, in the style of Frederick the Great of Prussia; breeches of white kerseymere, and gaiters of black cloth, extending to above the knee. His hair was white, and cut very close, his hands well formed; his bearing severe but refined; such was my impression of the prince. With extremely courteous manners, he had a noble and serious, almost sad, expression, and he seemed to suffer from gout.

After having slowly read through the *Tzar's* letter, during which time I was looking at all this curious and warlike collection, the prince said, in very good French, without the least accent: "A severe attack of gout has prevented my going to Frankfort to pay my respectful homage to the Emperor of Russia. I am grieved that this great sovereign should come to see me first. In conformity with His Imperial Majesty's wish, I will receive him as a relative; this will somewhat distress the grand duchess, but she will accept the order with resignation. I am sending her the kind letter you have just brought me, and you will go to her apartments, and make arrangements for tomorrow's reception. It is her province, and it entirely rests with her. It is long since I took any part in such details."

Having been conducted to the apartments of the grand duchess by the chamberlain on duty, I was dazzled by the graceful and dignified bearing of this princess, still very beautiful, in spite of her age. She received me most kindly, but I found it difficult to dissuade her from the idea of an official reception. I was obliged to tell her that His Imperial Majesty had ordered me to insist on this point. He was coming to Darmstadt to enjoy the pleasure of family life, of which he had so long been deprived, and not the ceremony of a court. As I withdrew, after receiving an invitation to return to dinner, I said, with the view to arouse the curiosity of the beautiful princess:

> I am charged by His Imperial Majesty to ask a host of questions with regard to the personnel of the charming Court of Darmstadt, one of the most brilliant in Germany, thanks to the august princess who is its model, and indeed its chief ornament, uniting so many noble qualities in her person.

The soldier could become a courtier. This compliment won for me a gracious smile and the reply: "Only a French noble could give a graceful turn to such direct flattery. I thank you. Count." I bowed low and withdrew. The chamberlain, who had announced me, handed me over to a gentleman-usher, who had been charged to show me to my room. I strolled about the magnificent park adjoining the palace, and then returned to dress. At four o'clock I entered the large drawing-room. The grand duchess soon appeared, and we passed at once into the dining-room. The chamberlain introduced me to an elderly lady, and asked me to take her in to dinner. Covers were laid for twenty— the hereditary grand duchess, the high dignitaries of the little court, the ladies in attendance, etc. The grand duke always dined in his own apartments, and the prince, his son, was travelling at this time.

My neighbour was a Frenchwoman, a Canoness of Bavaria, who had been lady-in-waiting to the grand duchess ever since the Revolution. She said: "You are commanded by your sovereign to obtain information with regard to the Court of Darmstadt. I have been charged to answer your inquiries. Question me."

I learned, first, that the hereditary princess was the sister of the Empress Elizabeth and the ex-Queen of Sweden, and was therefore the *Tzar's* sister-in-law, and not his cousin. I promised to inform the Emperor Alexander of this near relationship.

As my intelligent *cicerone* was unable entirely to satisfy my curiosity during the dinner, our conversation was continued in the drawing-room, and she put me in a position to give the emperor, next day, most confidential information. I saw that my mission had become known among the ladies of the court, for during the evening, in the drawing-room, I was surrounded by pretty women who, in order to attract attention and make themselves known, availed themselves of every possible pretext to talk to me about the Emperor Alexander.

The next day the *Tzar* arrived at two o'clock. I gave him all the information I had received from the lady-in-waiting. A delightful ball followed the dinner. The emperor charmed every one by his amiability. Giving his arm to the grand duchess, as they passed through the rooms, he said: "Are you satisfied, *Madame*, with my young ambassador? Does he not promise well?"

"He is a very pleasant flatterer," she replied.

As we returned to Frankfort, the emperor expressed his satisfaction at the way in which I had discharged this pleasant duty. On such a cheerful note did I bury the year 1813.

Now I come to that famous year 1814, so full of memorable events, which changed the face of Europe, by re-establishing the Bourbons on the thrones of France and Spain, while destroying an empire that appeared powerful, but which was overwhelmed by the number of its enemies, in spite of the military genius of its ruler, then in all its splendour, in spite of the valour of those old regiments, for so many years the conquerors of Europe, now crushed, and well-nigh decimated by two years of disasters unparalled in history.

On January 3rd, the Russian headquarters were moved across the Rhine at Bâle, reached Altkirch on the 13th, Vesoul on the 17th, passing by Montbéliard and Villersexel, finally arriving at Langres on the 26th.

Two days later I received news of the death of my brother Louis, who was killed at Lignol, a village not far from Bar-sur-Aube, on January 26th, at two o'clock in the morning, three days before the bloody Battle of Brienne. We had been separated by the chances of the campaign in Saxony, but we had met on the bridge over the Rhine at Bâle. My brother had begged me to obtain from the emperor a change of corps for him; he could no longer remain the chief of staff to Count Sacken.

The count had a great regard for him, but exacted an amount of work above human strength. His chief of staff must see everything for himself, and never be satisfied with reports. At Villersexel I had an opportunity of speaking to the emperor, and I had begged him to take Louis on his staff. He promised to bring us together again, and to give the necessary orders to Prince Wolkonski. Thus, I was awaiting the fulfilment of his promise, when, on the 28th, my brother's servant came into the room that I shared with Rapatel, and told me, amid his sobs, that his master was dead.

Having been sent on a reconnaissance, one very dark night, Louis had come upon a French main-guard, who retreated, firing by platoons and crying out, "Cossacks." My poor brother had been struck by eight bullets. Taking advantage of the enemy's retreat, the Cossack, who accompanied Louis, placed his body in front of him across his horse and brought him back to Count Sacken's headquarters. I was the more distressed, as I reproached myself with not having pressed the emperor for the immediate fulfilment of his promise.

It only remained for me to render the last honours to the companion of the struggles of my childhood. Not being able to leave, for we expected every moment the order to advance, I asked someone in Langres to go to Lignol and arrange for a suitable funeral for my brother, and to tell the parish priest that I would pay for everything as soon as possible. In the month of July, I sent the *curé* of this little parish his fees and the money required to erect a gravestone with Louis' name, rank, and the date of his death.

Ever since we entered French territory Rapatel and I had tried to promote the restoration of the Bourbons. The twenty-four years of constant wars, and, above all, the disasters of the last two years, and the continual appeal for recruits, all these causes had led to general discontent and disaffection towards Napoleon. I believe I may affirm that with the exception of government officials, the purchasers of national property, and some enthusiasts for the rule of the sword, the nation was wearied, disillusioned and discouraged by so many sacrifices, and frightened at the thought of the misfortunes that were about to fall upon the country.

Some Royalists from Paris, among others Count Alexis de Noailles, the Comte de Wall, the Comte de Virieu, the Marquis Quinsonnas, met together at the house of the Marquis de Chalencey, where the Emperor Alexander was staying. Their aim was to sound the emperor on his intentions with regard to the Bourbons. Before arousing a demonstration, before declaring themselves and inducing their friends to declare themselves, it seemed essential to have not merely the assent, but the support of the Emperor of Russia, M. de Chalencey begged us—Rapatel and me—to be present at this meeting. We drew up a memorandum on the spot that I was charged to present to the emperor the next day. (The memorandum, signed by the Comte de Rochechouart, is given in full in the original French edition.—Tr.) I asked for an audience, which was at once granted. . . ,

Having read the memorandum, the emperor said:

I understand, and I approve of the steps that you and de Rapatel have taken, but we are not yet sufficiently sure of victory to
come to a decision. Wait for the result of the next battle, which
cannot be long delayed. If fortune favours us, I will grant you
the permission you ask. There is no doubt as to my feelings
with regard to the family of your ancient kings, but I cannot act
without my Allies; I can only let things take their course; it is
quite another thing to act alone. Meanwhile, let the French declare themselves; then many difficulties will be smoothed away.

I communicated this reply the same evening to the Royalist meeting; it was decided that we should act. We drew up a letter to the King,
Louis XVIII, in England, and another to the Duc de Berry. These
letters, which were signed by each one of us, were entrusted to M.
Mallet, a Swiss colonel.

★★★★★★

These two letters are given in the French edition. M. de Rochechouart adds that they knew the Duc de Berry was in England, but they did not know where the Comte d'Artois might
be, and they understood the Duc d'Angoulême had joined the
Duke of Wellington in the South of France.—Tr.

★★★★★★

After these letters had been sent off, we separated; some went to
Burgundy, some to Franche-Comté, and a few remained at our headquarters. Quinsonnas and the Abbé Reluquet returned to Paris; Alexis
de Noailles and Virieu went to Dijon.

On February 7th we were at Troyes, where other Royalists joined
us.

I shall not describe the manoeuvres of our staff, forward, backward,
and to the side; I will refer the reader to the work of M. de Koch.
I shall confine myself to the negotiations with the French princes
which were entrusted to me, on the one hand by the Emperor Alexander, and on the other by the Comte d'Artois.

From the time of his arrival in France the Comte d'Artois found
himself in a very delicate position, being in direct contact with the
Austrian Army, the leaders of which, with the exception of Prince
Schwarzenberg, were more than cold, obeying the instructions of
Prince Metternich, who did not conceal his aversion to the Bourbons.
So, knowing the part I had taken at the first meetings of the Royalists,
Monsieur charged the Comte de Wall to give me the following letter:

Vesoul, January 21st, 1814.

I had intended, *Monsieur*, to send a letter to the Emperor of Russia by the Comte de Wall . . . but on the one hand I am so much touched, so deeply moved by the reception I have met with from the French people ever since I crossed the frontier, and especially here, and, on the other hand, I am so much astonished at the conduct of the Austrian general, Hirsch, the commandant of this town, that I am afraid of expressing my feelings too strongly. I confine myself, therefore, to sending the Comte de Wall to you; he will explain to you in detail what has taken place, and I beg you to inform His Majesty the Emperor of Russia. . . .

Charles-Philippe.

I communicated this letter to the emperor, who charged me to recommend patience to the Comte d'Artois, and, above all, to dissuade him from coming to headquarters, if he expressed any intention of doing so. The time had not yet come openly to take the side of the Bourbons, a course which was not equally pleasing to all the Allies.

In my reply to *Monsieur* I thought it necessary to explain the steps we had taken before his arrival, and my position with regard to the *Tzar*. (this memorandum is omitted in the English translation.—Tr.)

This report shows the difficulties that fettered the Royalist party, how little favour was shown to them by the Allies, and, consequently, how false is the assertion, "The Bourbons were brought back by foreign bayonets." On the contrary, it was the French who compelled the Allied sovereigns to recognise the rights of the Bourbon dynasty, when all their predilections inclined in another direction.

CHAPTER 8

The Allies Advance on Paris, 1814

In the middle of January, a Congress met at Châtillon-sur-Seine with the object of negotiating a peace. I will not enter upon the causes which prolonged the conference till March; the negotiations were suspended or accelerated according to the progress of military events. . . . After the Battle of Brienne and other slight defeats, Napoleon charged the Duc de Vicence to communicate to the Congress his final concessions; after long debates, they were accepted by Russia, England, Austria and Prussia. The peace appeared to be concluded; it only remained for Napoleon to ratify it.

★★★★★★

A few years later, at St. Helena, Sir Hudson Lowe refused to give Napoleon the title of emperor on the ground that his government had never recognised him as such, but only under the name and title of General Buonaparte. . . . The official documents of the Congress of Châtillon, signed by all the Plenipotentiaries, proved the falsity of this assertion. . . .

In the name of the Most Holy and Indivisible Trinity, Their Imperial Majesties of Russia and Austria, His Majesty the King of the United Kingdom of Great Britain and Ireland, His Majesty the King of Prussia, acting in the name of all the Allies, on the one part, and His Majesty the Emperor of the French on the other part: desiring to cement the future repose and well-being of Europe by a solid and lasting Peace on land and sea, and having to attain this salutary aim assembled their Plenipotentiaries at Châtillon-sur-Seine, to treat of the conditions of this Peace, the said Plenipotentiaries have agreed upon the following clauses:

Art. 1.—There shall be Peace and Amnesty between Their Majesties of Austria and Russia, His Majesty the King of the United Kingdom of Great Britain and Ireland, and His Majesty the King of Prussia, acting at the same time in the name of their Allies, and His Majesty the Emperor of the French their heirs and successors in perpetuity, etc., etc.

Six articles follow in which the same titles and descriptions are continually repeated. These articles are ratified by the following signatures:

Châtillon-sur-Seine, February 17th, 1814.

Caulaincourt, Duc de Vicence, Aberdeen, Cathcart, Count Razoumowski, Humboldt, Count Stadion, Charles Stewart.

Thus, the English Plenipotentiaries then recognised Napoleon as Emperor of the French, and even recognised his heirs and successors in perpetuity.

★★★★★★

We were at Vandoeuvre, having retreated after the last success of Napoleon, when the news reached us of the signature of the peace at Châtillon. Some of our friends were with us; there were assembled Armand and Jules de Polignac, Alexis de Noailles, Rapatel and I. Pozzo came to inform us that peace had been signed, he had seen the ratification of the Allied Powers; but, suddenly rising and striking the table with his fist, he said with all his Italian fire: "No, gentlemen, it is not all ended, the Corsican has not signed." The expression "the Corsican," thrown out so unexpectedly, amused us greatly, coming as it did from another Corsican; it remained to see what meaning he attached to it. These prophetic words were confirmed two days later. Napoleon, blinded by some success, refused to ratify the conditions accepted by his minister, the Duc de Vicence; he put forth exaggerated claims. The plenipotentiaries rejoined their Sovereigns; diplomacy declared itself powerless; it was necessary to resort to the chance of the battlefield. . . .

After the negotiations at Châtillon had been broken off, the Emperor Alexander, wearied with the delays of the *generalissimo*, Prince Schwarzenberg, resolved on a more vigorous campaign. A whole week was spent in a series of successes and checks, marches and counter-marches. At last the armies met at Arcis-sur-Aube. Severe fighting took place. Napoleon, having sustained enormous losses, withdrew to

Vitry-le-François. The Russian Army followed him. The combat was renewed with varying fortune.

Suddenly Napoleon effected a manoeuvre that has been differently criticised, blamed by many, approved by a few. The actual result was to bring about the fall of the great leader within a few days. The manoeuvre consisted in passing to the rear of the Allied armies in order to cut off their communications. Napoleon hoped that they would follow him and thus be drawn away from Paris. The Allied armies divided; two Russian and Prussian corps remained to watch Napoleon, the rest of the army, under the *Tzar* and the King of Prussia, and the Army of Silesia, as it was called, under Field-Marshal Blücher, marched directly on Paris, driving before them the corps of the Maréchal Marmont, Duc de Raguse, and of the Maréchal Mortier, Duc de Trévise. In this sudden and rapid movement, the Emperor of Austria became separated from his allies, an apparently unimportant incident, which deprived Napoleon of the protection of his father-in-law, and of Prince Metternich, at a very critical moment for himself and his dynasty.

Napoleon, aided by the valour and devotion of his troops, carried out the most skilful manoeuvres and passed from point to point with bewildering rapidity; nothing could avert his ruin.

All the writers of that day throw blame on such and such a manoeuvre, such and such a decision; on the inaction, incapacity or faint-heartedness of such and such a general. Undoubtedly the Marshals of the Empire had not the military genius of Napoleon; they were very brave, but too much accustomed to receive their master's orders, and without initiative. Napoleon's manoeuvre was therefore dangerous; it separated him from the generals under him, and thus deprived them of the inspiration of his genius and of his eagle glance that saw at once the advantage to be derived from the enemy's position.

Moreover, every victory hastened his downfall by the price it cost. France no longer provided recruits; the old army, the veterans who had conquered on all the battlefields of Europe, lay dead amid the ice of Russia. If the greatest general of modern times was deceived in his calculations, the reason is that there comes a day when human power and wisdom are of no account. Let men call it destiny, fate, or invent some other name, what can they do against the will of Him who moves the heaven and the earth?

On March 25th, we met a French column at Fère-Champenoise. I will give the narrative in the words of M. Koch, adding a few details, as I took part in this fierce encounter:

ALLIES ADVANCE INTO PARIS, MARCH 19, 1814

The column, whose appearance caused so much astonishment and alarm to the Allies, was formed of the Pacthod and Amey divisions that had reached Bergères on the 24th. General Pacthod, in haste to join Marshals Marmont and Mortier, had sent an orderly officer to Marshal Mortier, and, without waiting for his return, began to march on Vitry at daybreak. Arriving at the outskirts of Villeseneux at ten o'clock in the morning, he received a message to remain at Bergères (where he was supposed to be) until further orders.

This division, which escorted a large convoy of supplies and munitions, had been marching during part of the night; the horses were dropping down with fatigue. General Pacthod, believing he was out of danger, thought there would be time to rest at Villeseneux. But he had scarcely settled down there when he was attacked by General Korf, who was following the road from Châlons to Etoges. General Pacthod at once formed his troops: the right supported by the village, the left covered by an immense square, the convoy in the rear.

M. de Beauchamp gives further details:

The convoy was in itself of extreme importance, as is evident from the number of troops accompanying it. It was observed by Maréchal Blücher's cavalry. The *maréchal* at once detached the cavalry generals, Korf and Wassiltchikoff, to attack it. At the sight of the enemy, the column and convoy fell back on Fère-Champenoise at the very moment when the cavalry of the Russian Grand Army reached this point, by the road from Vitry. On receiving news of this encounter, Prince Schwarzenberg had hastily recalled part of the cavalry from the pursuit of Mortier and Marmont; at the same time, the Emperor Alexander ordered the Russian artillery of his Guard to advance. Pursued and attacked on all sides by troops under the immediate command of the Sovereigns, the French column formed in several squares, and prepared to make the most heroic resistance; it was composed entirely of young, soldiers and National Guards, but nothing could intimidate these novices in warfare.

The squares continued to fire and retreat, braving the cavalry charges, rejecting the repeated Russian summons to a truce, refusing to lay down their arms. In vain did Colonel Rapatel, a distinguished officer, the same who had received the dying

Conantray
Cauvrey
Conantray
Marsh.
St Gond
Vassoldnkeff
Onizeux
Constantine
Aulnay
Pahlen
Korff
Pet.^e Morin
FÈRE CHAMPENOISE
Rajetsky
Pierre Morin
Gourganson
Euvy
Ecury le Repos
Conantray
Le Clou
Norme
Pachod
Nostitz
Clamange
Lenharrée
Vassunont
Villeseneux
Montepreux
Maxmont
Sommesous
From Arcis
Saudron
La Chalons
Vatry
Mortier
Poivre
Bussi Lettrée
Bonmartin
Soude St Croix
Soude

BATTLE OF
FÈRE CHAMPENOISE
25th March 1814.
A.K JOHNSTON F.R.S.E.
French ___ Allies
Cavalry ___ Infantry ___ Artillery
S C A L E S
Military Steps 2½ Feet each.
English Miles

message of his former chief, General Moreau, advance alone to bring to an end the useless struggle. 'My friends! My fellow-countrymen!' the colonel called to them, 'cease fighting! You have won enough honour! The Emperor Alexander will restore you to liberty.' Scarcely had he spoken these words than he fell, struck by two bullets, and died, honoured by the army, and by the *Tzar*, to whom he was *aide-de-camp*.

Artillery alone could conquer this handful of brave men struggling against a whole army. The batteries opened fire, breaking through the squares; simultaneous charges completed the work, carrying death and disorder into them; it was necessary to surrender. Generals Pacthod and Amey, five brigadier generals, twelve cannon, 4,800 infantry and the entire convoy fell into the power of the Allied armies.

The following are the details which I will add to these two narratives:

On the first appearance of the French column there was, in fact, a moment of bewilderment in the Allied army; to what corps did it belong? What was the cavalry that appeared on the right? We were in the midst of an immense plain; the artillery of the Guard received orders to advance, when suddenly we saw the distant cavalry charge the column, which at once formed the infantry in squares and opened a vigorous fire of artillery. There was no longer any doubt; the column belonged to the French Army; orders were given to the Russian artillery to attack, and the whole of the cavalry also began to advance. Rapatel, believing that two of his brothers were with the opposing forces, from information received from some prisoners taken that morning, went forward to assure himself of the fact, and to persuade the column to yield to such superior numbers.

What became of him? I did not know. The order to charge having been given to the cavalry, our staff had not time to move aside to let them pass; we were compelled, under pain of being crushed, to follow the torrent. In two minutes, the Emperor Alexander and the King of Prussia found themselves in the midst of the enemy column, borne along by a cavalry charge of 16,000 Russians, Prussians and Austrians, *cuirassiers*, dragoons, hussars and Cossacks. Never again shall I see such a *mêlée*. I can scarcely relate it, the confusion was so great, the incidents so many and strange; it was all over in less time than it takes to write it.

Premier-fait

Viaspre

Macdonald

Pouare

Moulin Neuf

Vilette

St. Etienne

St. Remy

Nozay

Kaisaroff

Barclay

Menil. la Comtesse

Wrede

Cadois

Ney

Torcy

Le Chene

Oudinot

Ormes

ARCIS

Position after the Battle

To Lire Champenoise

To Trin

Vaupoisson

BATTLE OF
ARCIS-SUR-AUBE
21st March 1814.

A.K.JOHNSTON, F.R.G.S.

French   Allies
Cavalry   Infantry   Artillery
SCALES
Military Steps 2½ Feet each
English Miles

The column of 9,000 men had in a moment 4,000 dead or wounded, lying on the road they had taken in the hope of reaching a wood not far away, where they would have been protected from the cavalry attacks and the ceaseless firing of thirty cannon. This column, as I say, was escorting a numerous convoy of supplies and munitions for the French *Grande Armée*; from afar it seemed much stronger than it really was, and this is the reason that such powerful forces were sent against it. The wagons were drawn up in the centre with the carriages, notably those of General Pacthod, who was commander-in-chief. The defence was heroic, and the more praiseworthy as the troops were conscripts or mobilised National Guards, hastily gathered together; only the artillery was served by old soldiers recently come from Spain.

At the moment when I found myself in the midst of the principal square, together with the Emperor of Russia, the King of Prussia and the officers of their numerous staff, carried away by the charge of the hussars and Cossacks of the Guard, I saw a French officer near me, struggling with some Cossacks, who were trying to despoil him in spite of his cries and protests.

"Take me to my brother; I have a brother in the Russian Army."

"What is your brother's name?" I asked.

"Rapatel," was the reply.

I threw myself between him and the Cossacks, ordering them to leave him alone. I said: "Your brother is my comrade. Come, that I may have the pleasure of taking you to him."

I had scarcely spoken, when Brozine, one of my colleagues, came running to me and said: "Oh! Rochechouart! What a misfortune! The emperor has just heard of the death of poor Rapatel; he has sent me to look for his body."

Could there be a more pathetic scene? The poor prisoner, miraculously escaped from the massacre of his troop, learning the death of his brother at the very moment when he was. looking forward to receiving help and consolation from him. Tears ran down his face, which was still black with the smoke from the powder. I grasped his hands, saying: "You are my prisoner; you will not leave your brother's comrade."

I obtained a riderless horse for him, and asked him, "Have you any belongings that can be saved?"

He answered, amid his sobs, "As I was a *commandant* of artillery in the Pacthod Division, all I possess is in a caisson."

I set out with him to find the caisson. It was intact; the Cossacks had pillaged the carriages, but had left the artillery and caissons alone.

The five prisoner generals got into General Pacthod's carriage; the emperor had just given it back to him. He had also returned to these generals their swords, saying: "Gentlemen, when you can use them so well you ought never to be separated from them."

Just as we were setting out for Fère-Champenoise we found hidden under the carriage a charming little girl of eight or nine, weeping bitterly. General Pacthod asked her how she came to be there. She pointed to her father, a demobilised National Guard, whose body had been cut in two by a cannon ball.

"I followed him," she added, "so that I might not be alone in the house. My mother is dead; I do not know that I have any relations. After my father was killed, I slipped under the carriage to avoid the cannon balls."

General Pacthod took her up on the box of his carriage, saying, "Little one, if all this ends well, and soon, I will take care of you."

He kept his word; being unmarried, he had the poor orphan brought up in a good school. In 1824, I was one day dining with him; she had grown tall, and very pretty. I believe she married the nephew of her benefactor, and General Pacthod left her a part of his fortune.

In the evening, I presented Captain Rapatel to the emperor, who, as usual, was most kind. He expressed great regret at the death of his brother, whom he valued highly, and asked Captain Rapatel his plans.

"I beg your Majesty to set me at liberty, but, at the same time, I beg that you will allow me to wait for a favourable moment to enjoy it. I will remain with my brother's comrade and friend, M. de Rochechouart, who has promised to be a brother to me in his stead."

"Be it so," said the emperor. "When peace is signed, if you would like to fill the post of *aide-de-camp* that I gave to your poor brother, it will rest entirely with you; you are in good hands until then."

So, I took Captain Rapatel with me; I had already Armand de Polignac, who had been charged by the Comte d'Artois to accompany the Emperor Alexander, in order to take advantage of every opportunity of speaking to him. Two days later another Frenchman serving in the Russian Army, the Marquis de Montpezat (formerly a captain on the staff of the Duc de Richelieu, at Odessa) arrived from the blockade of Hamburg, and begged me to add him to my companions. The gravity of events prevented his receiving any reply to the despatches he carried. As we were so near Paris, he naturally wished to be at the Allied headquarters at the moment when everything was to be decided; he shared my carriage with Rapatel.

My suite was further increased by. a young French non-commissioned officer, named Boutet, who had been saved on the battlefield of Tarantino, in Russia, in 1812, by the Lieut.-Colonel of the Cossack Eegiment of the Guard, who had picked him up when he was seriously wounded, and had his wounds dressed. This young man wrote a very beautiful hand; he suggested that I should keep him with me and make use of his services, at least until our entry into Paris. He retained a grateful recollection of the colonel of the Cossacks, but for whom he would have died at Tarantino; but, he thought, I could be of more assistance to him. Later, he became *aide-de-camp* to Armand de Polignac.

On March 29th, there was fighting at the gates of Paris along an immense line. The Russian Grand Army, and the so-called Army of Silesia, formed an effective force of at least 150,000 men. To these the French could only oppose from 25,000 to 30,000 men, and these were disheartened by the recent defeats. They were under the command of the Marshals Marmont and Mortier, but the generals did not agree and would not act in concert. There was a third leader, Joseph Buonaparte, invested with the title of Lieut.-General of the Empire. The confusion was great and the capture of Paris inevitable.

Many brave deeds were done, but the sacrifices served only to delay the fall of the town a few hours.

The Allied Army was marching on Paris in the form of a semicircle; only the route to Orléans was open, and along this route the Regent, the Empress Marie Louise, with her son, her ministers, the Council of Regency, and Prince Joseph. Buonaparte, retired. They took up their residence at Blois, thus leaving the capital without government, and a prey to all the elements of intrigue that were within it.

On the 29th the general staff passed the night at Bondy. On the 30th, as we were crossing Pantin, I sang to my comrades "*Que Pantin serait content*," etc. A grocer, standing at his shop door, was watching us pass. He called out, "Hi! Here are Cossacks singing our old song."

During the day the Prés-Saint-Gervais, the Buttes-Chaumont and Belleville were occupied after a vigorous resistance and many casualties on both sides. Towards 2 p.m. the Emperor Alexander arrived on the Buttes-Chaumont, whence he could look down on Paris. We could hear a terrible fire of musketry in the direction of Montmartre and Vincennes, and incessant discharges of powerful artillery. At this solemn moment the emperor dismounted, in order to get a better view of the impressive scene. He asked me to point out the principal buildings; then his face became grave, he ceased to question me, and remained rapt in deep thought. Of what was he thinking? God only knows. He seemed no longer to hear the cannon or the fusillade or the murmur of the great city at our feet. I withdrew discreetly, and I, too, gave myself up to strange reflections.

The emperor was soon aroused from his dream by the arrival of a messenger with a flag of truce, brought by Count Nesselrode.

The *Tzar*, the King of Prussia, the generals and ministers present, assembled in Council. At the end of a quarter of an hour the emperor signed to me to come forward.

> Go and find the Comte de Langeron; he should be at the foot of Montmartre; tell him that I have just granted an immediate suspension of hostilities. Consequently, let him give orders to cease firing at once, and that no soldier shall attempt to enter Paris even if the barriers should have been captured. I shall hold him personally responsible. Go, as quickly as you can.

I set off at a gallop, but what a terrible and perilous mission! In order to take the shortest route, I had to pass through narrow streets where furious fighting was still going on. From every house, transformed, as it were, into a fort, there came a murderous fusillade; at every step, cannon, on one side or the other, enfiladed the streets, the roads and by-paths. I said to myself: "I shall never reach my destination through this hail of balls and bullets. I shall be killed ten times over."

Happily, and by miracle, I came through without a scratch. I fastened a white handkerchief to the end of my sword, and all the way as I went I waved my flag, and shouted in Russian, French, and German: "Cease fire, by order of the *Tzar*. My friends, do not fire any more, there is a suspension of arms. I am going to announce it to the whole line."

As a rule, they listened to me, except in some places where the struggle was too fierce, or the noise too great for me to be heard. At last, after unheard-of dangers, I found M. de Langeron at Montmartre. I repeated to him, word for word, the instructions of the emperor. He immediately gave orders to cease fire, laid down some severe regulations, and forbade, under pain of death, that anyone, no matter who, should leave the ranks, or enter Paris. The advance guard of his division was already in occupation of the barriers Rochechouart, des Martyrs, Blanche, and de Clichy.

Two hours later firing had ceased along the whole line, and I returned to inform the emperor that his orders had been carried out. He said: "You have done well, you have lost no time."

★★★★★★

A few days later, remembering this dangerous mission, the emperor signed my brevet of Commander of the Order of Saint Vladimir with these words: "In reward for his conduct at the Battle before Paris from March 18th-30th, 1814."

★★★★★★

PRUSSIANS IN PARIS

PART 4: IN THE SERVICE OF LOUIS XVIII

CHAPTER 1

Commandant of Paris, 1814

The *Tzar* made his way back to Bendy, where his presence was needed for negotiations that were prolonged far into the night. Armand de Polignac, Montpezat, Rapatel, Boutet (the Comte de Rochechouart's "suite"—Tr.), and I took the road towards Belleville, where we were to have supper and spend the night. As we followed the boulevards outside the barriers of La Villette and Pantin, we entered into conversation with many of the inhabitants, terrified at the thought of the morrow . . . and we distributed the Proclamation of Louis XVIII wherever we could.

As the day was closing in we left the barriers and entered Belleville, where everything was still in confusion; there had been street fighting during the day, but, strange to say, no damage had been done, either by the French or the Allies, beyond that which necessarily follows from fighting in the streets—broken windows, branches broken off the trees, etc.

We ordered supper at one of the more prosperous inns of the suburb. The landlord, with his wife and children, his cook and cash-box, had taken refuge in Paris, leaving the head waiter, a wide-awake fellow, in charge of the establishment, with two assistant cooks.

The Comte de Lambert, whose division occupied Belleville, and the Baron de Damas, had joined us, so we were a large party of Frenchmen. The waiter, hearing us all talking French, without a word of Russian, could not conceal his astonishment. Folding his arms, he said: "Oh come! For Cossacks, you chatter away fast enough in French, and the best French, too!"

We answered with a merry peal of laughter, and Boutet gravely remarked: "You need not wonder at that, waiter, we learned French when we were put out to nurse."

Towards eleven o'clock my companions and I withdrew to the house where we were billeted, a pretty country residence belonging to a wholesale dealer of the Marais. The gardener, who was caretaker, had been threatened with having to billet Cossacks, and was delighted to receive an *aide-de-camp* of the *Tzar*.

On March 31st, I mounted my horse early to return to Headquarters at Bondy. On my way, I learned that the emperor was near the barriers. Turning in that direction I met Colonel Brozine, the comrade who had told me of Rapatel's death at Fère-Champenoise. He exclaimed: "Where have you been hiding? They are looking for you everywhere."

"What for?"

"You are appointed *commandant* of the Fort of Paris, and General Sacken, governor. Make haste; they are waiting for you."

Before I had recovered from my astonishment I heard General Sacken himself calling me:

I was despairing of coming across you, but we have no time to lose. I am glad the *Tzar* has chosen you because you are a Frenchman, and it will show the Parisians that he wishes them well. As for me, I rejoice to have near me, working with, me, the brother of one who was for two years my chief of staff, and whose death I greatly deplored. You will take the command of three battalions of Russian Guards. They are drawn up near here; I have added two cannon. You will go to the Hôtel de Ville, and take possession of it in the name of the *Tzar*.

You will leave your cannon and two battalions there, and with the third battalion you will go to the Elysée, which is assigned as a residence for the Emperor of Russia and his ministers. Afterwards, you will consult with the Prefect of the Seine, and the Municipality of Paris, with regard to billets, rations, forage, and accommodation for our sick and wounded at the hospitals. Two officers of the National Guard will be in attendance to guide and protect you, but act prudently and avoid any collision. You will choose a suitable residence for me, and come and tell me where it is. Go, be prudent, and firm.

Imagine my astonishment, delight and confusion! Surprised by a command, totally unexpected. Beside myself with joy, that I should thus make my entry into this great city that I had left ten years before under such sad circumstances—all alone, separated from my relations who had been dispersed by the Revolution and ruined by their devotion to the Royal Family; obliged to be content with the *panier* of the diligence . . . I was returning *commandant!* There was neither time nor possibility for reflection; I was carried along by the torrent of affairs.

I made my entry by the Rue du Faubourg-Saint-Martin; I chose Montpezet as *aide-de-camp*, and M. de Zasse, Major of the Fort; I met him accidentally at the moment. . . .

Just as I was about to give the word of command to my battalions: "Forward! March!" one of the officers of the National Guard referred to by General Sacken came forward to escort me. What was our mutual surprise! I recognized Albert de Brancas, later Duc de Cerest, and he found an intimate friend in the Russian officer charged to take possession of the Hôtel de Ville in the name of the *Tzar*. We had seen a great deal of each other when I stayed in Paris after my return from Portugal. We greeted one another most cordially; then M. de Brancas, turning to the crowd around us, said:

Parisians! The Emperor of Russia gives you a pledge of his good will towards this great city. He has just appointed this officer, his *aide-de-camp*, as *commandant*. He is a fellow-countryman, a native of Paris, a friend, whom I have found again, and I present him to you as a friend of yours.

A murmur of approval greeted these words; my name flew from mouth to mouth, and as we were quite close to the barrier, and the street, Rochechouart, the effect was complete. The other officer of the National Guard was the handsome Count Albert d'Orsay, also a good friend of mine; he had just been thrown from his horse on the pavement of the Faubourg Saint-Martin, and was being carried home on a stretcher. I pressed his hand as he passed.

I reached the Hôtel de Ville without opposition; I drew up my troops in order of battle on the Place de Grève, and went up to the rooms of the Prefect, the Comte de Chabrol. He received me very coldly, and made difficulties to everything I asked. I therefore felt obliged to speak severely. . . . M. de Chabrol at once adopted a different tone, and assured me he was quite at my service. I asked him to assemble the twelve mayors of Paris, while I went to carry out the orders of the governor, General Sacken.

I left M. de Zasse at the Hôtel de Ville, with the two battalions, to arrange about billets and rations, and with my third battalion I took possession of the Elysée. I installed the emperor's military household in this palace, I chose the residence of General Hulin, the late Governor of Paris, on the Place Vendôme, for my staff and myself, and finding nothing suitable for General Sacken near the Elysée, I selected for him the house of M. Roy, rue de la Chaussée d'Antin.

All these arrangements being completed, I rejoined the *Tzar* and the King of Prussia, on the Place Louis XV. The *generalissimo*, Prince Schwarzenberg, was parading the Allied Army before their Majesties. Napoleon's latest reports had represented this army as exhausted, disorganised and reduced to inefficiency. Instead of this, the Parisians, who gathered in crowds, watched for three hours the Russian Guards, in splendid uniform, marching past; the Prussian Royal Guards, less numerous, but equally fine troops; the entire corps of Hungarian grenadiers in martial array; at least 20,000 Cossacks, or Kalmuks; 35,000 Regular Cavalry of the three nations, followed by four hundred cannon with all their train.

This display of overwhelming force seemed to make a great impression on the Parisians. The most numerous and brilliant staff ever assembled completed the picture. Add to this, an electrified crowd, shouts from more than a hundred thousand voices, "Long live the Emperor Alexander! Long live the King of Prussia! Long live the King! Long live the Allies! Long live our Deliverers," mingled with words of command in Russian and German, the sound of carriages and horses, the tramp of infantry; the scene is indescribable. A single incident among a thousand remains in my memory. A young woman having contrived—how I know not—to raise herself on to one of the stirrups of the *Tzar*, shouted frantically in his ear: "*Vive l'Empereur Alexandre.*" The sovereign took hold of her hands to keep her from falling, and said in his gracious manner: "*Madame*, cry '*Vive le Roi,*' and I will cry it with you."

After having reported to General Sacken the arrangements with regard to houses, I was about to withdraw, when he told me of a decision that had just been taken by the Allied sovereigns. The Russian general, Count Sacken, was retained as Governor of Paris, and three *commandants*, Russian, Austrian and Prussian, had each four *arrondissements* under their orders, in which they should billet the officers of their nation. . . . My command remained the most important. I alone was charged with communications with the *prefecture*, the Provisional Government, and the staff of the National Guard.

I will describe in some detail the change of government which re-established the Bourbons, to the exclusion of the Napoleonic dynasty. I learned these particulars from the Duc de Richelieu, who received them from the Emperor Alexander himself; it would be impossible to draw from a more authentic source.

The first conferences were held early in April at the house of M. de Talleyrand, in the Rue St. Florentin, where the Emperor of Russia was living, as the Elysée was not ready for his reception. The departure of Marie-Louise for Blois with her son, and Napoleon's ministers, and the absence of the Emperor of Austria, who was only able to arrive when all was over, had left the field free to the enemies of the Empire.

I wish to show how false is the statement, so often made by French Liberals:

The Bourbons only came back by means of the bayonets of the Allies, and not by the will of the nation.

Nothing is less true: to be convinced of this, it is only necessary to follow the acts of the Allied Sovereigns. They prove, (1) That it was their express intention to leave the French to declare what form of government they desired. (2) That never has a more frank and honourable declaration been made.

The *Moniteur* of April 2nd, 1814, publishes the following:

Proclamation

Paris, 1st April, 1814.

The armies of the Allied Powers have occupied the Capital of France; the Allied Sovereigns welcome the expression of the will of the French nation.

They declare:

That if the conditions of the Peace must include strong guarantees where it is a question of restraining the ambition of Napoleon, they ought to be more favourable when France herself, by a return to a wise government, offers the assurance of tranquillity.

The Allied Sovereigns, therefore proclaim that they will no longer treat with Napoleon, or with any member of his family; that they will respect the integrity of ancient France, as it existed under her legitimate kings; they may even do more, because they always maintain the principle, that the happiness of Europe requires that France should be great and strong.

That they will recognise, and guarantee, the Constitution which France shall give to herself. They, therefore, invite the Senate to appoint a Provisional Government, to provide for the needs of the administration, and to prepare a Constitution suitable to the French people.

The intentions which I have just expressed are common to me with all the Allied Powers.

Alexander.

For His Imperial Majesty, the Secretary of State: Count Nesselrode.

This Proclamation, clear and positive without restriction or ambiguity, is official.

During the night of March 31st—April 1st, the first Conference met in the apartments of the *Tzar*. The King of Prussia, the Prince de Schwarzenberg. Count Nesselrode, General Pozzo de Borgo, Prince de Talleyrand, Baron Louis, Mgr. de Pradt, Archbishop of Malines, were present. Talleyrand, Baron Louis, and Mgr. de Pradt declared themselves openly in favour of the exclusion of the Napoleonic dynasty, and of the recall of the Bourbons. But they held that the mandataries of the nation, the Senate and the *Corps Législatif*, should meet and appoint a Provisional Government. The Prince de Talleyrand, as Vice-Grand Elector, convoked the Senate for the following day, April 1st.

The Senators appointed to be members of the Provisional Government, and empowered to draw up the Constitution, were:

The Prince de Talleyrand, President.

General Beurnonville.

The Marquis de Jaucourt.

The Duc de Dalberg.

The Abbé de Montesquiou.

Monsignor de Pradt, in his memoirs, recounts in great detail all that took place in the *Tzar's* room. According to him, the whole of the initiative for the recall of the Bourbons, was taken by the French; the Sovereigns merely gave their approval of the discussion, without influencing the decision.

On April 3rd, the Senate and *Corps Législatif* pronounced the dethronement of Napoleon in these terms:

The Senate resolves and decrees:

Article 1.—Napoleon Buonaparte has forfeited the throne, and the hereditary right established in his family is abolished.

Article 2.—The French people, and the army, are released from their oath of fidelity to Napoleon Buonaparte.

Article 3.—This Decree shall he transmitted by a special message from the Provisional Government, to be sent immediately to all the departments, and to the army, and proclaimed, at once, in all parts of the Capital.

The long preamble to this decree enumerated the grievances of the nation against Napoleon.

It was only after these Acts had received the adhesion of the *Corps Législatif* and the *Cours de Cassation des Comptes-d'Appel*, &c., that the Comte d'Artois entered Paris. The enthusiasm of the Parisians defies description. I drew a favourable augury from it . . . the sequel shows how little importance should be attached to these outbursts of popular feeling.

On the 15th, the Emperor of Austria, at length, arrived. The *Tzar* and the King of Prussia went to meet their Ally; *Monsieur* received him at the head of the National Guard. There was much cheering, a grand parade and review, and march past of the troops. This programme was repeated at the entry of each Prince or Sovereign. On the 20th, the Duc de Berry arrived from Rouen. . . . On the 23rd, the Prince Royal of Sweden came to offer his homage to the Comte d'Artois, almost in these words:

My Prince, I congratulate you most sincerely on your return to your country; it is a country difficult to govern. It needs an iron hand and a velvet glove.

Monsieur repeated these words to me himself a few days later, when describing his conversation with Bernadotte.

I have nothing further to relate until the solemn entry of the king, on May 3rd. The Constitutional Charter, which was signed in the evening of May 2nd, at the Château of Saint Ouen, where Louis XVIII passed the night, was not published until June 5th, after the departure of the foreign armies. The Emperor Alexander, without escort, and attended only by a single *aide-de-camp*, went out to Compiègne, on May 1st, to congratulate the king, and to dine with him. Thus, showing his sincere regard for the French nation, a regard which he never ceased to show us under all circumstances.

What shall we say of this entry of the king, except that it was a scene of wild, unheard-of enthusiasm? Everything seemed to promise a long duration of prosperity, assured by a complete reconciliation with all Europe.... What became of it all? How long did it last?

Splendid sunshine greeted this memorable day; the houses were garlanded with *fleurs-de-lys*. More than twenty thousand guns of the National Guards held bouquets of *fleurs-de-lys*. I was present at the solemn *Te Deum* sung in the Cathedral, but I was not able to remain till the close of the ceremony; another duty called for my presence elsewhere.

The Duchesse de Richelieu had come from Courteille, where she was living with her mother, the Comtesse de Rochechouart. She had begged me to obtain an audience for her with the *Tzar*, as she greatly desired to be presented to him. In granting me this favour, the emperor questioned me as to the lady, and her family, and the reason why the duke, her husband, had never lived with her.

I answered the questions fully. Then he said:

The only time I shall be free is next Tuesday, the day of the entry of Louis XVIII, and I should not like to deprive her, or you either, of the pleasure of seeing the procession. Arrange to bring the Duchesse de Richelieu to me here, in my study, before the king's return to the Tuileries.

In order to see the procession, the duchess had taken a window on the Quai des Orfèvres. It was arranged that I should come for her in my carriage before the end of the ceremony, and take her to the Elysée. The audience lasted three-quarters of an hour, and the Emperor Alexander then took leave of her most kindly. I drove her home, and she talked all the way of the handsome emperor, his gracious manner, his kindness and intelligence; she raved about him, at which I was not at all surprised, knowing by my own feelings, the fascination exercised by this great sovereign.

The next day, I went for orders. The emperor drew me within the embrasure of a window and said:

Now I understand the conduct of the Duc de Richelieu with regard to his wife. Oh! My dear Rochechouart, how ugly, how frightful she is! I think her very intelligent, and she has many great qualities, but, at twenty, it would have required superhuman courage to pass over such ugliness."

The poor woman was, in fact, terribly ill-favoured by nature: deformed both in back and chest, a huge nose, long arms, out of all proportion to her very short stature; she had the most solid virtues, great intelligence, and, unhappily for herself, a most loving heart.

Matters were becoming very serious for me. I needed a friend, the Duc de Richelieu, to advise me. I was alone, young, and my head a little turned by the high position I occupied. I yielded too readily to the impulse of the moment, without fully weighing the consequences. Regardless of what courtesy required, which I ought never to have forgotten, I left the service of Russia, to enter that of the king. This is how I decided, but too hastily.

A few days after the restoration of Louis XVIII, the question of a general Peace came under discussion. It would naturally be preceded by the departure of the foreign troops, and the surrender of the capital to its rightful sovereign. It was decided that the troops should leave on June 1st, and that the *Moniteur* should publish the Conditions of the Peace on June 2nd. The Emperor Alexander had fixed his departure for June 3rd; he intended to go, first, to London, and then to Russia.

I begged General Sacken to convey to His Imperial Majesty my resignation of my commission in the Russian Army. Monsieur had promised that, if my resignation were accepted, he would admit me into the French Army with the rank of major-general. Having received this promise, I ought to have said nothing about it, and to have accompanied the emperor back to Russia. I certainly owed him this mark of devotion in return for all the favours he had bestowed on me. I felt it too hard to leave my country again, now that I had found life there so pleasant. I was wanting in gratitude. General Sacken carried out my request with kindness and zeal. Two days later he said to me:

> The emperor is not pleased with you; as far as I can understand, he had thought you were more attached to him. He will, however, discharge you with the honorary rank of major-general, but he will not receive you to take leave of him. This is all that I could obtain.

I understood then, but too late, the full extent of my fault; it was now irremediable.

I will close this phase of my life with a letter from the Duc de Richelieu:

> Odessa, June 25th, 1814.
> I have received your letter, my dear friend. The first part delighted me, as I believed you were still in the service of Russia; but what you tell me further on, shows that you have made your decision, and this is confirmed by what I hear from my

wife and my sisters. I am grieved about it. Loaded and over-whelmed as you have been with favours from the emperor, you ought, at least, to have shown him the courtesy of accompanying him home, especially as you were attached to his person as *aide-de-camp*. However, it is done now. Do not let us speak any more about it.

As for me, as soon as the emperor returns to Russia, I will ask permission to go to St. Petersburg to see him, and I shall obtain leave of absence to enable me to go to Paris. I do not much wonder that he has not granted it at the request of my family, for there are many things connected with these Provinces which he must wish to discuss with me, and I should like to see him for the same reason. . . .

R.

CHAPTER 2

The Hundred Days

At the time when I quitted the service of Russia so suddenly, General Dupont was Minister of War. He had been born in the Charente, not far from Rouchechouart, and was very kind to me. He took the first opportunity to ask Louis XVIII to admit me into his service, as major-general; and informed me of His Majesty's consent in a letter dated July 22nd.

On August 29th, the Comte d'Artois received me as a Knight of Saint-Louis, and also appointed me Lieutenant to the 2nd Company of Musketeers of the Royal Guard, called the "Black Musketeers."

In November, the Duc de Richelieu wrote to me from Vienna. The *Tzar* had, at length, granted him temporary leave of absence, that he might visit France, offer his homage to the king, arrange his private affairs, and see his family from whom he had been separated so long. . . . He announced his approaching arrival, and asked me to find him rooms.

In reply, I begged him to stay with me in the Rue Royale, where I had rented a furnished flat from the Baron Louis; it was large enough for us both, as well as for the duke's *aide-de-camp*, my old comrade Stempkovski. I pressed the good duke to let me have the pleasure of giving him hospitality, as we had so many things to say to one another.

Thus, at the end of November, I had the happiness of embracing him after a separation of two eventful years.

At this time, the family of the Duc de Richelieu consisted of: (1) The Maréchale de Richelieu, the third wife of his grandfather; (2) The Dowager Duchesse de Richelieu, the second wife of his father; (3) His two sisters, Madame de Montcalm, and Madame de Jumilhac, daughters of his father's second wife; (4) His mother-in-law, the Comtesse Louis de Rochechouart; (5) His wife.

Having devoted a few days to the first part of his family, he wished to go to Courteille to see his mother-in-law and his wife, who had continued to live there even during the Revolution. The thought of this visit worried him a good deal, and he insisted on my going with him, to which I gladly agreed.

It was the middle of December when we reached this beautiful *château* near Verneuil. The warm welcome of these two intelligent women made the days pass quickly that we were able to spend with them; we were obliged to return to Paris for the official visits on New Year's Day, M. de Richelieu as First Lord of the Bedchamber, and I, to present my platoon of Black Musketeers.

Louis XVI had allowed M. de Richelieu to succeed to the office held by the *maréchal*, his grandfather. The duke could not discharge its duties while remaining in the service of Russia; on the other hand, he could not abruptly leave the service of the Emperor Alexander; he was attached to his provinces of New Russia, and especially to Odessa. He hesitated the more to come to a decision, as the course taken by the new government gave him great anxiety. He doubted its stability. A new generation had sprung up under the Revolution, differing in manners, habits and ideas from the former generation, and there was little sympathy between the two. A desire had been expressed that M. de Richelieu should enter the King's Council. He united a long experience of public affairs to a conciliatory spirit, occupying a position between the two generations, to each of which it may be said that he belonged.

He merely answered:

I am incapable of governing this country. The other members of the government would be strangers to me, as I am a stranger to them. I have only general ideas; would they be in harmony with theirs?

In talking intimately, he would say:

How, my dear friend, can you ask me to mix myself up with this squabble? What can I think of certain persons whose present words and acts are in direct contradiction to their past? For instance, what can I think of our Minister of War, Maréchal Soult. A child of the Revolution, to which he owes his whole career, instead of maintaining a dignified silence with regard to certain acts of the Revolution, he now becomes, himself, its accuser.

Thoughtful men foresaw grave events, but no one took steps to prevent them.

The news published in the *Moniteur* of March 8th created a deep impression in Paris:

Buonaparte left Porto-Ferrajo, on February 26th, at nine o'clock in the morning in very calm weather, which lasted till March 1st. He went on board a brig, which was followed by four smaller vessels, *felluccas*, etc., transporting 1,000 or 1,100 men, at most, consisting of a small number of Frenchmen, and the rest Poles, Corsicans, Neapolitans, and natives of Elba. The vessels have anchored in the Gulf of Juan, near Cannes; the troops have landed, etc., etc.

If it be asked: What was done after the news of the landing of Napoleon? I should be puzzled to answer. The only result was to bring Napoleon within twenty days from the Gulf of Juan to the gates of Paris, and to oblige the king to leave his kingdom.

On March 18th, when coming in to dinner, M. de Richelieu said to me:

All this will end badly, they have lost their heads at the Tuileries. I do not blame them, for, in truth, the march of events has been so rapid, and the defections are so numerous, that it is impossible to check them. Although neither the king nor his ministers have breathed a word to me about it, I think they will withdraw before the torrent, perhaps to Lille, and there await the decision of the Allied Sovereigns, still in congress at Vienna. I cannot honourably leave the king, though he has not taken me into his confidence. I shall remain with him to the end. Stempkovski is leaving at once, with my valet, my carriage, and belongings, and will wait for me at Frankfort. You have three horses; you will lend me one of them. I have been able to raise 10,000 *francs* in gold; if you have any money turn it into gold and make your preparations. We may have to leave in a few hours.

Having dined hurriedly, I went to the Celestins, the barracks of the "*Mousquetaires noirs.*" Our captain, the Marquis de La Grange, had received no orders; he advised us, however, not to leave our house, as the order to mount might arrive at any moment. I returned home, and put my most precious possessions in my carriage—a dressing-case containing 8,000 *francs* in gold, my entire fortune, and M. de Richelieu's portmanteau—only keeping 500 *francs* in my purse. I left my plate, table-linen and wines in Paris, in charge of my valet.

The next day was spent in the same state of anxiety; the most disquieting news kept coming in. Our musketeers, confined to barracks, with their horses saddled and bridled, were waiting for the orders that did not come. After dinner, M. de Richelieu went to the Tuileries, where he had the privilege of entry as First Lord of the Bedchamber; he returned at nine o'clock, and said:

Let us mount our horses. There is not a moment to lose; let us be off. I had half an hour's talk with the king. He did not say a word about his plans or intentions, but the Prince de Pois, Captain of the Bodyguard on duty, whispered to me: 'They are leaving in an hour; the relays are ready; we are going to Lille; come and join us there.'

Just at this moment, the Marquis de La Grange sent me the following order:

The Four Red Companies will meet at eleven o'clock at the Barrière de l'Etoile.

In his haste to mount, M. de Richelieu placed the belt containing his 10,000 *francs* upside down, so that the openings of the little pockets were downwards; the motion of the horse in trotting caused the gold pieces to shake out into his riding-breeches and boots. When he reached Beauvais next morning, he put them all back in their place, but one may imagine the discomfort and bruises resulting.

We were obliged to halt at Beauvais after our fifteen leagues' ride by night. The King's Household troops consisted of part of his bodyguard, *gendarmes*, light horse, Grey and Black Musketeers; the infantry comprised the Swiss and four cannon under the command of Casimir de Mortemart, and, finally, a few hundreds of the so-called Royal Volunteers, accompanied by Louis de La Rochejaquelein with some of his grenadiers on horseback. This little army was commanded by *Monsieur* and the Duc de Berry. They had left Paris very late, and in great haste and confusion, with no clear idea of the road they were to take; so that the number who lagged behind, or lost their way, was very great. We were therefore obliged to wait for them to know the strength of our army. It amounted to 4,000 men.

During the night of the famous March 20th, a courier from Paris arrived with the news that Napoleon had entered the Tuileries in triumph, escorted by the troops that had been sent out the evening before to fight him. At the same time, we heard of the arrival of Louis XVIII at Lille, where he was well received by Maréchal Mortier, Duc de Treviso. During the day, the order reached us to rejoin the king as soon as possible.

On March 21st, we spent the night at Poix, on the 22nd at Abbeville, on the 23rd at St. Pol, on the 24th at Béthune. A profound sense of discouragement fell upon our little army when *Monsieur* communicated to us a Royal Despatch, drawn up almost in the following terms: "The king obliged to leave Lille, being unable to rely upon the fidelity of the troops forming the garrison finds himself reluctantly compelled to retire to Belgium. He thanks all those who have remained faithful to him, and urges them to return to their homes to await better days. The king charges the general officers to disband the corps, which cannot enter a foreign country with their arms."

General Comte de Lauriston disbanded the *Maison Rouge* at Béthune. Many general officers resolved to continue their way. I naturally took this course. We proceeded to Estaire, to reach Ypres, the place assigned as a rendezvous to all Frenchmen who were willing, or able, to follow their princes, as individuals.

We spent the night of March 26th at Estaire, a little town on the Lys, surrounded with marshes and peat-bogs. Our convoy was crossing the difficult ground when a courier announced that General Exelmans, with a column of cavalry, was pursuing us, in order to scatter us, and drive us from French territory. The news caused a general panic, and, wishing to take a short cut, our convoy left the causeway, and plunged into the peat-bog. My dressing-case contained a considerable sum, and my servant wished to take it away, but the coachman, who had not been with me long, joined with some other worthless fellows, and threatened to kill him. My carriage and several others were pillaged and destroyed. Thus, I found myself in the same position as at the crossing of the Beresina, with nothing but what I was wearing, and what I had in my purse, except two saddle-horses and my cloak.

Worn out with fatigue and excitement, we reached Ypres on March 27th. We went at once to hear Mass, as it was Easter Sunday. On the way, M. de Richelieu said to me:

Come with me, my dear friend, I will make your peace with the Emperor Alexander. We will go back to Odessa, and never leave it.

After the Mass, I was returning to my rooms, feeling inclined to go with the good duke, when I met François d'Escars. He said:

The Comte d'Artois is distressed to learn that you have lost your luggage at Estaire; he thinks you could be of great service to the king, and begs you to go at once to Ghent. We are all making our way there to rejoin the king. You may need money for your journey, so *Monsieur* has charged me to give you this purse; Goodbye, till we meet at Ghent tomorrow.

The purse contained 3,000 *francs*. I related this conversation to M. de Richelieu, and added that, after this kind attention, I could not leave the king. I must stay with him to the end. M. de Richelieu replied:

Since they count on your services, your duty is clear: absolute devotion, the sacrifice of your personal interests, even of your life. God alone knows what the future has in store for us. I am writing to the *Tzar*. I shall not mention you. I leave this evening for Vienna to rejoin him. I will write to you; you will do the same to me. I understand the services expected from you. The support of the Emperor Alexander is more necessary now than ever. They know I am going to him, so I shall be your intermediary.

A few hours later, we parted with heavy hearts. The future was very dark.

On March 29th I arrived at Ghent, and went to thank the Comte d'Artois for his kindness. He ordered me to go to Alost, where the Duc de Berry, with the consent of the King of the Netherlands, had established his head-quarters. The number of officers was considerable, and might form the cadre of a little army, which the Royalists hoped to raise, but nothing had been arranged. The Duc de Berry urged me to return to Ghent.

I arrived there on April 5th, and had scarcely dismounted when I received orders to go to the Duc de Feltre, Minister of War, the only minister who had followed the king—I am not counting M. de Blacas, the minister of the King's Household, who had been the companion of Louis XVIII during the emigration. I went at once. The Duc de Feltre said, "I have recommended you to the king as my Chief of Staff. Will that suit you. General?"

"Of course," I answered: "Nothing could be better, *M. le Duc*."

"In that case, come tomorrow morning, and I will install you officially." He added:

I shall have great need of your services, for upon you will fall the whole work of the Ministry I am organising. The officers mentioned in my letter will help you. You will assign to each one the duties to be undertaken, according to his aptitudes. I have chosen you for two reasons. The first is the illustrious name you bear, and your relationship to the Duc de Richelieu and the Duc de Mortemart, which affords a double guarantee of your fidelity to the king. The second lies in your former connection with our Allies. *Monsieur* has told me of the services you rendered to him last year with the Emperor Alexander.

No sooner had I taken up my duties than I wrote to the Duc de Richelieu, as we had arranged. A few days later I received his answer, enclosed in a despatch-box sent from Vienna by the Prince de Talleyrand.

Vienna, April 14th, 1815.

You may be glad to have news of me, my dear Leo. I arrived fairly comfortably, except that I was kept under arrest for thirty-six hours by a tiresome Prussian captain, who insisted that I might be an agent of Buonaparte. He had me escorted to Aix-la-Chapelle by a *gendarme*. I found the traffic on the roads congested by troops. The emperor received me with his usual kindness. Nothing could exceed the good dispositions that I find here. Unfortunately, some time must elapse before the troops, numbering more than 250,000 reach the frontier of France.
The heads of the columns are in Bohemia, divided into five great Army Corps of 50,000 men each, under Sacken, Langeron, Doktoroff, Yermoloff, and Rajewski. The emperor reckons that more than 800,000 men will be arrayed against France. I begged him to allow me to accompany him on this campaign, and he very graciously assented. I have said nothing of you so far, but an opportunity will come; I shall seize it, as you may well believe. I do not know yet when we shall leave; it will be known later.
You would not recognise the Austrian Army. It is complete, more than complete; over 300,000 men will enter upon the campaign. Every day immense regiments, perfectly equipped, pass through the town. It is impossible—at least, unless it were

done on purpose—that the affair should not end soon, and well. Although *Monsieur* must know all this already, tell him, and offer him my homage. . . . On this 15th, I have just received your letter. We are better informed about the South than you are. *Monseigneur* le Duc d'Angoulême has gained some successes. He should, by this time, be before the gates of Lyons. Still, I am anxious about him, unless reinforcements can be sent to him soon, and this affair of Murat renders it almost impossible at present. . . .

R.

He writes again:

Vienna, May 3rd, 1815.

The war will be waged with extreme bitterness. The Allied armies appear irritated to the last degree against a nation which seems thrown in the midst of Europe to do harm. I greatly fear that, whatever care we may take, it will not be possible to exercise as great moderation as during the last campaign. All this, dear friend, and many other things, do not promise us a happy future, so we must live from day to day, and be resigned to our lot.

R.

On June 15th we were informed of the opening of hostilities between Napoleon and the Anglo-Prussian and Belgian Armies. On the 16th one of those fugitives, who always bring bad news reached Brussels; he reported that part of the Prussian Army had been defeated with severe loss, and the English Army completely routed; its baggage was retreating through the Forest of Soignies. The news soon reached us at Ghent. I hastened to the Duc de Feltre for orders, and he took me to the king, whom he found surrounded by people urging him to fly. Louis XVIII, calm and resigned, answered:

Gentlemen, I have received no official intimation. If the misfortune were as great as you say, I should have been told. I shall not move from here unless compelled by circumstances. Let those who are afraid leave.

That evening a great many did leave; the more timorous went to Nimewegen with their own horses, for I had transmitted an order from the Minister of War that no post-horses should be allowed to go out.

On the 17th better news restored calm to our little court. It was said that the French had gained a slight success, but of no importance. Finally, on the 19th, we learned the result of the Battle of Waterloo. As I was not present, I will not speak of the battle, and I am thankful that I did not witness this terrible disaster for the French army, though it was to put an end to our exile.

The king hastily made preparations for returning to France, and I spent twenty-four hours in dictating the order of the march of our little army, tracing the route, sending word beforehand to the local authorities, and arranging for supplies and billets.

The king, the Comte d'Artois, and the ministers left Ghent on June 22nd; our little army left Alost on the same day. Louis XVIII spent one night at Mons, and entered France on June 24th; the staff of the Minister of War, under my command, formed the escort.

At Mons, while the Duc de Feltre was dictating some orders to me, the Comte de Blacas came into the room in great grief; he had just left the king, and hastened to inform his former colleague of the step he had taken. Rightly or wrongly, the Comte de Blacas had been blamed for all the faults of the government after the First Restoration. The accusation was generally credited in France, and even in foreign countries, and it had not been altogether rejected at court, so ready are people to throw the responsibility for all misfortunes on a single individual.

On the eve of the return to France, M. de Blacas, who felt deeply this injustice, had not hesitated to go to the king and say that, desiring before all things the happiness of his master and his country, and fearing that his presence would be injurious to his august person, although he did not form part of His Majesty's Council, he would withdraw to a foreign country, and wait until public opinion should do him justice. Sacrificing his own happiness that he might not give a pretext to the disaffected, he submitted to the unjust accusation without a murmur, only too glad to be able thus to prove his devotion to the king. Ready as he was to sacrifice his life, he did not hesitate to sacrifice his good name. He had left without giving Louis XVIII time to reply. He went away from us in tears.

I did not lose a word of this interview, and when M. de Blacas had gone the minister and I looked at one another in silence, full of admiration of this noble act. I am glad to make it known, for such disinterested conduct is rare in these days.

A few moments later the conversation turned on the formation of the new Ministry. Strange rumours were afloat; it was said that Fouché, Duc d'Otrante, would enter the Cabinet. The Prince de Talleyrand, head of an unscrupulous school of politicians, had proposed this step to the king, who would thus avail himself of the services of a man, perfidiously clever, it is true, but whose past should have excluded him from the King's Council and the Bourbon family. . . . The Duc de Feltre admitted to me that he felt a great distrust of Talleyrand, and had not attempted to disguise it.

This feeling had been inspired by Napoleon, who said to him one day:

> Clarke, I forbid you to associate with the Prince de Talleyrand, for he is nothing but He will sully you.

After repeating these more than forcible words with regard to the too famous diplomatist, the Duc de Feltre spoke of Fouché:

> I could never endure that man. Napoleon only made use of him reluctantly, and got rid of him on the first opportunity. In justice to Napoleon, it must be said that all those whom he dismissed from his service or from the army deserved it. . . .

I urged the minister to take the first opportunity to enlighten the king as to the character of those whom he proposed to employ and the effect of such a choice upon honourable men. But the Duc de Feltre, perfectly honourable himself, a hard worker, solely occupied with his duties, and a very good administrator, hated talking. He owned to me that he durst not speak to Louis XVIII about such things. Just at this moment we saw the king's carriage pass, on its way to the frontier; it took the road to Cateau Cambresis, avoiding Valenciennes, and the other fortresses invested, or besieged, by the Allies.

There was nothing to be done now. Talleyrand was with the king, and the intrigue had been so skilfully managed that the Duc de Feltre could do no more than follow in silence.

The *Tzar*, and even the Austrian Cabinet, were well disposed towards Louis XVIII. The Prussian generals and the Duke of Wellington, on the contrary, lost no opportunity of doing us an ill turn. Prussia, crushed at Jena, had been subjected to endless humiliations. Napoleon had driven away Queen Louise, who was respected and beloved by her subjects. Having now an opportunity of revenge, the generals seized it, with little moderation, and certainly little generosity. . . . If these powers had got possession of our fortresses, they would have carried away, or destroyed, all our war material. To avoid this humiliation and loss, the Duc de Feltre sent to all the commandants the order to hoist the Royal Standard and submit to the king, with whom the Allies were not at war. In this way General Bourmont, at Lille, and General Reille, at Valenciennes, saved all the war material in their forts. We spent the night of July 1st at Saint Denis. Just as I was going to bed the Duc de Feltre sent for me.

I want first to thank you, my dear Rochechouart, for your help during the time we have been together, and for your kindness to me, and then to tell you that the king has accepted my resignation. I am retiring because I cannot remain in the Ministry with colleagues of whose policy I disapprove. I have the satisfaction of knowing that I have done my duty. I entered the Ministry at a time of danger, at a crisis of which it was difficult to foresee the end. I leave it now the king is in safety. Besides, in tendering my resignation, I am only anticipating the wishes of M. de Talleyrand, the new President of the Council; we should never have got on together. I know the Maréchal Gouvion St.-Cyr is to take my place. I am sorry he is not here, or I would have spoken to him of you; but here is a letter which you will give him with this portfolio. I am assured beforehand of the good reception you will meet with tomorrow in Paris. *Adieu*, my dear friend! Embrace me, and God bless you.

Then he took me in his arms, and we both had tears in our eyes. A carriage was waiting for him; he got in quickly and disappeared.

On Saturday, July 8th, the king made his entry into Paris. The Comte d'Artois had arranged the procession. First, and in command. General Maison, the newly-appointed Governor of the First Military Division, with his staff; next the staff of the Ministry of War under my command; then the Marshals of France, and the generals who had accompanied the king to Ghent, or who had joined him since the abdication of Napoleon; lastly, our little army from Alost.

As the king passed to the Tuileries he was received with deafening acclamations, louder and more enthusiastic than at his first entry; at least equal, I am told, to the cheers that had greeted Napoleon three months before.

CHAPTER 3

The Richelieu Ministry

I followed the king to his apartments; there I found the Maréchal Gouvion St.-Cyr, to whom I delivered the portfolio of the Minister of War and the letter from the Duc de Feltre. The *maréchal* begged me to come early to breakfast with him on the following day, so that we might talk more freely. I complied punctually with the order and invitation. The *maréchal* received me most kindly, and frankly told me that I could be very useful to him, not only by informing him of what had taken place at Ghent, but by making him conversant with the persons surrounding the king and princes, seeing that he was a stranger to court life, he added:

> So, I ask you, to retain the position you held under the Duc de Feltre. I also count on your help during the delicate negotiations we shall have to conduct with the Allies, negotiations requiring great prudence and firmness; lastly, your presence here will be most valuable on account of your relationship with the Duc de Richelieu, who will shortly be called upon to play an important part. I beg you to come every day at the same hour; it is the best time to talk.

The *maréchal* suggested that next day I should present to him the officers on the staff of his predecessor. I replied:

> The reception will not take long, for they have all returned to their regiments, with the exception of the Marquis de Montpezat, lieutenant-colonel of the staff, an able and well-instructed officer. I should be grateful to you, *M. le Maréchal*, if you would leave him as my coadjutor.

"Granted," replied the minister.

On July 10th I was astonished to read in the *Moniteur* the list of the new ministers: the Prince de Talleyrand, President of the Council and Minister of Foreign Affairs; Baron Louis, Minister of Finance; Fouché, Duc d'Otrante, Minister of the Interior and of Police; Baron Pasquier, Minister of Justice and Keeper of the Seals; the Maréchal Gouvion St.-Cyr, Minister of War; the Comte de Jaucourt, Minister of Marine; the Duc de Richelieu, Minister of the King's Household.

During breakfast, I could not help expressing my surprise to the *maréchal*. I showed him M. de Richelieu's last letter, and added:

> I am convinced he will refuse. He is still in the service of Russia and attached to the Emperor Alexander. How could they assign him a post without consulting him, or even telling him beforehand! If I had been told before the notice appeared in the *Moniteur*, I would have informed you of M. de Richelieu's intentions, and thus spared the king a painful refusal, the Council the appearance of acting without consideration, and M. de Richelieu real distress, for he will find himself in a very false position with regard to the Emperor Alexander, and wanting in the respect due to him.

★★★★★★

Note:—In this last letter, dated Manheim, June 25th, 1815, M. de Richelieu says:

"I hope, my dear Friend, to see you soon again somewhere, but it will not be for long, and no human power can make me live with the people, whom I have unhappily learned to know so well."

★★★★★★

I did not venture to add that M. de Richelieu would never consent to be the colleague of Fouché.

The minister answered:

> This is incredible. Nothing was said at the Council with regard to the exceptional position of M. de Richelieu. I cannot imagine how they could act so carelessly. I will speak of it at the Council this evening. I am much obliged to you for the information you have given me. . . .

I hastened to M. de Richelieu on the day of his arrival, July 13th. He had not cooled down since he received the news of his appointment as Minister of the King's Household. He had at once gone to the *Tzar* to tell him of his absolute refusal, but the emperor replied:

I understand your refusal, my dear duke, and I am touched by your devotion to me. I should like to keep you in the service of Russia, and shall part with you with the deepest regret. Still, sympathising as I do with the King of France, I know that under the difficult circumstances in which he is placed, and those that I foresee are coming upon him, a man like you would be useful, perhaps even indispensable, to the maintenance of harmony between our two governments. We will speak about it again at Paris.

Having learned from the Minister of War the reasons of M. de Richelieu's refusal, the king accepted it; but he persisted in his desire that M. de Richelieu should form part of his Council, if not immediately, at least at no distant time.

The first act of the new Ministry was a report issued by the Minister of Police, and published in the *Moniteur* of July 26th, 1815, proposing two measures of extreme severity.

(1) Eighteen persons to be arrested and tried by court martial, Ney, Labedoyère, etc., etc.

(2) Thirty-eight persons to be expelled, some from France, others only from Paris. . . .

★★★★★★

Art. 12 of the Convention (July 3rd), between the Provisional Government and the Commissaries of the Anglo-Prussian Armies (Wellington and Blücher), provided that persons, houses and private property should be respected, etc. A remonstrance was addressed to the foreign generals with regard to the violation of this article; they replied that they had faithfully observed the Convention; no one had been disturbed or arrested in their names. The King of France had returned with full powers, and the remonstrance should be addressed to Talleyrand.

★★★★★★

The Minister of War related to me that Carnot, who was on the Duc d'Otrante's list of those to be banished, and who had been, together with Fouché, a member of the Provisional Government a fortnight before, was indignant at this act of his late colleague, and wrote to him:

To what place would you have me retire, Traitor?

Fouché replied at the foot of the same letter:

Wherever you like, Idiot.

This laconic correspondence in the Republican style gives a better picture of these men than ten pages of history.

Field-Marshal Blücher had determined to blow up the Bridge of Jena, although out of consideration for the feelings of the Prussians the name had been changed to the Bridge des Invalides. In spite of the protests of the Allied generals, in spite of the energetic opposition of Louis XVIII and his ministers, the day was fixed. There was danger of trouble, and perhaps of an armed rising on the part of the Parisians.

The Minister of War begged me to appeal to the King of Prussia. I went at once to the house where he was staying, in the Rue de Bourbon. As I knew all his *aides-de-camp*, I obtained an audience immediately. In a few words, I explained why I had taken the liberty of approaching him, and begged him to prevent one of his Generals from an act which could not do away with the fact that the battle of Jena had taken place. To my great surprise, the king replied:

> General, I had already been informed of Prince Blücher's intention, and I sent him word that I disapproved of it, and begged him to give up his project. I am sorry to find his answer is not in conformity with my wishes, and that he persists in his resolve 'for the honour of the Prussian Army,' as he says. I will send an *aide-de-camp* to him again, and urge him to be content with the change of name of this wretched bridge.

I saluted the king; but seeing that his answer was evasive, I hastened to the Duc de Richelieu to tell him what was going on. He went at once to the Emperor Alexander, who, indignant at such an act of vandalism, went to the King of Prussia. M. de Richelieu described the interview. Alexander declared that if Field-Marshal Blücher did not obey the order that he begged the king to send to him, he would go in person, and take up his position on the bridge, and would see if Blücher had the audacity to blow it up while he was there. He had not taken offence at the name of the Bridge of Austerlitz, and had not even asked that it should be changed.

The old *maréchal* was obliged to yield before these resolute words.

★★★★★★

According to Lord Stanhope, Blücher made one attempt and failed. The Duke of Wellington then wrote to him and posted an English sentry on the bridge and thus prevented its destruction. See Lord Stanhope's conversation with the duke.

★★★★★★

The Bridge of Jena was saved, and temporarily renamed, and, without waiting for the *Tzar* to express any wish in the matter, the Bridge of Austerlitz received the name of the Bridge of the *"Jardin des Plantes."*

. . . The Council of Ministers thought well at this time to grant decorations to the general officers of the military households of the Allied Sovereigns. If these decorations had been conferred under any other Ministry, the Allied Sovereigns would have welcomed them, and in return would have bestowed an equal number of cordons and crosses; but a heavy cloud had arisen between the *Tzar* and the Prince de Talleyrand. I did not know of it in time, or I should have told the *maréchal*, who would thus have been able to avoid an unpleasant check to the king. The Emperor Alexander did not refuse the decorations, but he did not give permission for them to be worn. The Prince Regent took the same course with regard to the British officers.

This is what had happened. The *Tzar* had just discovered that, during the Congress at Vienna, the Prince de Talleyrand had proposed to Metternich the project of a secret treaty of alliance offensive and defensive between France and Austria. The English Government was aware of the proposed treaty, the object of which was to counterbalance the influence of Russia in the affairs of Europe, an influence acquired by the part Russia had taken in freeing France from the yoke of Napoleon. Talleyrand had opened the negotiations unknown to Louis XVIII, hoping to obtain his consent if he should succeed in carrying them through. The events of March 20th put an end to the project; the secret became known to the *Tzar*, who did not conceal his displeasure at finding this same diplomatist directing the policy of France as President of the Council.

The claims of the Allies became daily more intolerable. Spain even took part, and threatened to exact heavy indemnities by armed force. The Duc d'Angoulême was sent to our southern frontiers to bring this grandson of Louis XIV to reason. Confusion reigned in our home affairs, the unrest was extreme.

The support of the Emperor of Russia became indispensable to the government in order to resist these claims. But how could this support be obtained after Talleyrand's attempt to repel the Russian alliance? The prince himself felt powerless to parry the blows that threatened to fall upon us simultaneously from all sides. The preliminaries of the Treaty of Paris revealed the most sinister intentions on the part of the foreign powers, a new map of France, from which certain provinces should disappear. We had not a friend to plead our cause. Our armies were destroyed, our treasury was empty, the nation was divided into three factions, the Ministry itself was not united.

The king, alarmed and convinced of the necessity of a government led by a man of unblemished reputation, turned to the Duc de Richelieu. He alone could bring the Emperor Alexander to undertake our defence. But M. de Richelieu continued to reject all overtures, openly declaring that he was incapable of guiding the affairs of France. Among his intimate friends he spoke, above all, of the want of accord between the Court of Louis XVIII and the friends of his brother, the Comte d'Artois. Negotiations with the Duc de Richelieu were carried on for three days. I was asked to add my voice to the entreaties that came in from every side; thus, I was present at all the conferences that were held at his house with this object.

On the eve of the day when he finally yielded, the Vicomte Mathieu de Montmorency literally threw himself on his knees before him with clasped hands; he begged him to make the sacrifice of his inclinations, his convictions, even his repose, to save his king and country, he said:

> Suppose you were on the battlefield, and that you saw it was imperative to charge, would you hesitate to put yourself at the head of your troops, even at the hazard of your life? This presents less danger, but the victory will be decisive for our country, without costing the life of anyone.

The duke, shaken in his resolution, still refused to make any promise; then a message came that the Emperor Alexander had asked to see him, and was waiting in his carriage. The duke hastened down, and the emperor made him take his place by his side, and gave orders to drive back to the Elysée.

The *Tzar* insisted, in fact, that the duke should become President of the Council; only on this condition would Alexander be again the friend of his king and country; he would do his utmost to save them both, to lighten the demands of the Allies, and restore France to the position she ought to hold in Europe. He concluded:

> Intriguers of the worst type have nearly brought about a quarrel between the king and me, by most unjustifiable means, hurtful to the true interests of France; I can place no confidence in them; in you alone have I sufficient confidence to enable me to forget this act of ingratitude. I release you from all your

engagements to me, on the sole condition that you will serve your king as you have served me. Be the bond of sincere alliance between the two countries. I ask it in the name of the safety of France."

After such words, the Duc de Richelieu could hesitate no longer. He returned to the king, and placed himself at his disposal. On September 26th, 1815, the *Moniteur* announced the formation of the new Ministry:

The Duc de Richelieu, Minister of Foreign Affairs, and President of the Council.
The Comte de Corvetto, Minister of Finance.
The Duc de Feltre, Minister of War.
Vicomte de Bouchage, Minister of Marine.
M. de Barbé-Marbois, Minister of Justice, and Keeper of the Seals.
M. Decazes, Minister of Police.

M. Barbé-Marbois refused at first on account of his age, but M. de Richelieu, who attached great importance to having him for colleague, on account of his reputation for strict integrity, pressed him to accept office so much, that he complied, saying that the insistence of the Duc de Richelieu did him such honour that he would gladly agree, and would work with him for the happiness of his country, for its tranquillity, and that of the king.

When the Prince de Talleyrand learned who it was that would succeed him at the helm of affairs, he exclaimed, with his caustic wit:

"Ah! The Duc de Richelieu—a good choice; he is the man in France who knows most about the Crimea."

To learn the true feelings of the Duc de Richelieu, we must turn to his letters to the Abbé Nicolle.

Paris, September 21st, 1815.
The lot is cast, *M. l'Abbé*, I have yielded to the king's command, the emperor's entreaties, and the voice of the people, calling upon me— I know not why—to take office at a most terrible time; it is this that has led me to accept. It would have been cowardice to forsake the unhappy king in the dreadful position in which he is placed. The emperor has been most kind. He has given me permission to keep my pension of 1,600 *ducats*, and devote it to the College of Odessa. I do not advise you to

return to France; we are on a volcano. *Adieu, M. l'Abbé*, pray to God for me. I have never been in greater need of His help. Poor France! Poor Odessa! Poor Crimea! Providence places man on the top of a high mountain, and pushes him, so that he rolls to the bottom without the power to stop; may I not fall down the precipice, and bring the Commonwealth down with me! I greet you affectionately.

R.

I anticipate by giving other letters from M. de Richelieu, as it is impossible to give a better description of the state of France.

Paris, January, 1816.

No, do not come here yet. With your gentle and conciliatory disposition, what would become of you in the midst of a people that is never calm for a moment, and carries everything to extremes. You would soon be as weary as I am. The life I lead is every day more and more intolerable; it clashes with all my tastes and habits, so that my whole being is on the rack. Party spirit is rife to such a degree that I can neither make myself heard, nor understand the language that is spoken to me, and, perhaps, I do more harm by not throwing myself into a party, and dragging the opposition to the scaffold, as I am urged to do every day. But as it would be impossible for me to follow the course advocated, I am losing ground every day; and it cannot be otherwise. Unhappy country where there is no choice between fanaticism and crime, and where the voice of reason is the only voice to which no one will listen!

I have begun this page ten times, but I must finish it. To resume, I would dissuade you from returning to France until I advise you to come. Although, in appearance, we are enjoying complete tranquillity, we are living on a volcano, and not to mention anything else, the death of the king would be the signal for a terrible revolution. Well, would you believe it, a certain party, strongly supported at court, is speculating on this event, and, I say it under my breath, regrets the delay. In their madness, they imagine that they would be able to re-establish everything that the Revolution has destroyed, and they do not see that the immediate result would be terrible bloodshed in France, followed by the abandonment of the country to the foreigner.

You cannot imagine the state of society today, an arena in

which people are ready to fly at each other's throats for slight differences of opinion. The unfortunate king is well aware of his position; he sees himself isolated in the midst of his family, attacked by his relations, attacked by his ministers, everywhere seeking rest, and not finding it; this state of affairs undermines his health. Often, the blood flies to his head, and considering the state of his legs, and that he is so stout, it is impossible not to shudder at the thought of the future! In the midst of all this, I will not speak of myself; I try to follow my line of combined firmness and moderation, but how difficult it is to keep to it! It is a struggle that calls for all my strength every hour of the day. Imagine my weariness! One must employ all one's strength and ability to maintain the government in office, and there is neither time, nor possibility, of doing anything useful. So, there is no compensation for all the trouble and anxiety that must be endured; it is especially hard for me, as I have no one here to whom I can open my heart. See then, if there is not some merit in my asking you not to come; but one must first love one's friends for their own sakes; it is a duty I am fulfilling, but with regret.

.... Last week, I was thinking of throwing everything up; but, unless I am absolutely obliged to do so, I feel bound in conscience to remain, as long as the king supports me, and they do not force my hand, by insisting on my leaving the path I have felt it my duty to take. Heartiest greetings.

R.

Paris, January 23rd, 1816.
My letters will have enabled you to grasp my situation, which does not become any easier. Struggling against the follies of some, the criminal enterprises of others, and worries of a hundred and fifty thousand foreigners under whose guardianship we are placed; meeting at every step with obstacles on the part of those on whose support we had a right to rely, I do not think a man has ever been in a more painful position.... Yet in spite of all the efforts to disturb the country, whether by the criminal plots of the revolutionaries, or the extreme projects of the ultra-Royalists, who would re-establish everything in a day, France is tranquil, even beyond our hopes.
I am convinced that, if the princes would come into line with

the king, or if the king had the courage to insist on their doing so, matters would go on fairly well. But we are far from that state of things, and with the differences at present existing, I do not see how we can answer for anything. Under these circumstances, it would be madness to ask you to come back; it would be a martyrdom for you here, for I defy anyone who has lived for some years away from this irritation, to become accustomed to it. *Adieu*, etc.

R.

Paris, November, 1816.

Old Europe seems exhausted, physically and morally; even the soil refuses to bear, and the sun to ripen the harvest. The vintage has failed throughout almost the whole of France; the barley harvest is poor, hence, prices are extremely high, it almost amounts to a famine. I doubt if there exists, at the present time, a more unhappy nation than the French; humiliated, crushed with taxes, without commerce or industry, and bread at six or seven sous the pound. They suffer in silence, and thus merit respect by their resignation. No one shows any energy here, except in hatred.

Society is intolerable, and passions as violent as in 1792. Those who think a Revolution that has lasted for twenty-seven years can be undone by two or three decrees, are furious that we do not lend ourselves to such an easy task. They called me to power, thinking to make me the tool of their extravagant ideas, and finding that I do not fall in with them, but on the contrary, seek to save them, in spite of themselves, by following a wise and moderate policy, are enraged against me, and say as much evil of me now, as, before, they said good; and, probably, in either case, more than I deserve. Truly this is a little thing, but when the estrangement comes from the class among whom you are destined to live, and when their errors may have such grave consequences, it is impossible not to deplore them.

The spectacle of France exposed to pillage is far from cheering. It is only the Russians whose conduct is admirable, as that of the emperor is a model of chivalry, honour, and wise policy. But the other armies exercise cruelly the right of reprisal, the English, however, excepted; the Prussians, Austrians, and Bavarians vie with each other in using, and abusing, the fruits of victory.

France is literally expiring under the weight of Europe that is crushing her. The march of an army corps through a province exhausts the country to such an extent that those who follow can hardly procure subsistence. Most people in the country places are living from hand to mouth, with nothing laid by.

I have just seen a Prussian Corps pass through Corteille, on the way to Brittany. Although I did everything humanly possible to prevent some of the evils, and the general was an old friend of mine, and a very kind man, I shudder at such a calamity in a country so poor, and with men as exacting and wanting in discipline as the Prussians. Up to the present time, there is no sign of an end to this state of things, which (as indeed might be expected) is quite unlike the position last year. The emperor would be glad that it should be ended quickly and well, and that the hatred which has too long divided the nations of Europe should be quenched by a reasonable peace. God grant that he may succeed in his noble design. Believe me in my most sincere attachment.

R.

CHAPTER 4

The Comte de Rochechouart Again Commandant of Paris

I resumed the direction of the Duc de Richelieu's household as at Odessa, and in accordance with his wishes, and the finances of the country, I began at once to place it on an honourable but simple footing, without luxury.

The return of the Duc de Feltre to the War Ministry confirmed me in my duties of Chief of Staff. . . . About three weeks later, he reorganised the military commands on a more economical basis. He recommended me for the post of *Commandant* of the Department of the Seine, and the fortified town of Paris. The king and all his ministers agreed with the exception of the Duc de Richelieu. Through excess of delicacy, he was unwilling that, while he was President of the Council, one of his relations should receive such an important command, the highest that could be given to a major-general. The Duc de Feltre insisted that my relationship was no reason why I should be debarred from an appointment that I had already held to the general satisfaction. The Duc de Richelieu yielded to these representations.

In accordance with orders, I went to my new quarters in the Place Vendôme as quickly as possible, and began my duties on the following day, October 19tli. I still dined every day with the Duc de Richelieu, taking the place that would have been occupied by the mistress of the house; but wishing to do credit to my position, I gave a grand luncheon every day to the staff, the officers on duty, and some foreign officers whom I knew well, not to speak of my friends and relations.

I have already referred to the secret desire of the Prussians to get possession of the contents of our arsenals and other fortified places. The arsenal of Vincennes contained a considerable amount of war material. . . . The difficulty was to obtain entrance to the fort, the gates, fortunately, being guarded by the brave General Daumesnil, Governor of the Castle of Vincennes.

Baron von Müffling, Commander-in-Chief of the Prussian Corps occupying Paris and the environs, tried his utmost by persuasion and diplomacy to obtain access to the castle. At the first summons, General Daumesnil raised the Royal Standard with *fleurs-de-lys*, and replied that, unless he had a written order from the king, he would not allow anyone to enter the fort, being firmly resolved to defend it, and if necessary, to blow it up, rather than surrender. Being under Prussian surveillance, and unable to communicate with the outside world, he took advantage of the removal of a woman to the hospital, to conceal in her garter a note to the Duc de Feltre, asking for reinforcements, and for the visit of a superior officer, to whom he wished to make a communication.

The Duc de Feltre entrusted me with his verbal reply, and asked me what disguise I proposed to assume in order to reach General Daumesnil. I replied, "None; I will go on horseback in full uniform, with my *aide-de-camp*, and an escort."

I notified General von Müffling, who was personally known to me, of my intention of inspecting a fort placed under my command. He had the courtesy to take this quite naturally, and remarked, half in jest, half in earnest, "This General Daumesnil of yours seems a rough sort of man. I do not think he cares much about the Bourbons, for he does not like their allies."

Baron von Müffling readily gave a pass for the Prussian outposts, for me, my *aide-de-camp,* the Comte de Tamnay, and two orderlies. I made use of it early the following morning.

It is impossible to describe the surprise and delight of General Daumesnil when he saw me before the drawbridge of the castle; the chains were quickly lowered, and raised again as soon as I had crossed the moat. When I reached his room, I told him that the Minister of War, feeling acutely the difficulty of his position, had charged me to say how greatly the king appreciated his firm and courageous conduct, and to assure him of His Majesty's satisfaction; to inquire further, how it would be possible to send him the reinforcements he asked for; and finally, to receive his communication with regard to the project that he had not dared to mention to anyone. The following dialogue took place:

The General: "I should need more men. My garrison consists only of fifty veterans, thirty-six dismounted cavalry, and fifteen engineers, besides a score of officers."

Rochechouart: "The Prussians will never allow reinforcements to enter."

The General: "I am certain of it; but now that I am assured of the support and approval of the king, I will struggle on, fully resolved to carry out the project which I communicated to the Prussian colonel yesterday, in reply to his demand that I should deliver up to him the castle and arsenal."

Rochechouart: "Can you tell me what the project is?"

The General: "I brought the colonel into the very room where we are; it is my bedroom; you notice the furniture (it was a 24-pounder cannon, on its carriage; the large window of the room, formerly occupied by Anne of Austria, served as its embrasure; on one side was a pile of cannon balls, on the other, cartouches of grapeshot), then I told him that without a written order from the king, I would not surrender the fort, the defence of which had been entrusted to me. I would repel every attack, and, finally, if resistance were no longer possible, I would make use of my last resource. Then I showed him the little trapdoor, beneath your feet, and lifting it up, I warned him that it was connected by means of a tin pipe, which had been laid some days before, with the main powder-magazine below us. I would throw a lighted fire-brand down it, and it would blow us all up."

Rochechouart: "What was the effect of the threat?"

The General: "The tone in which I spoke showed him that I had quite made up my mind to carry it out. The colonel went away, saying that I was taking a great responsibility on myself. I said: 'I am not concerned about that. What responsibility can a dead man incur? But I shall die gloriously, giving my country the last proof of devotion within my power, for I shall die with all that is dearest to me in the world.'"

Rochechouart: "It is a sublime act of self-sacrifice, my dear General. But to what did you refer in your last sentence?"

Without answering, the general rang the bell, and said to the orderly: "Ask my wife to come here with her child."

Two minutes later a beautiful young woman came in, holding in her arms a fine boy, three or four years old. Continuing, or rather completing his train of thought, the general said:

I could have sent my young companion away to Paris, with our only child, but I know her well enough to be certain that she shares my feelings, and my love for France. At the moment when I am blown up, she will be at my side, holding her son as she is holding him now, and one grave will cover all three of us.

Tears came to my eyes as I listened to these simple and touching words, spoken without bravado, and in a tone of great earnestness. I grasped his hand warmly, as also that of his young wife, and told them I sincerely hoped they would not be driven to that extremity. I took leave of this brave man with deep respect for his noble conduct, and assured him I would faithfully report to the Minister of War. . . .

I conclude this year, 1815, with the narrative of a great and terrible event—the trial, sentence, and condemnation of Maréchal Ney. It was my duty, as *commandant* of the fortress of Paris, to superintend the carrying out of the sentence. Many versions of the last moments and tragic end of Maréchal Ney have appeared; all are different, or incorrect, for not one of these authors was present, and, moreover, they have all deemed it necessary to add, or suppress, certain details, at the expense of the truth, in the interest of the political party to which they belonged.

I have spoken of the report presented by Fouché, Minister of Police, on July 26th, 1815, asking the king to order the trial by court-martial of eighteen persons, who had played an active part during the Hundred Days. . . . In accordance with this report, Maréchal Ney was brought before a court-martial, presided over by Maréchal Moncey; the latter, however, excused himself on the ground that he and Maréchal Ney had formerly been on bad terms, and, therefore, as a man of honour, he ought to decline to be his judge. (The Council of Ministers, on the recommendation of Fouché, condemned the Maréchal Moncey to six months' imprisonment in a fortress, with the loss of his pay and suspension of his rank.)

By order of the king a new court-martial was constituted, composed of the Marshals Jourdan (President), Massena, Augereau, Mortier, Lieutenants-Generals the Comte de Gazan, the Comte Clarparède and the Comte Villate, the Chief Commissary Baron Joinville, Commissary of the King, Major-General the Comte Grundler, Judge-Advocate, and M. Boudin, Clerk (of the Court). The court-martial was held on November 9th, and declared itself incompetent. Ney's advocates, MM. Dupin *ainé* and Berryer *père*, had pleaded that the title of *maréchal* was not a rank, but a dignity, and that the Chamber of Peers alone had the power to try one bearing the title. This legal opinion cost the life of Ney. The four Marshals of France, and two of the generals who formed the court martial, had all more or less taken part against the king, and were, therefore, little less guilty than Ney. General Clarparède said to me:

I can affirm that the majority of the court is in favour of acquittal, the *maréchal's* advocates are mad or foolish to raise the question of incompetence that had not occurred to anyone.

In the result, five out of the seven judges hastened to declare themselves incompetent, glad to escape the snare that had been laid for them, nominally by the king, but really by the infernal cleverness of Fouché, joined to the astuteness of Talleyrand. . . . The Chamber of Peers delivered the sentence on December 6th (1815). . . . On December 7th, an *aide-de-camp* of General Despinois, who commanded the First Military Division, and was my immediate superior, awakened me at three o'clock in the morning, and delivered to me a sealed letter. (The Comte de Rochechouart gives this letter in full in the French edition.)

I mounted my horse, and, attended by my *aide-de-camp*, I went to the Palais du Luxembourg; in accordance with General Despinois's instructions I went first to M. de Semonville, (*Grand Référendaire de la Chambre des Pairs.*) who told me he was awaiting me with great impatience, being in haste to rid himself of responsibility for his prisoner. He delivered up the prisoner at once, conducting me to the room occupied by the *maréchal*; two cavalry grenadiers of the Royal Guard were with him. The delivery took place without the *maréchal* taking any notice; he remained in conversation with M. de Canchy, the Secretary Archivist of the Chamber of Peers. . . . I then took up my quarters in a large room on the ground floor, in order to be at hand to receive and carry out any fresh instructions.

A few moments later General Despinois sent me word that the king had allowed the *maréchal* to receive three persons only—his wife, his lawyer, and his confessor. I went up to the prisoner's room and Colonel de Montigny, having read the Royal Authorisation in my presence, the *maréchal* said to me:

I will first see my lawyer; he is probably in the Palais waiting for permission to see me; then I will see my wife and children; as for my confessor, let them leave me alone, I do not want any priests.

★★★★★★

Note:—Colonel de Montigny, the Adjutant of the Palais, who was left in the post he had occupied before the arrival of the Comte de Rochechouart, according to General Despinois' instructions.

★★★★★★

At these last words one of the old grenadiers rose and said: "You are wrong, *maréchal*," and showing him the stripes on his uniform, he went on: "I am not as distinguished as you, but I am as old. Well then! I never went so bravely under fire as when I had first commended my soul to God."

These few words, spoken with much feeling and solemnity by this colossus, seemed to make a strong impression on the *maréchal*. He went up to the grenadier, and, laying his hand on his shoulder, said gently:

"Perhaps you are right, my brave man; it is good advice you are giving me."

Then, turning to Colonel de Montigny: "What priest can I send for?"

"The Abbé de Pierre, Curé de Saint-Sulpice, he is a distinguished priest in every way."

"Ask him to come, I will see him after I have seen my wife."

The advice of the old soldier had prevailed.

The notary was brought in, with the usual precautions; he did not remain long, having probably received his instructions beforehand. The Maréchale Ney then came in, with her three children; the Comte de Tamnay, my *aide-de-camp*, carried the youngest in his arms, up the stairs to the prisoner's room, which was at the top of the Palais. The poor child did not understand what was going on, and wondering at the sight of so many soldiers, began to play with Tamnay's moustache.

The distressing interview lasted about an hour; the *maréchal* being unable any longer to struggle against his emotion, put an end to it himself. He could only prevail upon his wife to leave him by promising to see her in the morning, which he well knew would be impossible. They parted with many tears. Soon afterwards the *Curé* of Saint-Sulpice was brought in, and remained with the *maréchal* a full hour, during which time I ordered the two grenadiers to remain outside the room; the good priest promised to return at the fatal hour.

During this time I received in succession (three further orders—these letters are given in full in the French edition—Tr.) . . . These clear and precise orders provided for everything. I, therefore, followed them exactly. I did not know the place appointed for the execution, but supposed it to be in the Plaine de Grenelle, the usual scene of military executions; I was about to send an officer to reconnoitre the ground, when, only half an hour before the sentence was carried out, I received a verbal order to make the arrangements between the Observatory and the gate of the garden of the Luxembourg, facing a wall, which is still standing, at the left as you go out of the garden. The police had learned that there would be an attempt at a rescue near Grenelle.

I was much perplexed as to the choice of an adjutant to carry out the sentence. . . . . I finally selected the Comte de Saint-Bias, an excellent officer, a Piedmontese by birth. ("His mother was Maid of Honour to the late Queen of Sardinia,"—Letter of de Rochechouart to General Despincis.) I was delighted to spare a Frenchman this painful duty.

A new message from General Despinois—I received them every quarter of an hour—informed me that the execution should be at nine o'clock in the morning, early enough to prevent there being too many spectators, but late enough to ensure a certain number.

After the Abbé de Pierre had left, the *maréchal* threw himself, fully dressed, upon his bed and slept quietly till a quarter past eight. Five minutes later the *curé* returned. I begged him to tell the prisoner that his last hour had come. The good priest, though prepared for his sad duty, was seized with a nervous trembling, which lasted till the execution was over.

As soon as he appeared on the threshold, Maréchal Ney said: "Ah! *M. le Curé*, I understand. I am ready." He knelt down and received absolution, and then went calmly down the stairs.

I had taken upon myself to order a carriage without consulting the prisoner. (He was to have a carriage if he asked for one.—Tr.) The *maréchal* saluted us. I was greatly relieved to see him in a blue coat, white cravat, short black breeches and black stockings, no decorations. I was fearing he might be in uniform, and it would have been my duty to cause him to be degraded, and his orders, epaulets and buttons taken off. Noticing the bad weather, he said with a smile: "What a wretched day!" Then turning to the *curé*, who had stepped aside to allow him to get into the carriage, he said: "Go first, *M. le Curé*, presently I shall go first." The two officers of the *gendarmerie* also got into the carriage, taking their seats in front.

A few hundred yards from the iron gate of the Luxembourg, in the Avenue de l'Observatoire, the procession stopped. As the carriage door was opened, the *maréchal*, who expected to go to Grenelle, and probably was aware that a manifestation would have been made there in his favour, said: "What! there already!" He, of course, refused to kneel down and be blindfolded; he merely asked the Commandant Saint-Bias to show him where he should stand. He stood facing the platoon, who held their guns ready to fire. Then, in an attitude that I shall never forget, it was so noble, calm and dignified, without bravado, he took off his hat, and availing himself of the moment when the adjutant stepped aside and gave the signal to fire, he said these words which I distinctly heard:

Frenchmen, I protest against my sentence; my honour . . . .

As he said these words he placed his hand on his heart; the volley was fired, and he fell. A rolling of drums, and the shout of "*Vive le Roi*" from the surrounding troops closed the mournful ceremony.

Such a death made a deep impression on me, and turning to Auguste de La Rochejaquelein, Colonel of the Grenadiers, who was beside me, and who, like me, deplored the death of the *bravest of the brave*, I said:

There, my dear friend, is a lesson how to die.

The words spoken by the *maréchal* in face of death have been incorrectly reported, both by journalists and by so-called spectators; it was even said that the *maréchal* had given the order to "fire." The events happened as I have stated. I have no interest in disguising the truth. I distinctly heard the *maréchal*, who was not far from me, and whom I was watching most attentively. Having been ordered to give a report of the execution to General Despinois, I was on horseback and overlooking the crowd; I heard and saw better than anyone. The body not having been claimed, for it had not been possible to let the family know, was taken to the place named in Order 4. ("*L'Hôpital de la Maternité*."—Despinois; Order 4). Having carried out the orders given to me, the rest being out of my province, I withdrew; but before returning home I went to the Duc de Richelieu to give him an account of my sad mission, and to tell him of two untoward incidents that I had not been able to prevent. During the quarter of an hour that the body lay on the ground, before it was removed, an Englishman suddenly put his horse to the gallop, made him leap over the

THE DEATH OF MARÉCHAL NEY

body, and after this revolting act, was gone like the wind, so that it was impossible to stop him.

In the second place, I had been greatly surprised to see a Russian general, in full uniform, among the spectators, and I recognised Baron van B—— of Dutch descent, who had been for a long time in the service of Russia. He had been Governor of Mitau. Impelled by curiosity, he had diligently followed the trial, and not wishing to miss the sight of the execution, he had remained all night in the vicinity of the Luxembourg. His uniform and numerous decorations had enabled him not merely to move about freely but to secure a good position to see everything. After hearing my report, the Duc de Richelieu thought it his duty to mention the fact to the Emperor Alexander.

The noble sovereign was very indignant, sent for the inquisitive officer, and said:

Give thanks to God that you are not a Russian! But for that I would have made you a private soldier on the spot. You are a foreigner. I dismiss you from my service. Take off at once the Russian uniform you have dishonoured, and never set foot in Russia again.

I learned these details from the *aide-de-camp* on duty.

CHAPTER 5

The Liberation of the Occupied Territory

The Duc and Duchesse d'Angoulême, who had been married a long time, had no children. It therefore appeared a matter of urgency that the last son of the Royal House of France should marry, and thus secure the crown to the elder branch of the family. The Duc de Berry was thirty-nine years of age, and had contracted a secret marriage while in England without the king's consent. This union was declared null, and the king made suitable provision for the two daughters born of the marriage, as well as for their mother. (Later, the elder daughter married the Prince de Lucinge, and the younger, the Baron de Charette.)

The Duc de Richelieu was anxious that the prince should marry the Grand Duchess Anne, the sister of Alexander. The negotiations failed, however, because the king and the Count d'Artois desired that the princess should renounce the Orthodox religion before her marriage, while Alexander insisted that this so-called conversion should not take place until some months after, in order that it might not appear that the Grand Duchess had yielded to pressure from the French Court.

The project was abandoned, and on June 17th, 1816, the Duc de Berry married the Princess Marie-Caroline, granddaughter of Ferdinand, King of Naples. There were brilliant *fêtes* on this occasion which were continued for a whole month. But soon torrential rains destroyed the harvest and brought about a terrible famine. Further sacrifices were needed to provide food for the people, and for the foreign armies, who occupied a large part of French territory.

On account of the deplorable state of the national finances, economy was strongly urged upon all the Ministries. My staff appeared too large; the post of Colonel Chief of Staff was suppressed, and I was left with only twenty-six officers, instead of thirty-four. I particularly regretted the Count de Beaumont, my former Chief of Staff, a friend on whom I could rely. His departure greatly displeased the Duc de Berry, and was the cause of one of those violent scenes, when he seemed unable to control himself at the moment, though he soon regretted it, and sought to make amends.

On this occasion, as he was driving down the *boulevard*, he saw me, beckoned to me, and then said angrily:

"So, you have sent away that poor Beaumont. It is because he is known to be a friend of mine. All your ministers are only —— Say so to the Duc de Richelieu from me," and he raised the whip he held in his hand as if he would strike me.

I sprang out of the way, and replied: "*Monseigneur*, such messages are only delivered directly, and not through an intermediary," and I bowed low and went on. On the following Sunday, at the reception given by the princes of the Royal Family, he came up to me, and said with his usual kindness:

"Rochechouart, I think I spoke too hastily the other day. I am sorry to have hurt you, but I was very fond of the Count de Beaumont, and annoyed to see him left without a post." Then, taking my hand, he said: "Forget that moment of anger."

No one can form any idea of the difficulties that confronted the government unless, like me, he had enjoyed the intimate friendship of the Duc de Richelieu. The task was laid upon the Ministry of carrying out the provisions of the Treaty with the Allies, signed on November 20th, 1815; and, unless we were to lose a part of our territory to satisfy the greed of Prussia, we must pay a War Indemnity of 700 million *francs*, thus divided:

To	Russia	..	.. 130	million.
„	England	..	.. 130	„
„	Prussia	..	.. 110	„
„	Austria	..	.. 110	„
„	Bavaria	..	.. 55	„
„	Baden	..	.. 35	„
„	Other States	..	130	„

In addition, there was the cost of the subsistence of 150,000 Allied troops, who were to be in occupation for five years; it was calculated at 150 million a year, but the cost rose in 1816 on account of the bad harvests.

The Chamber of Deputies was divided into three parties—the

Royalists (who were subdivided into Ultras and Moderates), the Liberals (nearly all of whom had formerly been Revolutionaries), and the Doctrinaires. The antagonism of these parties prevented the ministers from seeking a remedy for the dangerous financial position. M. de Richelieu frequently said:

> I am incapable of struggling against these difficulties; I am deeply discouraged, and if I did not feel that I am, perhaps, the only minister who can obtain the liberation of our territory, I would retire; once that object is attained, nothing shall keep me at the head of affairs; my health cannot withstand the strain.

I will explain in some detail the measures taken for the liberation of the territory; first, because I believe they are little known, and next, because the relations established at this time between the Duc de Richelieu and M. Ouvrard led to my marriage.

In November, 1816, the Treasury was empty. The Council of Ministers deputed M. Decazes to see the well-known financier, M. Ouvrard, and ask for a loan of sixty million . . . M. Ouvrard replied:

> No one can lend sixty million in the existing state of affairs, but I will undertake to procure a milliard to free us entirely from the Allies.

M. Decazes looked upon this idea as an absurd paradox, but, out of politeness, he begged M. Ouvrard to draw up a memorandum explaining it. The next day the Duc de Richelieu received the memorandum, and having read it, sent the following note:

> I beg M. Ouvrard to be so kind as to come and see me tomorrow, at three o'clock, to discuss the memorandum he sent me.
> Monday.   Richelieu.

At the appointed time the Duc de Richelieu, Count Corvetto, the Minister of Finance, and M. Ouvrard, had a long conference. The principle of finding a milliard, instead of sixty million, was accepted. It remained to come to an understanding with regard to the security given by the government, and the use to be made of it.

M. de Richelieu anxiously awaited the suggestions of the financier. "You must issue a hundred million of *rentes*," said M. Ouvrard. Count Corvetto, taken aback, exclaimed: "Issue new *rentes*! Why, I have the entire issue of six million *rentes*, granted by the Chamber in 1815. I cannot make use of them at any price."

"Then, you will have a hundred and six million," said M. Ouvrard, "and I will undertake to get them taken up. At present, it is known that you are compelled to borrow; people wait, hoping for more favourable terms; by borrowing a hundred and six million *rentes* you declare the ledger finally closed; you will see the result."

M. de Richelieu understood the main outline of the project, but, alarmed at its boldness, he came to no decision at this first interview.

A few days later the Treasury suspended payment to the Allies. M. de Richelieu, regardless of the ridicule that had been thrown on the project of M. Ouvrard, sent for him again, and authorised him to carry it out.

He went to London to consult Messrs. Hope and Baring. The question was to induce the Allies to accept payment of the indemnity in *rentes*. Messrs. Hope and Baring undertook to sell these *rentes* for a commission. It was also necessary to obtain funds for the payment of the subsistence of the Armies of Occupation. Messrs. Hope and Baring at once agreed to advance the sum required at 5 *per cent,* interest, plus a commission of 1 *per cent.* The Council of Ministers had given the contract for these supplies to M. Doumerc; it was payable in *rentes*, a great advantage under the existing circumstances. It only remained to prevail upon the Allies to accept payment of the indemnity in *rentes*, at a fixed value. M. Ouvrard sought an interview with General Pozzo di Borgo, the Russian Ambassador, who advised him to see the Duke of Wellington, as he enjoyed the confidence of the Allied Sovereigns.

The duke was at Brussels, much disturbed at the suspension of payments by the Treasury, and uneasy as to the supplies for his army. He received M. Ouvrard on December 5th, 1816. The financier explained his plan, and added:

> I have addressed myself to Your Excellency, knowing the weight of your advice with the sovereigns of Europe; moreover, I am convinced that the value of the *rente* will rise rapidly, as soon as the banks realise that the Allies accept these *rentes* in payment.

He concluded by asking that the Army of Occupation should be reduced by one fifth, as the surest way of calming the French nation, soothing their pride, and restoring their credit. The Duke of Wellington asked for twenty-four hours to consider the matter. The next day he informed M. Ouvrard that he agreed, and that he hoped to be able to bring over the other Powers to his opinion. He wrote the same day to Lord Castlereagh, the British Prime Minister, asking him to consult

Mr. Baring.

Paris remained in a state of anxiety, which was shared by the Duc de Richelieu. It was thought that the negotiations would fail and the hopes of success prove illusory. The Bank of France openly declared that it would not take a *sou* of the Loan.

On January 9th, 1817, the Duke of Wellington arrived in Paris. Taking up his quarters at the house of M. Ouvrard, the Hôtel de La Reynière, Rue des Champs Elysees, he begged him to come down to his room when the Duc de Richelieu and M. Corvetto called on him. It was decided that a written statement of the project should be drawn up by M. Ouvrard, and that the Duke of Wellington should take the paper to the Conference of the Allies. The same day the plan was accepted by the Ambassadors of the Powers and sent by special couriers to their Cabinets.

On February 11th, the Duc de Richelieu was able to announce to the Chambers that the Allied Armies would be reduced by thirty thousand men, which would lessen the expense of their support by thirty million a year. . . . The choice of the foreign bankers excited a happy rivalry among the French bankers, confidence was restored, the *rente* rose; Messrs. Hope and Baring wished to become purchasers instead of agents. Thus, as M. Ouvrard had told the Duke of Wellington would be the case, the intervention of the Allied Powers had assured the full success of the Loan. When the first agreement with Messrs. Hope and Baring was signed the *rente* was at 53 *fr.* 5 *c.*

A month later it had risen to 65 *fr.* Then, the capitalists, the French bankers and merchants, who had rejected with alarm any financial operation with the Royal Treasury, saw by the examples of the foreign bankers that *rentes* could be bought with, safety and advantage. From that time, all begged the favour of sharing in the Loan. It was necessary—a strange and novel precaution—to call out the military to maintain order among the crowd that besieged the doors of the Treasury to buy *rentes.* . . .

During the summer (of 1818) M. de Richelieu opened negotiations for the meeting of a Congress to settle definitely all the questions pending in Europe, and especially the duration of the occupation of French territory by the foreign Armies. He hoped this occupation might be reduced to three years, as was permitted by the provisions of the Treaty of November 20th, 1815. M. de Richelieu, who represented France, arrived at Aix-la-Chapelle, where the Congress was to be held, on September 26th, 1818. . . . I will not enter into any details with regard to the Conference—that belongs to history. I will merely say that, thanks to the support of the Emperor Alexander, the Duc de Richelieu succeeded in fixing November 30th as the date for the withdrawal of the Allied troops. . . .

He dreaded the end of the Congress and his return to Paris, so greatly did he fear that the king would not accept his resignation. He wrote to me:

> Aix-la-Chapelle, Nov. 20th, 1818.
>
> I thank you for your short letter, my dear friend. I expect to be in Paris on Thursday or Friday. I wish to see the emperor and receive his blessing, and then to plunge into that frightful abyss of passion, vice and corruption. Pity me, in spite of the medley of Orders with which I am decorated, and the snuff-boxes with which I am overwhelmed. I would give it all to be free to go to Ursuff. . . .
>
> R.

As soon as he arrived in Paris M. de Richelieu asked the king to allow him to retire, now that his task—the liberation of the territory—had been accomplished. The king begged him to remain and help him with his advice. . . .

In December, the Chamber was discussing a new Franchise Bill. The Duc de Richelieu remained for a short time alone in the Ministry, the other ministers having resigned; but being unwilling to assume such great responsibility, and feeling his health shattered by the strain he had undergone, he renewed his request to the king, and his resignation was at last accepted. The king publicly expressed his regret, appointed him a Minister of State, and Master of the Royal Hunt, and called upon M. Decazes to form a new Ministry. . . ,

On January 4th, 1819, M. de Richelieu, who was far from well, set out for the south, leaving me a power of attorney to manage his affairs. His *aide-de-camp*, Stempkovski, whom he had sent for when he was at Aix-la-Chapelle, accompanied him. M. de Richelieu went first to Courteille, and we kept up a regular correspondence while he was away. . . . At last, on December 2nd, 1819, I welcomed him home at the Royal Huntsman's residence in the Place Vendôme, now the Ministry of Justice. Everything was in order—the cook at his stove, the footmen in the ante-room, the horses in the stable. He embraced me affectionately, after an absence of eleven months. For me this year had been uneventful, as, following the ceaseless advice of M. de Richelieu,

I had kept entirely away from politics and remained a soldier.
. . . From this time, I resumed the direction of his house. The months of December and January passed quietly; the king appointed the Duc de Richelieu to represent him at the Coronation of George IV of England; we were making preparations for this important mission, when a terrible event overthrew our plans.

The storm was rumbling; only the king, reassured by his minister, and favourite, Decazes, remained unconscious of danger. . . . On February 13th, the Duc and Duchesse de Berry were present at the opera. During the interval, while the prince was seeing the princess to her carriage as she was not well, a workman named Louvel stabbed him with a dagger, and he died during the night. . . . The distress throughout the whole of France may be imagined. I spent the night in going backwards and forwards between the Rue Richelieu and the Place Vendôme, making arrangements to maintain order, and seeing that they were carried out, hearing reports from the officers returning from patrol. The town was much moved, but quiet.

A general outcry arose against the Decazes Ministry; it was accused of allowing a free hand to the revolutionaries by its Liberalism, and thus endangering the country. The king appealed to M. de Richelieu, begging him to form a new Ministry. After hesitating for a few days, he accepted the Presidency of the Council without portfolio, on February 20th, feeling he could not refuse anything to the king and the Royal Family who appealed to him in the midst of their sorrow.

I will leave M. de Richelieu to discuss the Franchise Bill, and to meet the new Chamber in 1820, true to my principle to take no part in politics; they formed, however, the chief subject of conversation at his table. . . .

On September 29th, 1820, a hundred and one cannon-shots announced that the Duchess de Berry had given birth to a son, who received the names of Henri-Dieudonné, and the title of Duc de Bordeaux. . . . The news caused great enthusiasm throughout France, as was shown by numerous addresses to the king. . . .

I have mentioned that the negotiations for the liberation of the territory had led to frequent interviews between M. de Richelieu. and M. Ouvrard. During the summer of 1821 the marriage of Mlle. Elizabeth Ouvrard and Raoul de Montmorency had been arranged; it was about to take place when his uncle, Thibaut de Montmorency, died as the result of a carriage accident. Raoul thereupon gave up the project of marriage with Mlle. Ouvrard.

This lady, who was very agreeable, but not remarkably beautiful, pleased me greatly. I begged M. de Richelieu to obtain her father's consent to our marriage. The Abbé Nicolle, who had returned from Odessa, and was now the Director of the College of St. Barbara (later, the College Rollin), kindly undertook the negotiations. M. Ouvrard, gratified at the thought of having a relative of the President of the Council for son-in-law, gave his consent. I wrote to the king to ask his approval, and to beg him to do me the honour of signing my marriage contract. . . .

At this time M. de Richelieu was much occupied with the Address to the Throne. The majority wished to insert the following sentence:

> We congratulate you, Sire, on your friendly relations with Foreign Powers, confident that a much-valued peace has not been purchased by sacrifices incompatible with the honour of the nation and the dignity of the Crown.

M. de Richelieu maintained that such an insinuation was in itself an offence to the dignity of the Crown. The Chamber, having voted in favour of retaining the sentence, he resigned on the Saturday evening.

On the Sunday, after the Mass, he was present at the signature of my marriage contract by the king. In the evening, he left for Courteille, whence he wrote to M. Ouvrard:

> Courteille, December 25th, 1821.
> The Abbé Nicolle has given me the letter you have done me the honour to write. It was no merit on my part to delay my journey in order to be present at the signature of the marriage contract, but great merit on the part of the young people to wait for me till the 5th of January; I am very grateful to them. . . . I will return, without fail, on January 3; it is essential that I should avoid the New Year's official visits. . . .
> Richelieu.

On January 5th, I was married at Saint-Roch; I was truly the happiest of men. . . . The good Stempkovski, who had just been placed on the retired list, obtained permission to take my place beside his former general, thus giving up his whole future to devote himself entirely to him. (After the death of the Duc de Richelieu, Stempkovski returned to Odessa.)

The Duc de Richelieu had taken a great liking for Courteille; he often went there to rest from the fatigues of his political life in that quiet home with his wife and her mother. There all the new books were read, literature and philosophy discussed with a few kind and intelligent neighbours—politics only being taboo. The time passed quickly.

In May, after a heated discussion in the Chamber of Peers, the Duc de Richelieu went to Courteille. On the 22nd, feeling unwell, he returned to Paris, arriving at four o'clock in the afternoon. I hastened to receive him and embrace him; an hour later he fell down unconscious in an apoplectic seizure. The Abbé Nicolle was informed at once, and hastened with me to his bedside, where he sought to assure himself that his friend was able to follow the prayers we were saying; while the Abbé Feutrier, Curé of the Church of the Assumption, administered the last sacraments. Just before his death, M. de Richelieu seemed to understand the prayers of his friend; he pressed his hand, and tears fell from his eyes, already veiled by death. At eleven o'clock in the evening he breathed his last. He was fifty-five years old and a few months.

I went out of the room crushed and broken-hearted. I had loved him as if he had been my father, and he had a great affection for me, and never ceased to give me proofs of it since my arrival at Odessa. His wise counsel had guided my youth, and I was losing his support at the very moment when it would have been most useful to me. I mourned him sincerely.

He was buried at the Sorbonne, where all the Richelieu family had been buried since the time of the cardinal. The Duchesse de Richelieu claimed his heart, desiring that it should rest near her, for she had never ceased to love him devotedly. I could not entrust this precious relic to anyone else, and carried it myself to the Church of Courteille. The Duchesse de Richelieu died in 1830, and was interred in the same tomb, which thus united, after death, two hearts that had been separated during life.

Later Years & Rochechouart's Death

NOTE BY THE TRANSLATOR

The military career of General de Rochechouart practically ended with the year in which the Duc de Richelieu died.

On December 31st; 1822, he received a letter from the Minister of War, the Duc de Bellune, informing him that, by an Order signed by the king on the previous day, he had been placed temporarily on the unattached list, and the Comte de Wall had been appointed Commandant of Paris.

A few months later the armed intervention in Spain, by an expedition under the Duc d'Angoulême, brought about the financial ruin of M. Ouvrard, who had been employed by the commander-in-chief to provide supplies for the troops.

The Count de Rochechouart writes:

> As the fortune which Madame de Rochechouart would have inherited from her father was swallowed up in consequence of this expedition, I cannot enter into details with regard to the agreements with M. Ouvrard for the purchase of supplies and the manner in which they were carried out. I should be accused of partiality.

The count had, however, received a million *francs* as his wife's dowry at the time of his marriage, and in 1828, with part of this money, he bought the Château of Jumilhac in the Dordogne, which became henceforth his home.

While living there with his family, he was recalled to the army in 1830 in consequence of the expedition to Algiers. The troops under his command, a brigade of reserves, had actually embarked at Toulon on July 8th, when, on the following day, a telegram announced the surrender of Algiers. The troops returned to their quarters to await further orders. Meanwhile grave events were happening in Paris, and after the Revolution of July 27th-29th, Charles X abdicated, and embarked for England.

On August 10th, General de Rochechouart was placed on the unattached list, and in the following March retired on a pension. The length of his service having been calculated as 16 years, 3 months and 28 days, he received a pension of 2,000 *francs* a year up to 1839.

In 1832 the Duchesse de Berry landed in France in order to promote a rising in La Vendée in favour of her son. Being unable to help her, as he had no family connections in La Vendée, the Count de Rochechouart offered his services to Charles X. In reply, he was asked to go to The Hague with a view to obtain from the King of Holland permission for the exiled Royal Family to live in his territory. Later he was sent on a somewhat similar mission to the Emperor Nicholas. On this occasion, the Count de Rochechouart added a request on his own behalf:

> I do not know what may befall us in France. I would beg His Imperial Majesty, if the necessity should arise, to allow me to come to Russia with my family.

To this the Emperor Nicholas sent the reply:

> Not only will H. I. Majesty receive you and your family with pleasure, but, knowing your military services, he will accept them at once if they are offered.

Having re-established good relations between the *Tzar* and the Duchesse de Berry, the count returned to The Hague, where he remained as her representative at the Court of Holland. After her reconciliation with Charles X, whose sympathies had been alienated from her by her secret morganatic marriage with the friend of her childhood. Count Lucches-Palli, there was no longer any need for the Count de Rochechouart to remain at The Hague, and on May 16th, 1834, he returned to his wife and four children after an absence of two years.

His son, who edits the *Memoirs*, adds the following note:

> After his return from The Hague, the Count de Rochechouart withdrew to the Château of Jumilhac; no longer in the army, avoiding politics, he divided his time between the education of his children and the management of his estate, devoting his leisure to minute historical

research. He wrote the *History of the House of Rochechouart*, and employed his later years, almost up to the time of his death, in revising and completing the *Recollections* of his childhood and youth. He never recovered from the shock of his wife's death, which occurred on July 20th, 1857, after a long illness. On February 21st, 1858, he had an apoplectic seizure, from which he died on the 28th, just as one of his most ardent wishes was about to be granted—the marriage of his eldest son to Mlle, de La Rochejaquelein. Before he died, he had the consolation of knowing that it had been arranged.

LEONAUR

ALSO FROM LEONAUR
AVAILABLE IN SOFTCOVER OR HARDCOVER WITH DUST JACKET

OFFICERS & GENTLEMEN *by Peter Hawker & William Graham*—Two Accounts of British Officers During the Peninsula War: Officer of Light Dragoons by Peter Hawker & Campaign in Portugal and Spain by William Graham .

THE WALCHEREN EXPEDITION *by Anonymous*—The Experiences of a British Officer of the 81st Regt. During the Campaign in the Low Countries of 1809.

LADIES OF WATERLOO *by Charlotte A. Eaton, Magdalene de Lancey & Juana Smith*—The Experiences of Three Women During the Campaign of 1815: Waterloo Days by Charlotte A. Eaton, A Week at Waterloo by Magdalene de Lancey & Juana's Story by Juana Smith.

JOURNAL OF AN OFFICER IN THE KING'S GERMAN LEGION *by John Frederick Hering*—Recollections of Campaigning During the Napoleonic Wars.

JOURNAL OF AN ARMY SURGEON IN THE PENINSULAR WAR *by Charles Boutflower*—The Recollections of a British Army Medical Man on Campaign During the Napoleonic Wars.

ON CAMPAIGN WITH MOORE AND WELLINGTON *by Anthony Hamilton*—The Experiences of a Soldier of the 43rd Regiment During the Peninsular War.

THE ROAD TO AUSTERLITZ *by R. G. Burton*—Napoleon's Campaign of 1805.

SOLDIERS OF NAPOLEON *by A. J. Doisy De Villargennes & Arthur Chuquet*—The Experiences of the Men of the French First Empire: Under the Eagles by A. J. Doisy De Villargennes & Voices of 1812 by Arthur Chuquet .

INVASION OF FRANCE, 1814 *by F. W. O. Maycock*—The Final Battles of the Napoleonic First Empire.

LEIPZIG—A CONFLICT OF TITANS *by Frederic Shoberl*—A Personal Experience of the 'Battle of the Nations' During the Napoleonic Wars, October 14th-19th, 1813.

SLASHERS *by Charles Cadell*—The Campaigns of the 28th Regiment of Foot During the Napoleonic Wars by a Serving Officer.

BATTLE IMPERIAL *by Charles William Vane*—The Campaigns in Germany & France for the Defeat of Napoleon 1813-1814.

SWIFT & BOLD *by Gibbes Rigaud*—The 60th Rifles During the Peninsula War.